WHEN IN ROME

Penelope Green

WHEN IN ROME

Chasing
la dolce vita

HODDER

HODDER AUSTRALIA

Published in Australia and New Zealand in 2005
by Hodder Australia
(An imprint of Hachette Livre Australia Pty Limited)
Level 17, 207 Kent Street, Sydney NSW 2000
Website: www.hachette.com.au

Reprinted 2005 (five times), 2006

National Library of Australia
Cataloguing-in-Publication data

Green, Penelope.
   When in Rome.

   ISBN 0 7336 1903 7.

   1. Green, Penelope. 2. Women journalists - Italy - Rome -
   Biography. 3. Minority journalists - Italy - Rome -
   Biography. 4. Australians - Employment - Italy - Rome -
   Biography. 5. Rome (Italy) - Social life and customs -
   21st century - Biography. I. Title.

945.632093092

Cover design by Christabella Designs
Cover photograph of Penelope Green by Fabio Cuttica/Contrasto
Other photographs by Penelope Green
Text design and typesetting by Bookhouse, Sydney
Printed in Australia by Griffin Press, Adelaide

Hachette Livre Australia's policy is to use papers that are natural, renewable and recyclable
products and made from wood grown in sustainable forests. The logging and manufacturing
processes are expected to conform to the environmental regulations of the country of origin.

A Oriel Green e Maria Minchiatti ora fra le stelle

Contents

Reality bites

This is a small tale about what happened when I abandoned everything – career, apartment, family and friends – to chase a romantic dream I was praying might change my life for the better. Even if I had no idea what would make me happy.

I used to get a kick out of the smallest things: a stroll around Sydney Harbour, jogging in the leafy suburb where I lived, inadvertently seeing a couple share a sweet moment. But then all the street scapes started to look beige. I felt as though I was living in a cross between *The Truman Show* and *Groundhog Day*.

I wrote list after earnest list of Things To Do. But I was so sapped that I couldn't muster the energy to start. I began sticking self-affirmation notes around my flat before recoiling in horror. How Oprah! I was doing things recommended by self-help books, which I loathe.

I looked at friends who seemed happy with their lot and felt picky and ungrateful, because I knew I was ridiculously fortunate.

I couldn't help wondering, was this it?

And so it was that on a pleasant autumnal afternoon in April 2002, just after my twenty-eighth birthday, I found myself with Carmen, a Pranic healer-cum-clairvoyant recommended to me by a girlfriend who, like me, also happened to be in the throes of a Generation perpleXed what-the-hell-am-I-doing crisis.

Fighting back cynicism, pessimism and every negative *ism* in the dictionary, I entered the good witch's studio. Rock crystals, bowls brimming with rose water, trippy karmic prints and dippy oceanic music underwhelmed me. Only desperation made me stand my ground. The appointment was part of my erratic plan to calm the surging professional and personal tumult I was suffering. According to a chick magazine I once flicked through, there's an alleged astronomical phenomenon, called Saturn Returns, that forces major life crises for anyone between the ages of twenty-eight and thirty, when Saturn returns to one's birth planet after a long hiatus in someone else's Uranus.

I suspected it wouldn't take Carmen long to channel my aura of disarray.

Barely a month earlier I had thrown in my job as Communications Director at a chic PR and events firm in Sydney, despite the fact it was a job some might kill for and that I was, while by no means a millionaire, earning the biggest wage of my life.

With big brand fashion and design clients, my average week might involve helping launch a new clothing range spruiked by Serena Williams, attending a magazine shoot involving international supermodels and Hollywood stars, flying around Australia with VIPs to promote products, organising publicity for a key fashion festival and developing a PR campaign for a hip new residential design project in Sydney.

I adored my boss and colleagues – a fun bunch of twenty-something gals like me – and, while working hard during the week, enjoyed every weekend off and occasional long lunches.

Yet for all the good things about my job, which I didn't take for granted, I felt uninspired. I was lost in a room full of fashionistas and spin managers and couldn't relax and enjoy the job for the lark it often was. Worse, I felt like a fraud: I'm the last person to hyperventilate about the latest Collette Dinnigan collection. Unable to fake enthusiasm any more, I decided it was time to get out.

But what next? I'd hit career crossroads. Although I had nine years experience as a newspaper and magazine journalist, the thought of competing to get a new gig – of being sassy and winning at a job interview – filled me with fear. I just didn't have it in me.

Photography had always beckoned, but I had talked myself out of it due to a shortfall of funds and confidence. I wavered between being fiercely ambitious and so self-critical that I craved any desk job that would allow me to hide. This state of mind was cramping my every move. I was paranoid, android, numb all over. Something had to give.

It already had. Two weeks earlier yet another partnership I believed had all the promising signs of being a winner collapsed like Phar Lap. The fact it was hardly a surprise was little consolation. Within twenty-four hours of reaching Splitsville I'd used the average Australian's annual consumption of Kleenex.

My older sisters, Sal and Lisa, were new mums and, while I relished playing inept aunt, I found myself wiping away random tears as I nursed my two gurgling nieces.

It wasn't cluckiness – with next to no patience, a hedonist's selfishness and the attention span of a gnat, motherhood had never appealed to me. The thing that depressed me was that I couldn't imagine maintaining a meaningful, enduring relationship, let alone loving someone enough to want to procreate.

I can't stand girls (or guys, for that matter) who need to be attached to be happy. I've always been independent, from going to the movies alone to travelling solo. But I was starting to think there was something wrong with me. My relationship rate was threatening to overtake Elizabeth Taylor's.

I'd had loads of boyfriends but there was always some vital chemistry missing. Was it too much to ask for a smart, funny and, thus, sexy guy who adored me, was taller than me, had a touch of grunge-cool about him (but was still daggy enough to share my appreciation for the most forgettable musical hits of the eighties) and who had the crucial, inexplicable X Factor?

I wasn't looking for Ed Norton. I simply craved the company of someone who would make me think and laugh and *feel.* More than anything I just wanted to have a relationship that was balanced. I have as many hang-ups as the next person, but I seemed to have dated a bevy of men who were battling various demons or were just plain commitment freaks.

There are exceptions to every rule, but women are instinctive nurturers. We love taking a rough diamond and trying to polish it up, even if we get slashed to pieces in the process. I wasn't chasing bad boys for a thrill, I just had a tendency towards picking guys with serious baggage in some form (sadly inevitable, the older and more twisted one gets in the dating game), or who I probably knew deep down were wrong for me.

The process went something like this: meet Mr Potential; fall head over heels in lust, love or both. Turn into performing puppy, do anything to render myself adorable and to win points rather than just be me. Struggle to maintain my independence. Start to dislike who I have become but by this time it's too late – I've either sucked the life out of the relationship or turned into someone I would avoid having a beer with at all costs.

'You need to give up the Florence Nightingale act, Pen,' sighed my good mate Andrew, as we lay sprawled on Bondi Beach a few weeks earlier, nursing newspapers and mild hangovers. 'Stop trying to save people. Just look after yourself.'

And so I decided to do just that.

I had long entertained a pie-in-the-sky dream of living in Italy, a country I'd visited three times.

I was sixteen when I first travelled there, at the height of a bitter European winter and the 1991 Gulf War. With my middle sister, Sal, I spent thirty-six hours in Venice, part of our whistle-stop tour of Europe together. My imagination raced as I watched gondoliers appear then vanish into the blanket canal mist and we lost ourselves in the labyrinthine streets. Six years later I flew into Rome with my boyfriend at the time and spent two weeks in Tuscany, where my Australian uncle lives with his Italian wife and child.

Leaving Tuscany and the boy behind, I roamed Europe for four months, soaking up many glorious locales and cultures. In later years I travelled to countries closer to home, like Thailand and Nepal, but Italy was stuck fast in my heart.

Three years passed before I squeezed in a wintry trip to Sicily. I travelled by bus around the island, freezing in snow at the base of Mount Etna, admiring Greek ruins and pigging out on the ambrosial, ricotta-rich Sicilian sweets *cannoli* and *cassata*.

Mind-boggling history aside, every time I went back all my Piscean-tinted glasses could see was a slower life revolving around food and family life that appeared refreshingly devoid of stress. I wanted to live there, experience it first hand and find out if my fleeting, starry-eyed impressions were valid.

My plan had always played second fiddle to career moves, but now – languishing at work and strung out from another split – I was officially fed up enough to chase The Italian Dream.

Giving notice to my PR job, I hired removalists to take my life belongings from my studio flat in inner-city Sydney to my parents' house at Orange, in country New South Wales.

Just over a month later I spent my last week in Sydney wining and dining with family and friends who were envious of my seemingly spontaneous but actually long-planned escape. Happy to get caught up in their collective excitement, I didn't stop to analyse the ramifications of my decision. I had no idea how long I was going to be in Italy, I just wanted to get there. Asked by anyone what I was going to do once I arrived, I had a stock standard response: 'I'm going to learn the language and have a bit of a career break.' My actual plan wasn't much more detailed. I'd enrolled to do a language course in Perugia, in the region of Umbria. From there, I planned to head straight to Roma. If I was going to try to eke out an Italian existence, I wanted to try my luck in the capital.

I was secretly petrified that I had left it too late to go on the road again. To console myself, I filled my newly purchased backpack with more than a few of my favourite things. I was going to be a backpacker again, but this time I was going to do it with style. A slinky dress, some foxy tops and a smart handbag? Check. Good books, my Discman and thirty CDs painstakingly chosen so as not to remind me of my latest ex? Packed.

Finally, I flew to Perth, where Sal and her family live, for a short holiday with them and my mum, dad and Lisa, my eldest sister, and her family from Sydney. We spent a week shacking it on Rottnest Island, riding bikes, swimming and standing around a barbecue plate. Everyone seemed happy I was going away if not, I suspected, secretly glad to get rid of the ball of angst I had become.

Now here I was, eighteen hours before departure from Perth to Italy, staring into the gentle eyes of Carmen, a slight woman wearing a wise countenance and a rather unfortunate purple tie-dyed ensemble.

Asked to give a précis of my life, I blurted out enough to give her leverage.

'You have a strong life energy,' said Carmen, after a convincing minute of meditational silence. 'I don't think you will be coming back soon... You will discover your creative self and explore new avenues. You will have a very passionate relationship with a European. I see visa and immigration problems, marriage and children.'

My heart pounded. Fantastic, maybe I would become a photographer. And bring on Romeo and a Sicilian wedding. But kids?

Still, she was on the money about my relationship habits.

'You need to have more self-worth so you can learn to identify men who can give you more,' she said. 'Look at your body language,' she continued, pointing at my arms crossed tightly over my chest.

'Don't be too defensive when you travel. Be open to everything and trust your instinct, trust your heart – trust yourself.'

If she wasn't already, this woman should be on a retainer with Hallmark.

Desperate for direction, I lapped up Carmen's every word and twisted them to suit the dream I had packed up my life to chase. It was too late to turn back.

The next day I would be on my way to my favourite country. A land where no one knows my past, my mistakes, my foibles and idiosyncrasies. A place where I'll find the perfect job to get my creative juices flowing. A place where I'll follow my heart and not allow men to mess with my head. A place where, within reason, I'll heed the advice of a friend: Say yes to everything!

Ciao bella

Unable to sleep at dawn, I pull on my swimmers and tiptoe out of the house to walk to the Olympic pool nearby. The monotony of following a fat black line for two kilometres reduces, but fails to block out, my rising anxiety and excitement.

Crikey. Crumbs. Christ. This is it. No time for regrets.

'Sorry, Sal – I hate farewells,' I tell my sister as we pull into Departures at eucalypt-fringed Perth airport. Bear-hugging her on the footpath and giving a final squeeze to my niece, Lily, I hold back tears and stride into the airport.

The instant I walk through the sliding doors and into the cool rush of air-conditioning I feel a hundred times better, like when you vomit from seasickness then realise with one of the purest degrees of joy that you *will* survive.

Hovering in airports is one of my favourite means of escapism. It's real-life cinema. I meander happily, taking in the emotional scenes around me: the tender hugs of lovers reunited, the excruciating farewells, the disappointed or steely faces of people who hoped to have someone waiting for them only to find themselves alone at the baggage carousel, feeling as lonely as the unclaimed suitcases.

High on adrenalin, I board my flight and plonk myself in my aisle seat. Reality check. Why do I always romanticise air travel? The only time I have ever slept on a long-haul flight was when I flew First Class for a work conference to Taipei. I felt like a queen as I quaffed champagne while watching movies on a personal TV screen. Reclining my throne to a bed, I kipped for a record five hours. Once you've flown at the top of the plane, going back to economy is like being told Santa doesn't exist.

As the plane starts to roll onto the runway tiny shockwaves zap through me and questions start spinning around in my head. I take a few deep breaths and let my hopes lift with the plane. I'm going to be fine. Rueing my inability to nap sitting up, I reach into my daypack and grab my secret weapon for surviving long-haul economy flights – sleeping tablets.

Shuffling off the plane just after midnight in Singapore, I wander around like a zombie for two hours until I return to the boarding gate to meet Jo, a friend of a friend from Sydney.

A slight woman with big blue, startled eyes and her hair whimsically styled like Diana Spencer in her kindy-minding days, Jo not only happened to book her flight to Italy on the same day as me but, by sheer coincidence, is also on her way to Perugia, where I am enrolled in a three-month beginner's Italian course at the *Università per Stranieri* – University for Foreigners.

Years earlier, Jo did the same course and continued her Italian studies in Australia. Now fairly fluent, she's heading to Perugia to see Maria, the elderly Italian woman she boarded with during her stay. We met in Sydney a week ago and discovered our flights to Rome connected in Singapore, where we agreed to meet.

'I've booked a hotel for our first night in Rome, and Maria said you can stay with her until you sort out your accommodation,' says Jo, looking as haggard as I feel, as we reboard.

Relieved at not having to worry about finding digs upon landing, I thank her gratefully and find my seat. I pop another sleeping pill and pass out.

The cabin lights flicker on at 6 am and less than an hour later the plane bumps gently onto the tarmac at Leonardo da Vinci – Fiumicino, Rome's main airport. Following signs to the baggage carousel, I take in the scene around me as I wait for Jo.

Invariably petite and lean, young Italian women must all shop in the same department store: most wear tight jeans with heels and long black or white bomber jackets, and accessorise with designer handbags and buff boyfriends. Older women wrap themselves in a taxidermist's dream range of furs while their male sidekicks sport shiny leather shoes, belts and dapper suits.

Clutching minuscule mobiles, which beep or ring every two seconds, families, friends and lovers try to organise themselves with as much noise as possible.

'*Dai amore, su! Siamo in ritardo!*'

'*Ci vediamo presto piccolina. Stammi bene okay?*'

'*Aooooooo. Ti sto aspettando. Dove sei?*'

I feel like I am at the opera. The dialogue sounds so melodic.

Jo and I catch a train to Termini station, Rome's main transport hub. Stepping onto the platform, memories of my 1997 trip flood back as my eardrums fill with the sound of rolling luggage trolleys, grinding coffee machines, electronic announcements and even louder Italians who apparently all buy the same denim body-spray-paint. Looking at their jeans and jackets, I'm surprised they can even walk. Jets of exhaled cigarette smoke mingle with the waft of sweet pastries, coffee, perfume, aftershave and the stale body odour of the homeless camped in or wandering the station.

Ignoring men dressed in badly cut suits spruiking cheap hotel accommodation, we hop on the Metro and alight at Piazza di

Spagna, home to the Spanish Steps. Standing at the base, then, I remember how disappointed I was when I set eyes upon them for the first time. The mere name had me imagining the ridiculous: Spaniards dressed in bright Picasso-coloured costumes, leaping up and down. Instead I found a steep set of steps looking nothing like their postcard image which is covered in vibrant pink flowers. Today the steps are devoid of human life, except for a policeman with a whistle shooing away two Japanese tourists. Their crime appears to have been eating on the steps, but I notice the cop light up a cigarette within seconds of his scary policeman act.

I follow Jo up and we catch our breath at the summit before turning right down via Sistina. Old Vespas and modern motorbikes of every colour hurtle past us, brightening the dusty streetscape of crumbling facades and scaffolding.

Once checked into our hotel – a convent accommodating women or married couples only – by a moustached nun, we catch a tiny, Get Smart-style elevator to a spartan but squeaky clean room on the third *piano*, or floor.

Showering quickly, Jo and I head to the nearest bar, a word I remember refers to a place where one orders coffee more often than alcohol. Jo disappears into the peak-hour jam, telling me she has to pay first at the cash register then present the receipt at the counter for service. Nodding absently, I watch the squat barista in fascination. About fifty with stylish grey sideburns and a jovial demeanour, he handles the eight-cup coffee machine like a long-time lover, cranking it up and pushing all the right buttons without exerting himself. Occasionally he stops to inhale a cigarette that burns in an ashtray nearby.

Orders flood in as locals smack their receipts on the counter and wait for their coffees, which they drink standing at the bar. There are no tables in sight.

'Grab a *cornetto*,' says Jo, taking a serviette and mimicking the locals to open a container full of pastries nearby. She chooses a croissant with a telltale chocolate blob on top. I follow suit and grab a pastry splotched with orange.

I almost never eat pastries, because it flies in the face of the Healthy Food Pyramid I memorised in Three Unit Home Economics and I am fearful of the fat content. But today, drum roll, is the first day of the rest of my new life. And they look damn tasty.

Filled with apricot jam, my *cornetto* is more doughy than buttery. Convincing myself it's almost like eating toast and jam, I leave my guilt trip behind.

'Ohmygoddd,' says Jo, sounding like Meg Ryan in *When Harry Met Sally*. 'Mine has Nutella inside…it's amazing.'

The barista slides cappuccinos before us with an exaggerated gesture of achievement. I look down and see a gigantic heart shaped in cocoa atop the froth of my cappuccino. Jo has the same, yet a podgy local woman standing next to us hasn't attracted the same slick service. We stick out like tourists – and we are being treated accordingly.

I blush self-consciously and absorb the theatre going on around me. Two men talk heatedly about something, gesticulating excessively. Just as they appear to be on the verge of coming to blows, one gives the other a big backslap and they leave the bar laughing.

We walk back down to Piazza di Spagna, decorated with palm trees that seem out of place, and roam the grid of streets that run off the piazza, lined with the likes of Fendi, Dolce & Gabbana and Gucci. Perfumed shop assistants teetering on toothpick-thin heels unabashedly admire their reflections in wall-length mirrors. Fashion and beauty are as omnipresent as the shrieking of mobile phones and the American and English accents suspended in the air.

Within half an hour I feel frustrated by the attention I am receiving. On a fresh blue April day, I'm wearing a Chinese-style top with a slit down one side. It's a bit sexy, but by no means astonishingly revealing. As Jo and I enjoy a stroll, passing Italian men with bedroom eyes whistle and hiss their approval.

'*Buongiorno, signorina. Bellissima. Ciao, bella!*'

At first it's flattering, but soon I am annoyed. Who are these horny critters? Do they have girlfriends, partners, or wives? How can they possibly think any woman with all her marbles might fall for such platitudes?

'I know Italian men can be lecherous but this is getting ridiculous!' giggles Jo, confirming that I am not imagining things.

Looking at the women around me, dressed in winter wear despite the mild spring weather, I drape my jumper over my shoulders and adopt a don't-mess-with-me veneer.

The soft strain of nuns singing hymns in the chapel below our room stirs us well before my alarm clock sounds. Our morning train grunts through ugly suburbia – endless rows of concrete apartment buildings with little vegetation – then hurtles through lush countryside scattered with sunflower fields before pulling into Perugia three hours later.

Walking out of the station, I see an elderly, curvaceous woman wearing a stylish black dress, green cashmere shawl, bright red lipstick and orange Jackie O sunglasses. Her silver hair is pulled elegantly back in a bun and her smile is warm and wide.

'Maria!' Jo embraces her short frame and immediately starts to blubber like an infant.

Finally releasing Jo, Maria embraces me like a long-lost daughter, and I inhale the faint musty perfume that lingers in her scarf. There are only three perfumes I know by scent: Chanel No. 5, because I wear it; Issy Miyake, because an old boyfriend wore it, along with half of Sydney's gay population; and Anaïs Anaïs, worn by my beloved late grandmother.

Maria wears the latter and smelling her scarf immediately transports me back to childhood, sitting in my grandparents' kitchen and dunking Arnott's Milk Arrowroot biscuits into a cup of tea, making adult talk with my grandmother, Oriel. I'm overwhelmed by nostalgia.

Winding up a steep, long road lined with trees, our taxi flashes past a pretty piazza, where people sit on the steps of a massive church enjoying the sunshine, then pulls up abruptly on the slope of a narrow, cobbled street.

Using half my body weight to help Maria open two enormous wooden doors, we scale two flights of concrete stairs and pass through another set of big heavy timber doors into a small entrance hall. Full of a hotch-potch mix of furniture and miscellaneous bits and bobs, Maria's home is like her – worn but grandma chic. Explaining that she will share Maria's bed, Jo dumps her bags in the clean yet musty room nearest the front door. The imposing, sombre oil of Jesus Christ hanging on the wall opposite the bed is enough to make me pray I'll be camping in another room.

Maria ushers me along a corridor and past a formal dining room, and a kitchen full of heavenly scents, then opens a door leading to a big, bright room with sun filtering through a large window in an angled wall. There are two single beds with thick doonas on top – Perugia is at least ten degrees cooler than Rome – plus a wardrobe, a study desk and chair. Walking to the window, I look out to see a beautiful belltower and red-tiled rooftops petering out to make way for the green and gold Umbrian fields which roll into the horizon.

Jo tells me that an Australian girl, Olivia, currently rents one of the beds for 200 euros a month. In a few days her mother will arrive to take the second bed, but until then I can crash there.

We head into the kitchen, where Maria stands at the stove, stirring sizzling cubes of bacon and garlic in a large fry pan. At the round table, covered with a beautiful white embroidered tablecloth, sits a balding man with large black eyes and hound-dog jowls.

'Penny, this is Luca,' says Jo, giving me an 'I'll tell you all about HIM later' look.

'*Buongiorno!*' barks Luca gruffly in my direction.

I smile at him and nod politely.

'*Pronta!*' says Maria, motioning to us to sit down at the table. I watch as she drains water from a big pot of spaghetti, which she throws into the fry pan with the bacon and garlic.

She cracks three eggs into the pasta, mixing it swiftly before transferring it onto a large serving plate, which she places next to a breadboard loaded with a crusty loaf and a large chunk of parmesan cheese.

The only carbonara sauce I have seen in Australia has been enough to turn my stomach, a soupy mix of cream, greasy bacon bits and excess oil. Maria's version has no cream, but the eggs, oil and fresh parmesan add ample richness. I wolf it down quickly.

Through Jo's generous translation, I learn that Maria was born in a small town on Perugia's outskirts. She remembers the day the Nazis swept through the village, killing adults and children in their path. Her father hid her beneath the kitchen floorboards. Her family were among the lucky.

For forty years she has rented rooms to foreign and Italian students. She has hugged kids who have arrived home bawling their eyes out in frustration, struggling to learn the Italian language, seen a black shiny pistol in the suitcase of a shy young Russian woman who was a KGB operative, booted out heroin addicts, and protected her female tenants from the slimey advances of male students.

Luca, who has been silently chewing and drinking and refilling his glass of *vino rosso* with admirable speed, abruptly pushes back his chair and leaves the room. I raise my eyebrows at Jo, who explains that several times during past decades Maria has left Luca but never managed to get a divorce, due to complications linked to finances and the Roman Catholic Church. For better but more often worse, the cardigan-wearing pensioners have somehow remained together – although, says Jo, Maria had a long-running affair with a doctor she met when she was nursing her mother, who died of cancer.

'I don't understand,' I tell Jo, 'why she doesn't just leave…'

Jo translates as Maria rolls her eyes and answers in sentences punctuated with sighs. 'She says that sometimes it's easier to stay with someone than abandon them.'

'I disagree – life is short!' I retort, fuelled by the red wine and a sudden urge to be heard. Maria doesn't need Jo's translation to understand the gist of my outburst. When she drops her gaze, I fear I have offended her – until she cocks her head and looks at me cheekily. Her hazel eyes hint of adventures I crave to hear about.

'*Boh!*' she says with an exaggerated shrug of her shoulders.

Jo and I burst out laughing at Maria's turn of phrase, which sounds like a cross between a soft belch and a grunt, and can mean anything from 'I don't know' to a much ruder 'No idea – don't ask me!'

It soon becomes my favourite Italian expression.

With a week before I have to enrol and begin my language course, I decide to visit my Uncle Geoffrey, who lives with his wife and their daughter in San Gimignano, a small town overrun by tourists in Tuscany.

'*Buongiorno!*'

Heading out the door, I am intercepted by Maria as I walk past the kitchen. Dressed in a fluffy pink nightgown and slippers, her cheeks are as rosy as the kid in that Vegemite ad.

'I…go…San Gimignano now.'

Why is it that when I'm trying to communicate in another language I just bastardise my own? Maria kisses me on both cheeks and shoos me out the door.

Going to the tourist information centre in the pretty main piazza, I find the bus station and board the service to San Gimignano, sitting behind the driver's seat. A short, swarthy man with a tanned, weathered face climbs on and cranks the engine.

Before the bus has even edged out of the car park the driver whips a packet of Diana cigarettes out of his trouser pocket and lights up. Mounted to his right I note a large No Smoking sign.

'Where you from?' he asks in stilted English as the bus weaves out of the city.

'Australia.'

'*Ah, sì? Canguri, canguri!* Boing, boing, boing!'

With child-like excitement, the driver lifts one hand off the steering wheel and moves it up and down in a bouncing motion, laughing at his own cleverness.

Before I have time to respond, a mobile phone rings with the tune of the Guns 'n' Roses song 'Sweet Child of Mine'. Memories of drunken karaoke sessions come flooding back and my legs move from side to side, involuntarily impersonating the swaying motion of Axl Rose.

I look at the other passengers. No one moves.

'*Porca miseria!*'

Muttering in annoyance, the driver switches his cigarette from his left hand to his right, which he uses to steer, then reaches into his other trouser pocket to produce the phone.

'*Pronto*,' he sings out above the drone of the engine and traffic. '*Sì, sì –*'

Talk about multi-skilling. Lucky we're on a straight highway. After watching the patchwork countryside flash by, I change buses at Siena before we finally pull up just outside an archway in the old town wall of San Gimignano.

The last time I saw Geoffrey, one of my dad's five younger brothers, was in 1997. Somewhat of a gypsy who has tried his hand at everything from grape-picking to shiatsu massage, he was roaming the world years earlier when he stopped in San Gimignano to inquire about seasonal work.

Charmed by Anna, the cheery woman behind the tourist information desk, he decided to stay. They married and have one daughter, Bianca, who's now in primary school. Geoffrey has one other daughter, from a previous relationship, who lives in Australia.

Establishing himself as an artist, Geoffrey exhibits in galleries in San Gimignano, Florence, Vienna and other European cities. Fluent in German, French and English, as well as her native Italian, Anna now works in a ceramics shop at the start of the tourist track through the old town.

Following Geoffrey's instructions, I wander through the historic arch into the old town centre and find the ceramics shop. Petite, with sparkling cornflower blue eyes and spectacles, Anna squeals when she sees me, enveloping me in a hug. Full of beans at any hour, she hasn't changed since I saw her three years ago in Australia. Her generous affection and enthusiasm are contagious.

At 1.30 pm my timing is perfect – in Italy most shops, barring restaurants, close at this time and don't re-open until 3 pm at the earliest, and more likely four. Anna and I jump in her little Fiat Panda and vroom down-hill to park near a modern apartment building.

Entering the first-floor apartment, I am greeted with a shriek from Bianca and another hug from Geoffrey, whose paintings line the walls of the living room. A Whiteley-esque abstract featuring Sydney Harbour makes me think of home for the first time since my arrival.

'*Salute*,' says Geoffrey, raising his glass of red wine in a toast as we sit down to eat roasted guinea fowl and fresh artichokes pan-fried with garlic and herbs.

'So, Penny, you're going to study Italian in Perugia, eh?' he continues. 'Why Italian? Why Italy?'

'The quality of life here just seems better, slower, more relaxed, healthier... you only have to look at the old men sitting around the piazzas for evidence,' I say.

'They're probably dirty old paedophiles!' roars Geoffrey.

Gags, good food and conversation and sleep are the focus of my week in San Gimignano. Rising early most mornings, I go for a walk around the walls of the old town, enjoying views of the much-photographed Tuscany, arriving home to have breakfast with Geoffrey, Bianca and Anna before Anna rushes off to work.

During the day I play with Bianca and Geoffrey paints until the lunch hour nears, when he stops to prepare simple, healthy, but delicious dishes: pasta with fresh tomato and basil sauce, or garlic and olive oil; Tuscan soup chunky with vegetables, beans and bread; roast chicken and salads of fresh tomato and thin slices of fennel.

When Anna arrives home, the table is already set with a colourful cotton cloth and napkins. Water and red wine, sourced from a local vineyard and stored in a jug covered with wicker, is always in the centre of the table. Used to stuffing a sandwich in my mouth for lunch on the go, I savour the ritual of mealtimes and the hours Italians set aside to eat and catch up with loved ones.

This is what I came to Italy for, I keep telling myself with a rising sense of confidence. Mealtimes with Geoffrey, Anna and Bianca – who speak in English for my benefit – are never dull. It takes a while to adjust to the fact that when Geoffrey and Anna raise their voices at one another and seem to be on the brink of divorce they are, in fact, just having a good old-fashioned debate, Italian-style – like the two men I saw in the bar on my first day in Rome. Arms flail wildly and the conversation is liberally sprinkled with '*Allora*, Well, then,' and '*Boh*'. And just when I think one of them is going to grab their pasta fork and stab the other, they start laughing like maniacs.

Pretty soon I become adept at kipping for a good hour after lunch with the rest of the family.

Just before 4 pm Anna returns to work, leaving Geoffrey, Bianca and me to entertain ourselves until dinner time approaches, when the kitchen again echoes with the sound of knives on chopping boards, bubbling water and pans sizzling with garlic. Eating around 9 pm, none of us is in bed before midnight.

At the end of my stay, dosed up on food and love, I kiss the San Gimignano crew goodbye and head back to Perugia, heartened that I have a family nest only three hours away.

On the bus, I try to use my pidgin Italian with the driver, who doesn't smoke or talk on his mobile phone but proudly shows me photos of a new-born baby I assume is his son, cradled in his wife's arms or propped beside a teddy bear and the family labrador. I look at the big-bellied, smiling driver and feel strangely humbled, thinking of home.

Working crazy hours to get pay rises and kudos, I had turned into someone I didn't like, never seeing enough of the people I cared about. This was not just because I didn't have enough time, but because in Sydney it's standard practice to not commit to anything until the last minute – just in case a better offer comes up.

Raised to believe a handshake is a handshake, at first I was annoyed at the social game until I learnt how to play it.

After my first week in Italy, I am starting to think most locals – from the bow-tied baristas to the bus drivers – are more satisfied with their lot, working with a healthy amount of pride and pleasure, without killing themselves to scale the career ladder. Endearingly, they also make time to be with loved ones.

'*Ciao*, Penn-ee!'

Sitting at the kitchen table with an evening television game show on low volume nearby, Maria greets me with two kisses before we both smile blankly at each other, lost for words.

I retreat to my room, where I see an attractive girl with long, straight, blonde hair sitting on the other bed.

'Hi! I'm Olivia,' she says with a broad Australian accent.

Lissom with grey-blue, almond-shaped eyes, I imagine Olivia has the locals in a lather every time she sashays out the door in her tight Lee jeans. She has done a month of the three-month course I am set to begin. At twenty-three, she's having a break from her life in Sydney and her model boyfriend, whose bare ripple-chested torso adorns his agency call card, propped up near Olivia's bed.

We strike up an easy rapport. Olivia already seems like a gal about town, so I accept her suggestion to have a late night *aperitivo* at the Rock Castle, a pub lurking down a dark lane not far away.

At 10.30 pm the cavernous space below the arched, medieval brick ceiling is almost empty. The DJ cranks up the music and my head is spinning with Shakira, vodka and Marlboro Lights when a group of three twenty-something Italians approach us.

One of them has his heart and crotch set on Olivia, who flirts with the ease of someone young and beautiful. I look around and suddenly feel like a dinosaur in the Matrix. At midnight the nightclub is groaning with young students following a strict dress code: tight and tiny.

We eventually stumble home, Olivia's sexy heels clicking on the stone pavement. It was too cold to wear the pair of summer slip-ons I brought, and the only covered shoes I have are chunky white running shoes. As a compromise, I had decided to make do with what I had, teaming a pair of black socks with my black Birkenstock sandals. Before I left the house I'd convinced myself it was cutting-edge and even if I wasn't, what did it matter? The new and improved me follows instinct – not fashion trends.

Staring at my Birkies at evening's end I rue my decision. I look like I just escaped from a beer hall in Munich. I sink into the overused mattress on my single bed and attempt to focus on the revolving ceiling.

What the hell am I doing here again?

Olivia is stretched out on her bed like Barbie when I creep out of our room feeling decidedly dusty. Damn her. No matter how hung-over or tired, I always wake too early.

I have become addicted to having a daily *caffè* in a bar because I love the way the baristas seem to be on familiar terms with their clientele.

I want to find a local haunt where *I'm* greeted with a friendly '*Ciao*' rather than the more courteous *salve* or *buongiorno*. I want to listen to the talk of the town.

I pass a few aesthetically unappealing bars before I walk down a steep side street off the main drag. The soft, cosy lighting behind a polished glass and timber facade catches my eye. Pushing open the door of Bar Papaia, I see a curved timber counter and a wall of shelves, which are stacked to the ceiling with dusty bottles of wine. A cheery Italian pop song wafts from a radio sitting on a counter behind the bar, where a fit, Bruce Willis-bald man wearing a friendly smile and a plastic neck brace stands idly. He's the first barman I've seen dressed in normal garb. With large, expressive eyes, wide shoulders and sculpted arms, he's also my idea of a Sort. Beside him a sullen-faced weed of a girl is busy making *panini*, stuffing bread rolls with milky white buffalo mozzarella, prosciutto and sliced tomatoes as red as Coco Chanel's lips.

I order a cappuccino that arrives tepid. Going from being a skinny latte princess to a full-cream queen is one thing (Italian bars do not offer skim milk, unless they are located in a fine hotel), but I like the milk in my coffee so hot it almost burns the roof of my mouth. Drat. How am I going to explain myself? I know I am a tourist, but I don't want to sound like one. Especially not in front of this rather cute barman with fetching biceps. I flick through my mini-dictionary. *Caldo* means hot.

'*Scusi*,' I raise my voice to get the barman's attention. 'But... *non caldo*.'

'No problem, I make it hot for you. You can speak English. I speak little,' he says shyly.

Engaging in small talk, I learn that Piero has been joint manager of Bar Papaia for ten years. He is studying English and has travelled extensively. *Fantastico*. I recall Geoffrey's words of warning that if I date a local he must have seen the big wide world outside Italy.

'Otherwise they think like this,' Geoffrey said, his hands motioning in a straight line from his head. 'Their mothers do everything for them: cooking, ironing, the lot. They are *mammoni* or mummy's boys.'

As I pay for my coffee and *cornetto* I wonder if Piero lives at home with his *mamma*, or if he is a liberated Italian who lives alone – or with a girlfriend? I leave the bar with a spring in my step. I think I've found my 'Cheers' in Perugia.

Back at Maria's, I find Jo has returned from her trip to Torino. To my relief, she says she and Maria will accompany me to the university to help me enrol; find an apartment and get my *Permesso di Soggiorno* (Permit to stay), which all non-European Union residents visiting Italy must obtain within eight days of arrival.

The *Università per Stranieri* is an apricoty-pink building with an impressive Renaissance facade. Students mill about outside smoking, gasbagging and handing out flyers. At the enrolment office, where I present my papers and receive a student card, I let Maria and Jo do all the talking. I smile happily, still experiencing a child-like fascination with the sound of a new accent and all things foreign. We walk around the corner to the *Polizia*, where a man as camp as Liberace is processing the *Permesso di Soggiorno* applications of a queue of foreigners.

Before I left Australia I got a study visa because the Italian embassy in Sydney stressed it was necessary as a part of my course enrolment. Obtaining the visa was a nightmare, because at the last minute I discovered I had to prove I had previously studied Italian. By chance, shortly before my 1997 trip to Italy, I did a one-month, once-a-week TAFE beginners course, which empowered me to distinguish fish from meat on a dinner menu. The TAFE college had since closed and I only just managed to convince a faceless bureaucrat to fax me a document validating my course attendance.

Feeling super-prepared, I hand over my passport and student card.

'To yous thees visa you must leeve the country and reeturn on tha second of May,' says the man behind the desk wearing a Marco nametag.

'What?' I try not to let panic overcome me as Jo and Maria negotiate with him. I stare at his hands, slicing the air expressively like an orchestral conductor.

Finally, a resolution to the visa problem caused by things I do not understand is found: I will renounce the study visa in writing and instead get my *Permesso* using a tourist visa for which I require none of the paperwork I collected in a mad panic in Sydney.

Thanking Marco, we march to another office that handles student accommodation, where Maria talks to a lump of a woman who could have done stunts for Mrs Doubtfire. The woman, Anna, takes us to look at an apartment in a street near the university and Maria's house.

Small, with terracotta floors, white walls and Spanish-style arches, the apartment has a functional kitchen and dining area, a tiny bathroom and a bedroom facing the street. The ceilings are so low even Bilbo Baggins would have to duck. With good natural light, the bedroom contains a single bed with some shelves above it and a tatty reclining armchair. Opening the French windows, I see a flowerbox crowded with brilliant red geraniums. It ain't the Ritz, but it's sweet.

'I'm keen,' I tell Jo, 'but how much is it?'

Jo chats to Anna and tells me that the room costs 326 euros plus minimal expenses, about 200 dollars cheaper than the monthly rent and bills for my studio flat in Rushcutters Bay.

I look at the narrow bed as I walk out of the room and think of the luxuriously big, firm new mattress I bought a few months before I decided to pack up and leave Australia. Sleeping – let alone anything else – is going to be a challenge in my new home.

But there's no time to dwell on such matters. Tomorrow, university begins.

Io sono Penelope

Call me a nerd, but after being absent from a classroom for twelve years, it's all I can do to stop running to my first day of the course dressed in my jimjams.

Pulling on some clothes I hope look student cool and not too try-hard, I walk to Palazzina Prosciutti, one of the campuses of the *Università per Stranieri*. I can't help but take umbrage at the word *stranieri*, which means 'foreigners' in Italian but sounds a little like 'strangers' in English. Why not just call it an international university? *Stranieri* seems so us versus them.

Grey and ugly, Palazzina Prosciutti looks like a bomb shelter and the inside isn't much better. Devoid of any sign of human touch or warmth, paint peels off the walls and classrooms brim with messy arrangements of chairs and graffitied tables. I wasn't expecting 'Happy Days' but even the *Fame* kids would be burning their legwarmers in protest against the lack of ambience.

I find the right classroom, plonk myself in a chair and sneak curious glances at the students around me. Five minutes after 9 am, a keg of a woman walks in and drops her bag on the desk at the front of the classroom. Signora Fausta Alunno begins my first, two-hour grammar lesson. With a hint of moustache failing to sully her pleasant face, Signora Alunno begins speaking in rapid Italian. If she speaks English, she's not going to let on. Trying not to feel overwhelmed, I cling to words I recognise until we are asked to repeat simple phrases.

'*Io sono Penelope*,' I say self-consciously when it is my turn. I've decided to use my full name because if I pronounce Penny incorrectly I risk saying I am a type of pasta, *penne*, or a penis, *pene*.

Asked to declare where we hail from, I listen to my classmates give their answers: Tanzania, Korea, Switzerland, The Netherlands, Germany, China, Japan. Then it's my turn.

'*Vengo dall'Australia.*'

The same response is given by a tall, dark and devilishly handsome man who tucks his long legs awkwardly beneath the table-topped chair. We acknowledge one another with a smile.

An hour later a bell rings and we flood outside for a fifteen-minute break. In the queue to get an espresso at the uni bar, I stand behind two tall African women wearing iridescent smocks and headwear who dwarf four Korean nuns in grey and white habits ahead of them.

Nicki, a New Zealander, tells me she enrolled because her boyfriend, Gabriele, was born and raised in Perugia. They met in London and now they are staying with Gabriele's parents for a short time until they figure out what they want to do next.

'Why are you here?' Nicki asks, looking at me with interest.

'I always wanted to learn Italian and I was feeling restless at home, so I decided to throw my job in and come here for a break,' I say, hoping I sound adventurously flippant.

At 11 am we file in for a three-hour Italian exercise lesson with Signor Giovanni Rossi, a chimpish man who arrives ten minutes late to fill the room with putrid body odour. I notice our teacher wears the same jumper for the next three days. The afternoon flies as we practise simple sentences, but by two o'clock my head feels like lead. I walk back to Maria's after class and chat to the lanky Australian, Charlie, a doctor who used to live a few blocks from me in Sydney before we both left home. He got a job in Ireland, but when it fell through due to visa problems he decided to join his friend Simonne, also an Australian doctor, to do the course for fun.

That night Jo asks me to have dinner as it's her last night in Perugia. I'm grateful for the distraction from studying. Everyone keeps telling me the weather will soon be *caldo* but for now the May air is so *freddo* my nipples are constantly like bullets and I rue following the advice of my sisters to discard extra layers that were weighing down my backpack. I borrow a coat from Maria before Jo and I find the hole-in-the-wall trattoria Lo Scalino.

As we walk into the slightly dank but still homey establishment, I feel as though I am a talent scout for a David Lynch film. Cheesy cloths cover the simple tables with wooden chairs while a TV blares overhead. An old woman wearing a white apron and chef's hat kneads dough on a board. Her sagging bosom swings so low it threatens to hit the board at any moment. As she places a pizza in the wood-fired oven, she looks up. Some of her bottom teeth are either missing or rotting.

My frustration mounts as we stand and wait for what feels like twenty minutes before the lone, grumpy waiter takes us to a corner table and slaps down the menus. Venting my grievances to Jo, she laughs at my impatience, worsened by my rumbling stomach. When my blood sugar level is low, I feel capable of murder.

'Never, *ever* think you can rush an Italian. Everything is done *piano, piano* – slowly, slowly,' she says. 'Besides, Italians don't offer the level of service we're used to. They do whatever the hell they please.'

As Jo chatters away I try not to glower at the waiter, who seems far happier to talk to the locals surrounding our table. Finally he approaches to take our order.

It bugs me that he seems to treat us with less attentiveness because we come from another country. As he puts our pizzas on our table I decide to give him the benefit of the doubt.

'*Scusami, come ti chiami?* Excuse me, what is your name?'

Dropping his eyes to study me, the waiter looks amused before responding.

'*Mi chiamo Emilio.*'

Ecstatic at my progress, I continue. '*Io sono Penelope.*'

Emilio looks at me expectantly and my early menopause comes into play. I experience a hot flush twenty years too soon and my hands go all clammy.

'*Sei Greca?* Emilio says with apparent interest.

Having heard the word *Grecia* in class, I realise he thinks I am Greek due to the mythological significance of the name.

'No, Australia.'

'*Davvero? Che bello!* Really? How beautiful!' he responds, offering me a smile.

I am wondering what to stutter next when Jo returns from the bathroom.

'What did you do?' she asks, perplexed by Emilio's personality change.

Breaking into Italian, Jo chats to Emilio and learns that the woman shovelling pizza into the wood-fired oven nearby is his sister, Letizia. Together they have run the business for thirty-two years.

Merry from *vino rosso*, as Jo and I head for the door, I turn to face Emilio, who chats to a table of locals nearby.

'*Ciao, Emilio. Grazie!*' I sing out.

'*Buonasera, Penelope! A presto!*' he replies cheerily.

'What does *a presto* mean?' I ask Jo as we start to walk home.

'It means "see you soon".' she says. 'Looks like you've got a new mate.'

Saying goodbye to Jo the next morning, the dull feeling of loss that washes over me is compounded when I have to move to my new home down the road.

'*Grazie mille,*' I say, hugging Maria's small frame in the kitchen and suddenly wishing I could stay put. Even though we can't comprehend each other's languages, we have built a close rapport via hand gestures and eye contact. I want to stay and, as my language improves, discover more about her life.

That night, after class, I retreat to my new room to try to create a home from my backpack. I hang up my clothes in the wobbly wardrobe and place a bright scarf over the worn Jason recliner, which I drag near the window.

Making the bed with the sheets given to me by Mrs Doubtfire, who lives in the apartment upstairs, I ignore a sense of gloom upon spying the grey, prison-style blanket with a large cigarette-burn hole in it. Again, I try not to pine for my fabulous queen-size mattress in my parents' garage.

I place a few polaroids of family and friends on the shelf above my bed. Too sentimental at the best of times, I decided not to carry many memories of Australia with me. I don't want to miss people and start ruminating about issues I want to forget about for now.

I love my own space, content to fritter away endless hours on my own. But it occurs to me that – even if I wanted to – I don't have anyone to hang out with. Feeling detached from everything, I lie on my narrow bed and drown out the sound of cars and Vespas throttling below my window with my Discman.

Instinctively seeking routine to feel more settled, each morning before uni starts I go for rambling walks around the small historic town centre, taking in each new scene: smoke curling out of bar doors that swing open and shut during the breakfast rush; street sweepers combing Corso Vannucci; pigeons sleeping in nooks of the ancient city walls.

I've become friends with Nicki, the Kiwi in my class, and I have to stop myself from hugging her when she casually invites me over for lunch at the family home of Gabriele, her Italian squeeze.

Small and slim, Nicki has been whingeing that she's ballooning like Anna-Nicole Smith because she can't resist eating every mouthful of the home-cooked meals dished out at the family table at lunch and dinner. Sick of cooking for myself, I can't think of anything better than being fed by an Italian *mamma*. Better still, it's Sunday – the traditional family lunch day in Italy.

Sitting in my Jason recliner the following Sunday, I look over the geraniums in my window box to see Nicki and Gabriele wolf-whistling from the street below. Hopping into their car, I remember how Italians change personality the moment they are behind the wheel. They drive like Fangio, cursing at pedestrians and other drivers. It's no wonder around eighteen people die in car accidents in Italy each day.

We hoon out of the centre of town until we reach a two-storey brick farmhouse. Perched on the edge of a mountain, it overlooks a vegetable patch, chook shed and the sprawling valley below. Gabriele introduces me to his parents: Vincento, a small, fit man who spends his retirement gardening, and Severena, a little, cuddly woman wearing a floral frock and white apron.

Smiling and speaking words that wash over me, they motion me to sit down at the long table in the kitchen. I stare longingly at a plump chicken browning nicely on a rotisserie mounted above a coal fire nearby.

'This morning it was running around the garden,' says Gabriele with mock despair.

Severena fusses near the oven, draining and flipping home-made fettuccine into a large fry pan in which freshly picked wild asparagus sizzles.

I tuck into my pasta hungrily, savouring the full-bodied flavour of the pasta and the asparagus.

Turning to each other and Gabriele for encouragement, Nicki and I try to communicate, before embarrassment gags us.

'*Piano, piano,*' smiles Severena.

If one more person says '*piano, piano*' to me, I think silently, I am going to drop a baby grand on them.

Marinated with garden-grown sage, lemon and garlic, the chicken is delicious. I greedily ask for seconds before we eat *insalata mista* with our hands and Gabriele produces a tart he made hours earlier, filled with stewed orchard prunes. Squeezing in a slice, I realise how my eating habits are changing. At home I'd avoid salad dressings and follow the no-carb diet like every other bland, weight-watching chick I know. Now I'm pouring good olive oil over every salad and eating pasta most days. My love handles don't seem to have grown and I have more energy. Thinking of meals I enjoyed at San Gimignano, I realise Italians tend to eat simple and wholesome food, which reduces cravings for snacks. But when they do succumb to sweets, they seem to savour them as if they could be the last treat of their life – with an air of guilt-free bliss I envy.

As I pull out the chocolates I brought for the occasion, Severena begins clearing the table. Before, during and after the meal I notice Vincento and Gabriele don't raise a finger to help Severena, who seems to accept her role as cook and server.

'She waits on them hand and foot,' says Nicki in reference to Vincento, Gabriele and Marcello, one of Gabriele's two brothers who still lives at home at the age of thirty.

'Yesterday Marcello had a headache and Severena spent three hours worrying,' she adds, rolling her eyes.

Refusing to accept our offer to help clean up the kitchen, Severena takes off her apron and grabs a jacket.

'We're going asparagus picking,' says Gabriele, not realising how excited I am at the prospect. Of *course* we are going asparagus picking, because we're in Italy and it's all about skipping through fields in search of green things that will resurface later on our plates.

A short car ride brings us to a field full of thick bramble. We arm ourselves with white plastic supermarket bags and I follow Gabriele's lead, prodding bushes with a stick. I have never seen wild asparagus and presumed it would be easy to find, sprouting abundantly. Instead one has to first search for the nettle-like plant and then hunt around in the vicinity for a lone spear which blends in with the vegetation.

Cross-eyed twenty minutes later, I am eyeing the three asparagus spears in my bag when Mother Nature saves me. As it starts to rain heavily, we run back through fields strewn with red poppies to the car. Severena hands me her plastic bag and I am impressed to see it is weighed down by at least thirty spears.

When the weather clears, Nicki and Gabriele and I go for a stroll. As they walk ahead, I watch with envy as she tucks her hand into his back pocket and they chat as if they are the only inhabitants on earth.

Later, as the car winds through the dark countryside, I am suddenly ten years old again, sitting in the back seat beside my sisters and reaching for my mum's warm hand in the front seat as Dad drives along endless corrugated dirt roads leading to our country home. I wait for a pang of homesickness but it doesn't arrive.

I am more isolated than I have ever been, yet somehow I don't feel lonely. Stimulated by all things foreign, and slowly making new friends, I have barely thought of the life I left behind.

'*Buongiorno, cara,*' says Ivana, the matronly, bottle-blonde at the *pasticceria* the next morning, straightening out the creases in her white apron. Without a word she grabs my preferred loaf of grain bread, cuts it in half and deftly wraps it in brown paper. Grinning thanks, I fumble over my change, feeling stupidly happy.

In one small gesture she has made me feel like a local.

Returning home from a monotonous class with Signora Alunno, I find a note slipped under the door from Olivia, who I find flaked out on her bed at Maria's, recovering from a 5 am finish at a *discoteca* on the outskirts of town.

'In two weeks I'm going to Lake Como for a week, so if you want, you can take over my bed,' she says huskily. 'When I get back the other bed will be free, so you can just stay on. I've already spoken to Maria about it – she's cool.'

Thrilled, I find Maria sitting at the kitchen table, reading a newspaper. She envelops me in a huge hug and pushes a chocolate into my hand.

I pluck up the courage to tell Anna, the landlady, that I am already leaving, explaining my rent will be halved and I want to try to speak more Italian with Maria. I feel guilty because I had told Anna I'd be staying three months, but it's a dog-eat-dog world – and this is my opportunity to learn how to be more of a terrier. I tend to say yes to things I don't want to do, or worse, instinctively apologise for the most banal things – from passing through a door before someone, to coughing on the phone. Enough already. I will not say sorry when I think it's unnecessary again.

Operation John Howard has begun.

Hidden in a crumbling building just off the main drag of town, the morning produce market in Perugia has a rainbow-coloured range of fresh fruit and vegetables sold by craggy personalities who look like they double as scarecrows when they knock off work for the afternoon. Throughout Italy, fresh food markets spill out of piazzas in each town, selling fruit, vegies, meats, cheeses and seafood plus a random range of homemade products, clothing and footwear.

Busting to do my weekly food shop in the rustic ambience of the markets, my resolve crumbles as quickly as the stall-holders toss produce onto their scales.

'*Mi dispiace, non capisco,* I'm sorry, I don't understand,' I mutter, feeling vulnerable because I can't grasp the prices they bark at me. Chickening out, I head to a large supermarket near Perugia's train station. It's not as romantic as the market – but at least everything has a price tag.

Even at the supermarket I am flummoxed by the strangeness of everything. I stand for five minutes marvelling at the bizarre breakfast range, from 'Fitness' flakes with chunks of chocolate to every type of biscuit and cake imaginable and the omnipresent Nutella. I wouldn't be surprised if the Italians flavour toothpaste with the gooey stuff.

At the fruit and vegetable section I watch people around me and learn the ropes: I put on a plastic glove to put my selected goods in a clear plastic bag. Noting a code number written on a small sign near each item, I place my item on electronic scales and punch in the code. The weighed price prints out onto a barcode sticker, which I slap on the bag.

I weigh some bananas and apples and then grab some pears. Perhaps they are out of season, but reading the pears' price sticker, I can't help thinking my favourite fruit is far too expensive. I throw in an extra one before I knot the bag up. After all, everyone else around me is sampling the odd piece of fruit. What's a measly pear between friends? The deli section bustles with happiness like a real life Woolworths advert. The deliciously red legs of prosciutto are too tempting to pass so I get a small parcel before taking my heaving basket to the cash register and waiting patiently for the uninterested teller to scan my goods.

My eyes wander absently, observing the tight jeans of the woman behind me. In her early fifties, the same age as my mother, she's tanned and trim and showing a hint of her bright orange G-string, just like Kylie. My mother is trim too, but a G-string wearer she is not.

'*Signorina, signorina! Hai sbagliato –*'

I turn to hear the man at the cash register speaking to me. In his hand is the bag of pears. With horror, I realise the goods are weighed a second time at the cash register. I had assumed they'd just scan the price and drop the goods in a bag. A stream of angry Italian comes out of the man's mouth and I feel the eyes of the supermarket swivel in my direction.

'*Non capisco.*' Panicking, I feign ignorance as the man rants, until finally the woman in the vacuum-sealed pants turns to me.

'You mast weigh everytheeng properlee end poot the steecker on the bag,' she says, firmly but kindly.

I look sheepishly at the cash register man, who hrmphs and drops my pears from a great height into a plastic bag. I pay the balance and flee.

Charlie laughs at my idiocy when we meet later that afternoon.

'What *were* you thinking?' he demands.

'I don't know what overcame me,' I say, embarrassed at my erratic behaviour. 'I've never nicked a thing in my life, not even as a kid. It's weird, when you are in a foreign place you do stupid things you normally wouldn't because…you just feel free.'

'Yeah, I was thinking of rolling the local bank tomorrow,' retorts Charlie.

One afternoon Charlie, Nicki, Simonne, Gabriele and I drive to the nearby town of Gubbio to watch the *Corsa dei Ceri*, which translates as the race of the candles. This annual religious event, Gabriele explains, involves three teams of men representing rival saints who must lug fifteen-metre wooden candles weighing four hundred kilograms from the bottom of the town to a church at the top of a nearby hill.

Buying Peroni beer to keep cool on a summery May day, we wander the streets absorbing the mounting pre-race chaos. Sweating profusely under the midday sun in bright polyester uniforms, the competitors look like Melbourne Cup rejects. They swig from beer and wine bottles and smoke merrily before disappearing into three stable-like huts.

Minutes later, the three sets of wooden doors burst open and the teams emerge carrying the enormous candles sideways. Grunting and groaning, the men ease and push the candles, each topped with a figurine of the team saint, into a vertical position. A referee's whistle sounds and they are off and running – and we are drowning in a sea of human colour and sweat. Caught in the stampede tailing the race, we wind up hilly streets until, claustrophobic and exhausted, we abandon the idea of reaching the top and leap onto a small embankment to let the crowds pass.

Waiting until the human flow eases to a trickle, we get down off our perch and return to town, quickly drunk in the heat on Italian beer and the madcap festival spirit.

On the way home, we stop at a roadside trattoria where our young, good-looking waiter goes to great lengths to explain the Umbrian delicacies on the menu, including the house speciality: tagliatelle pasta with truffles. Italians are famous for their passion for food but I had no idea that they were so knowledgeable about the produce of their region. Everyone, it seems, can rattle off a list of their local cheeses, grains, meats and vegetables.

Two large steaming bowls of tagliatelle are placed before us and the waiter takes each of our plates and serves generous amounts, all the while bantering in Italian to Gabriele, whose presence, I suspect, guarantees us far better service than we *stranieri* may have received alone.

'*Buon appetito*,' says the waiter, commanding Charlie's attention long after he has left the table.

While Signora Alunno grows on me as much as Signor Rossi repels me, my favourite teacher is Daniela, the foxy forty-something woman who conducts our once-weekly *linguistico* session at the main university campus.

Arriving in class wearing a range of funky garb – from an Olivia Newton John 'Let's Get Physical'-style headband to tight jeans that show off her lithe figure, Daniela always manages to hold our attention despite the fact her class is the hardest. Sitting with headphones on, we must endure streams of Italian and repeat it, not only stretching our abysmal grammar but pronouncing the words with precision.

Though we call her by her first name, Daniela chooses to refer to us by country:

'*Australia, come va? Nuova Zelanda, tutto bene?*'

Struggling to keep straight faces, Nicki, Charlie and I watch the bodies around us lean over their desks in concentration.

A Libyan optometrist is doing the course because he is trying to expand his business exports to Italy, while three Chinese men are learning Italian to assist with their opera-singing careers. Everyone seems to have a sensible reason for attending school. Not a day goes by without Charlie, Nicki, Gabriele, Simonne and

I lamenting the fact that we have no idea what we want to do when the course ends. I take comfort from the fact that they are also in limbo.

That evening, I shower and head to Bar Papaia nervously, having accepted a dinner invitation from Piero, the cute barman who has become a friendly acquaintance. Admittedly it's a group dinner, but I can't help but feel there's a bit of healthy flirtation going on that could lead somewhere. Needing moral support, I ask Charlie and Simonne to come for a pre-dinner *aperitivo*.

Pushing open the bar door, I am reminded why I am attracted to Piero. Dressed casually in jeans and a blue shirt, he exudes warmth, kissing me on both cheeks. Charlie and Simonne arrive and offer their verdict as I follow Piero out the door.

'Jump him,' says Simonne, giving me an exaggerated thumbs up.

'If you don't, I will,' warns Charlie.

I hop in the passenger seat beside Piero as two other female students, an American and a German, hop in the back.

'Is this a new car?' I ask, noting the unmistakable smell of the upholstery.

'Yes, but it's not my car, it's Roberta's, my girlfriend,' he says.

My schoolgirl crush implodes. Damn. I knew he was too spunky to be single. He's just a good flirt. Looking at the young women in the back seat, I wonder if Roberta knows her boyfriend has a harem of admirers.

Piero turns off the highway that skirts along Lago Trasimeno, the lake located about thirty minutes west of Perugia. We arrive at dusk and the lake shimmers under the last rays of sun as we pull up at a rustic brick building. With beautiful terracotta flower boxes and manicured lawns, it looks more private home than restaurant.

Inside the entrance is a small room almost entirely filled by a long table where a large group of people are seated. After Piero kisses the others hello, I take a seat opposite him and try to concentrate on the conversation circulating around me.

Plate after plate comes out of the kitchen for the next two hours until finally we charge our glasses with *limoncello* – a strong liquor made from sugar and lemon – and Piero makes a toast to friends and foreigners, looking at me with an affection I try hard not to confuse with attraction.

Back home, I pack up my things ready to move back to Maria's in the morning before switching on the TV to brainwash myself with Italian. Soon I am hooked on a program that is a cross between 'Perfect Match' and 'It's A Knockout!' From what I can gather, the show features couples who have split up – but one of them wants to get back together. The 'Wooer' is given a brief period of time to try to verbally convince the 'Ex' why they should still be together.

In the final scene, the Ex stands on a mock train station platform and is given one minute to decide the outcome of the relationship before a small train painted like Thomas the Tank Engine chugs towards the platform – with the Wooer on board.

If the Ex decides they want to go back to their partner, they dramatically hit a signal 'yes', which brings the train to a grinding halt, allowing the Wooer to leap off and into their waiting arms. If unconvinced, however, the Ex hits the 'no' signal and watches as the train, carrying a wallowing Wooer, shunts slowly past the platform and disappears into a dark tunnel.

Lying in bed, I think of old boyfriends I'd like to send into an endless black hole before imagining Piero on the train, imploring me with those beautiful eyes.

School drop-out

Before I left Australia I was hunting for a small unit and preparing to apply for a First Home Buyer's loan. Now it's just me and my backpack, which doesn't have an ensuite bathroom but has a fabulous extra I love repeating aloud: expanding gussets. Yes folks, with a quick tug of two side zips, my pack expands from an average sixty-five litres to a mighty eighty litres. That's enough room to squeeze in two steak knife sets and a blender.

In addition to a childhood spent moving house, I dragged my accumulating adult possessions between rental properties in Sydney, Newcastle, Sydney, Perth, Canberra and then Sydney again, pestering friends and family with utes for help. With my backpack, changing addresses has never been so easy. And though my body strains slightly when I haul it on, my spirits immediately lift. Even if I'm not going far, I always have the sensation that I'm bound for an exotic new land. Without waiting for anything or anyone.

Walking through the front door of Maria's feels like slipping on a pair of Ugg boots. It's a bit daggy to be living with a granny, but I feel so comfy I don't give a damn.

My joy soon fades when Maria, showing me to my room, intimates through sign language that, while I can use the second fridge in the corridor, the kitchen is off-limits to renting students.

'Okay, *nessun problema*,' I say, feeling sick in the stomach at the idea of washing fruit or salad ingredients under a bathroom tap. Each morning Luca, Maria's husband, locks himself in one of the bathrooms and the house reverberates with the sound of him hoicking into a basin.

Dumping my bag in my room, I return to the kitchen to try to speak to Maria, desperate to use more Italian. While encouraged by the fact my written English is becoming erratic, surely a sign Italian grammar is starting to lodge in my brain, two months of university has flown by without any obvious benefits. Progress is being sabotaged by snowballing factors: Signora Alunno's class has quadrupled, leading to class protests and general chaos, and Signor Rossi has been away for two weeks because his mother is sick – but there has been no replacement. In Italy, that would just be *too* organised.

Increasingly frustrated, Nicki, Charlie and I go less and less, enjoying day trips around Umbria and memorising the drinks list at Birraio, our favourite brewery and wine bar, which offers a breathtaking sunset view over the Perugian countryside.

Getting sloshed in Italy makes me feel like a freak. I rarely see a local drunk. Ordering a second bottle of wine between four people, I often catch the waiter looking down his nose at we vulgar *stranieri*. According to my aunt Anna, since Italians grow up with wine on the table, they don't treat it like the forbidden fruit as populations in many Western countries do.

'We don't drink to get drunk like you Aussies, Yanks and Poms,' she told me at lunch one day as she added a dash of water into her glass of red wine – to me, like icing a chocolate cake with green pepper sauce. I later read a newspaper report with statistics showing that young Italians drink the least compared with other EU countries.

I soon find another unlikely drinking buddy in the surly waitress at Bar Papaia. By going to the bar each morning, I slowly prune the thorns off Sanja, a Croatian who fled to Italy in 1992 as civil war tore apart her homeland.

Meeting for the first time outside the confines of Bar Papaia one balmy summer's night, we buy some beer and sit on the steps of the *duomo* amid the throng of students and tourists.

With next to no English, Sanja speaks in Italian, which delights and confuses me at once. Repeating things often for my benefit, she reveals that she lived in her hometown, Split, without electricity or gas for ten months as residents bunkered down to avoid being bombed. Fleeing to Perugia, where she had a relative, she found the job at Bar Papaia, despite the fact she did not speak a word of Italian. Although she was on the verge of entering university in Croatia, she put off studies in Italy because just coping in a strange land, learning the language and building friendships, exhausted all her energy. She told me she enjoys the human contact at Bar Papaia and dreams of opening a tour business operating between Croatia and Italy.

Trying to make light of her previously snappy behaviour, she explains that she has just split with her Italian boyfriend of six years, with whom she was living. 'I have to start my whole life over again,' she says determinedly.

Walking home, I see Sanja scowl at the window display in a boutique, where the mannequins are dressed with khaki army print pants.

'Every day, *every day*, I saw that outfit,' she says, her voice filling with hate.

Kissing Sanja goodbye on both cheeks, I watch as she walks away down the hill, lighting another Marlboro Red that glows like a firefly in the dark. She's the same age as me, but I can't begin to contemplate the hardships she has endured in her life. Spending time with her is a breath of fresh air and a slap in the face – reminding me to count my blessings.

My diligent studying is beginning to pay off. Practising Italian with Sanja and Piero is resulting in small bursts of communication that bring ridiculous amounts of joy.

Hitting the books at home one day, I feel suddenly exhausted. As if it wasn't hard enough coping with present tenses, the past is a grammatically hairier place to be. Exasperated, I stand up suddenly from my desk for a break. Taking one long stride, I realise I have lost blood circulation in one leg from sitting down too long. With nothing to grab onto, I collapse like a gum tree in the centre of the room.

Hearing my shriek, Maria comes in and looks at my crumpled body with alarm before ascertaining I am somewhat sheepish but alive.

'*La mia gamba dorme.* My leg sleeps,' I say, telling her not to worry as I assess the minor damage – a jarred ankle.

Maria beckons me to follow her, so I hobble along the corridors, past the rooms of the two timid Polish girls who keep their door closed at all times, a tall earnest German boy and Michele, the chubby Italian *ragazzo*, until I reach her bedroom. Luca, who doesn't work and, when not eating food cooked by Maria, seems to loiter out in the piazza, sleeps in a room hidden just off the lounge room.

Pushing me gently into a sitting position on her bed, she hands me a bandage. I look at a framed photograph of a smiling young man on what looks to be his graduation day.

'*Chi è?* Who is that?' I ask, pointing to the photo.

In an instant her eyes grow misty. I hear the word *nipote*, which means 'nephew'. Jo once told me something about Maria's nephew dying of heart complications at a young age. Maria has no children of her own.

As the tears slide down Maria's cheeks, I feel helpless, wishing I could offer words of comfort. I say the first phrase I can cobble together in my head.

'*Maria, hai una famiglia – sei la nonna per tutti qui a casa.* Maria, you have a family – you are the grandmother for everyone here at home.'

Looking up at me with a tear-streaked face, Maria accepts a big hug, her small frame only reaching my shoulders. I feel her whole body heave a sigh and I struggle to hold her weight as my ankle throbs.

Impatient for my study injury to heal, I wait a few weeks before persuading Sanja to take me to the local pool one searing Sunday.

We meet at Sandri, the most elegant and oldest café in town. As I watch the waiter in a snappy red bolero jacket make my *caffè macchiato*, I gawk at the ceiling, decorated with colourful paintings like a mini Sistine Chapel, and the intricate homemade chocolates and sweets that fill the beautiful, polished teak and glass cabinets lining the long, narrow bar.

When Sanja and I arrive at the pool, nestled on the top of a hill on the outskirts of town, I hide my disappointment. Through the fence I can see that it is only twenty-five metres long. Call that a pool? Every second Australian country town has a council-run Olympic pool, but I will soon learn that *piscina* in Italy means a privately run pond that costs at least four times more to use.

Paying 8 euros, about 15 dollars, to get in, I raise my eyebrows again when Sanja tells me it is compulsory to wear a cap when in the water. Why are the law-flouting Italians sticklers for this particular rule? I am glad I brought my Speedo cap when the woman at reception motions to give me what looks like a blue and white striped life saver's hat shrunk three times in size.

Out by the pool, Madonna blasts from a stereo placed at the feet of a busty blonde wearing a barely-there bikini. Prancing up and down, her deep brown skin glistens with sweat as she barks orders at the aqua-aerobic class wading before her in the water.

Strewn across the all-concrete pool surrounds are tanned bodies adorned in itsy-bitsy costumes and big-brand sunglasses. There are more guys than girls and they all seem to pay just as much attention to waxing.

Excited at having my first swim since I left Perth, I slide into the pool immediately and start cutting up a lane. Just before I reach the end I see a body approaching directly in front of me. I keep going, assuming the imbecile will correct themselves at the last minute.

Thwack. My hand hits the body, belonging to a man with a Merv Hughes moustache who shakes his right hand in furious sign language I understand to be 'What the fuck are you doing?' And then the obvious dawns on me: like driving, I have to swim to my right. Apologising profusely, I avoid three near collisions before I get out of the pool almost an hour later, high on adrenalin.

Soccer fever grips Italy as the World Cup swings into action. If a bar or shop lacks a television, one soon appears from nowhere to be plugged in haphazardly, often dragged onto the footpath outside for all to see. For the next few weeks of World Cup fever I get a first-hand glimpse of the Italians' reputation for being *pazzi*, crazy, for soccer.

When Charlie, Simonne and I go to a pub to watch Italy draw with Mexico, my eardrums almost split when the home team nets a goal. While the level of play is brilliant, I'm more entertained by footage of the Italian coach, leaping up and down and reinventing the Italian code of gesticulation as he screams abuse and praise at his men, who seem more worried about their hairdos than the score.

Walking home to the sound of beeping car horns, I see an open-top Volkswagen speed past, the two male backseat passengers on their feet beating wooden spoons on the bottom of overturned saucepans. A traffic cop nearby turns a blind eye to the fact they have no seat belts on and the car is being driven like a Ferrari.

The afternoon South Korea knocks Italy out of the World Cup, Perugia fills with an eerie silence. The streets empty quickly and when I walk to Bar Papaia after class to see Sanja, a soccer freak, her stony face is that of the girl I met two months ago.

Inside the bar is a woman with a neck brace, just like Piero had the first time we met. Motorbike incidents in Italy seem common: I often see someone wearing a telltale neck brace. Sanja says the woman was riding her *motorino* home during the lunch hour when she had an accident. She was following a car driven by a man listening to the World Cup on the radio and failed to brake in time when Italy scored a goal – the driver had slammed on the brakes and got out of the car to do a street dance.

Later that evening I join Sanja and her friend, Rita, for a pizza. Rita complains of feeling bruised and sore. Maybe she's had a motorbike incident. I am alarmed to learn she is midway through a liposuction treatment for which she has paid a ridiculous sum.

'I have a problem here,' she says, screwing up her doll-pretty face and indicating her thighs which are naturally curvy but by no means unsightly. Trying to suppress my anger, I try to tell her she is beautiful and womanly – and how I think men prefer voluptuous women to haggard stick figures.

Sucking on a cigarette, Rita listens politely before pushing her half-eaten pizza aside. I want to frogmarch her to the beach on a scorching summer's day in Australia, where the full range of the human body is on display – including cuddly women who walk around oblivious to the orange-peel skin that coats their bums and thighs.

I've already noted a plethora of Italian TV shows focusing on health and beauty, while game shows typically feature young girls who look like dancing hookers. I am beginning to think Italy's fixation with looking good ranges from extreme to dangerous. Indeed, Rita is the first of many Italian women I will meet who are surgically *rifatte*, or redone, in various ways.

The Prime Minister, Silvio Berlusconi, sets no example. Eavesdropping on a conversation in Bar Papaia one day, through Sanja's patient translation, I am amused to learn that his new youthful appearance has been attributed to the fact he went under the scalpel. In Italy, appearance, wealth and success are admired and celebrated as a sign of power and strength.

I chew on my pizza in silence, staring at Rita's thighs in dismay.

Three weeks before my uni course is due to end, I quit going to class. The June heat makes it impossible to concentrate and our class has swollen to more than fifty distracted students.

I'm going to stay with Uncle Geoffrey in San Gimignano for a week before meeting two girlfriends from home to travel in Croatia and northern Italy, which fills my calendar until the end of July. But then the confusion begins.

I want to stay in Italy, because everything still feels so raw and exciting, and I fantasise about the day I will be able to communicate on my own terms with an Italian. But I am torn by the idea of leaving Perugia, which now feels like home and where I have made firm friends like Sanja and Piero, to head to Rome, though that was always my planned destination.

Location aside, my tourist visa has almost expired. When I re-enter Italy after the Croatian trip, legally I'll have to leave Italy every three months and return on a new tourist visa – until I find a more convenient solution.

As a stop-gap, Sanja suggests I go and pay a small fee to get a health sanitation card which will allow me to work in bars or cafés in Italy. So, in stifling heat, I trudge downhill to the hospital, which houses the sanitation office. Inside, a woman at a clerical desk hands me a form to fill out. Apart from the name and address, the rest is a mystery. I tick the 'no' box beside a list of words which are obviously diseases and sign it with the date, hoping I haven't just signed up to trial the new naturopathic version of Viagra.

I'm called to another room, where a sweaty man who looks like he wishes he was on a resort island motions for me to take a seat opposite him. He scans my form for a second before looking at me without interest.

'*Fammi vedere le tue mani*,' he says, holding out his hands to demonstrate he wants to inspect my hands.

My heart sinks. One of my worst habits is chewing the skin around my fingernails. Like most of my vices, it's one I picked up from my dad. When I am stressed I tend to chew my fingers more, without even realising I am doing it. Right now, trying to make decisions about what to do post-Perugia, my fingers are nibbled red raw.

I hold out my hands palms upwards, which raises no reaction, but the moment I flip my hands over the man snaps to attention, his forehead creasing with alarm. A stream of negative-sounding Italian slips from his mouth.

Blushing, I blurt out words such as 'stress' and 'tired' and chant '*Nessun problema*'.

Uttering more unintelligible words, he pauses to look deep into my eyes before stamping my papers with a perplexed shake of his head at the dodgy *straniera* before him.

Wondering why the sanitation test wasn't more rigorous, I walk happily back up the hill to Bar Papaia to show Sanja my accredited document.

When I return home that afternoon, Maria grabs me by the hand as I walk in the door.

'*Ti va un gelato?*' she asks, grabbing her handbag off her bed.

She's asking me if I want to accompany her outside to *fare una passeggiata* – or take a walk – and get an ice-cream. In Italy, especially on a Sunday, the streets fill from around 3.30 pm as lunch winds up and people enjoy a ritual stroll to digest and chat some more.

I take Maria by the arm and we wander up to the town centre, where she takes me to a *gelateria* I have never seen before, hidden in a back street.

Spoilt for choice, I ponder for five minutes before choosing three flavours: *nocciola*, hazelnut, *fico*, fig, and *Bacio*, which literally means 'kiss' and refers to the famous Baci chocolate made by the local Perugina factory, now owned by Nestlé.

Eyeballing each other over our mountainous cones, Maria and I are slurping happily when we bump into Fabrizio, a friend of Piero's, on the street. Sanja told me he is a bit keen on me, but I am not fussed and neither, it seems, is Maria.

'*Non è intelligente, non mi piace.* He's not intelligent, I don't like him,' she says moments after Fabrizio goes on his way.

'*Perché non ho ragazzo? Perché non sono fortuna?* Why don't I have boyfriend? Because I am not luck?' I ask Maria jokingly.

'*Perché le donne intelligente fanno paura agli vomini,*' she retorts.

I think she is telling me that intelligent women frighten men, but right now I feel as smart as a doorstop.

As we reach home Luca breezes outside, barking a few words to Maria, who rolls her eyes at me with mock exasperation.

'Why you are with him?' I can't help but ask her the obvious as he stomps off. My comprehension skills better than my lingual capacity, I know enough to understand her reply: 'When you speak Italian, I will explain everything to you.'

To kick off our last day in Perugia together, we have a fry-up breakfast at Simonne and Charlie's house. Nicki and Gabriele bring fresh eggs from the farm and wild asparagus from the fields.

'I wonder how Baz and Marge are going to cope without us,' says Charlie, looking over at the basil and marjoram pot plants we bought and tended throughout the summer.

Nicki and Gabriele have decided to spend another month in Perugia before going to Wellington to see Nicki's family and look for work. Simonne is off to London to suss out a few options and Charlie has accepted a short-term contract in a New South Wales hospital and plans to try to win an apprenticeship as a Qantas pilot.

While enjoying these last hours with my Perugian posse, I am feeling nervous about what to do after my Croatian holiday. There's no guarantee of a job in Perugia and though Rome is burning in my mind, I suddenly feel scared about just turning up there when I don't know a soul.

Booted out of Birraio at 3 am, we have a hugfest and promise to stay in touch. Swinging open the apartment door, I realise it's so late that Maria has switched off the light she normally keeps on so her students can make their way along the corridor. I smack various body parts against the walls before I finally feel my way to bed and pass out.

Less than seven hours later my backpack is at the front door. I find Maria in the kitchen and wrap my arms around her. She hands me a little parcel I know contains chocolate and gives me one last hug before I drag myself out the door and on to Bar Papaia, where I find Sanja and Piero in good form.

Slightly seedy, I have a cappuccino and *cornetto*, which Piero insists are on the house.

'Kiss me bye bye,' he jokes, unaware that if I had my druthers I would do much more besides. Playing along with his game, I plant a peck on each cheek before I turn to Sanja and immediately get choked up.

'*Tieni*,' she says, handing me a bag with a fresh *panino*, fruit and water, '*e prendi questo*.'

She shoves a 10 euro note in my hand, insisting I get a cab instead of going via bus. Knowing she works six days a week and has little money to throw around, I try to push the money back at her but she refuses to take it. I walk behind the bar and squeeze her tiny frame before I pull on my backpack and allow myself one final nostalgic look at Bar Papaia before heading towards the bus station.

Sleeping a record eleven hours on my first night back in San Gimignano, I settle into life with Uncle Geoffrey, Anna and Bianca, enjoying long lunches, siestas and late-night dinners.

Geoffrey and I work through the Perugia versus Rome situation. His advice is to take a day-trip to Florence, bigger than Perugia but far smaller than Rome, to see if it might be the change of scenery I am looking for.

Having visited the city in 1997, I familiarise myself again with the grey grid of streets hiding stylish boutiques and walk past the Uffizi and the Galleria dell'Accademia, home to Michelangelo's *David*, the sculpture replicated on a production line of cheeky plastic kitchen aprons flogged in Florence and across Italy.

As I climb back onto the bus, I've already decided I don't want to live in Florence. It has the same small-town vibe of Perugia, but at least in Perugia I have friends. Stopped at a traffic light, I watch a man on a motorbike ahead of the bus turn to his female passenger and, through his helmet, somehow give her a lingering kiss, all the while stroking her leg tenderly. My heart turns to pulp. *I want some of that.*

At the dinner table with Geoffrey, Anna and Bianca, I um and ah about where I should go. Geoffrey suddenly bangs down his wine glass.

'Penny, I love you because you are family, but sometimes you need a good kick up the bum,' he says belligerently. 'Go to Rome and work in a bar and learn the language, or stay in Perugia and do the same if it's easier – but for God's sake just do *something.*'

I choke back anger. Leaving my world behind in Australia was hardly *nothing*. Besides, doesn't he realise coming to Italy was a calculated choice so I could enjoy a slower life rather than work like an idiot for unmeaningful gains?

But of course he is right. No matter where I am geographically, I still have to work out what I want to do. I still have to earn a living.

Fed up with myself, I bang my fork on my wine glass and announce my intentions.

'It's Rome or bust,' I say, my resolution triggering a wave of nervous relief to wash over me.

'Thank God! Now, *vaffanculo!*' jokes Geoffrey, snorting at his own wit.

Home empty home

The Eurostar edges away from Milan's *Stazione Centrale*. Voluminous, with decorative ceilings and superb natural light, it is the most beautiful train station I have seen in my travels. As the train gathers speed, memories of my holiday in Croatia and northern Italy with my Aussie girlfriends dissipate. I have four hours and twenty-eight minutes to work myself into a tizz about what lies in store for me in Rome.

Through four degrees of separation I've found some digs for August, the hottest month in Italy and most of Europe. So far, details are sketchy, but there is a room available in an apartment near the Colosseum, so I assume the location is fairly central. The room belongs to an actor, Stefano, who will stay with his girlfriend, Patrizia, my original contact, while I rent his room. Speaking to Patrizia from a pay phone in Hvar, a tiny island on the Dalmatian coast, there was no time to ask who my new flatmates will be. I can only hope they will welcome a directionless, unemployed Australian with abysmal language skills.

Yet, despite the unknown, I feel good. Instinct tells me I'm doing the right thing. Carmen's dippy analysis is on rotation in the back of my head. *Trust yourself. Be open to everything.* The more I think about why I left Australia, the more determined I become. Perugia didn't even dent my appetite for all things Italian. It was merely an *aperitivo* to kick-start my Roman adventure.

Back in the present, I look around the Eurostar to check out the local talent. Three months have passed since I left home and I haven't even had a tipsy smooch, let alone a one-night stand. I've forgotten the joy of human touch and crave a little TLC.

While the idea of boy-hopping has appeal, I'm hopeless at games without guilt. But the beauty of moving to a new place is reinvention. In my imagination I see myself riding on the back of a *motorino* all Audrey-like, with one arm around Marco, the other hanging onto the scarf wrapped around my hair, on my way to the opera. And there I am again, sitting around the family table with Enrico, being told by his *mamma* that I cannot leave the house until I have another serving of her *torta*.

I stare at the word *Roma* on my train ticket and start to think about what I have to do when I arrive. *Piano, piano.* I calm myself with deep breaths. There's no need to worry unnecessarily about things that are, at least for now, out of my control.

I spend the last hour of the journey eavesdropping on Italian conversations I don't understand, flicking through my pocket dictionary when I identify the odd word. The train pulls up at Termini, Rome's train, bus and Metro hub. I swing my backpack onto my shoulders, thread my daypack straps over my arms, resting it on my gut, and prepare for the world outside the air-conditioned cocoon of the Eurostar.

My sneakers hit the concrete and I'm slapped by a temperature that feels about forty degrees but is probably just over thirty. There is not a skerrick of a breeze to soften the blow and at 3 pm, Termini is the chaotic pit I remember it to be. Bags, feet and cigarette butts blanket the ground. Hundreds of voices create a consistent hum that rises and falls in volume. Rome is twelve times louder than provincial Perugia and crasser than sophisticated Milan.

'*Aoooo!*' A skinny man with more hair than Meat Loaf greets his mate to my left. There's that weird word I heard at Rome airport when I was with Jo. It sounds like the noise I make when I knock my funny bone. It must be Roman dialect, because I didn't hear it in Perugia or in Milan.

I find a phone box and call Patrizia to warn her I am close. She gives me instructions to meet her and Stefano at his apartment, my new home. I must catch the Blue Line and get off at Colosseo, then catch the number 85 bus. I scribble the details on my hand.

Travelling with my Aussie mates, we took turns to navigate but now I'm on my Pat Malone again. It's more tiring fending for myself, finding accommodation and racing to make trains without losing sight of my backpack for a second.

Down in the Metro station I go to a ticket machine. One ticket lasting seventy-seven minutes upon validation costs seventy-seven cents. How can it be – why choose a sum so difficult to source change for? Why not round it up to eighty? I haven't got any of the brown one and two cent coins to make the right sum so I try a one euro coin. The machine spits it out as stubbornly as I push it in. Around me, other tourists are having the same problem. Frustrated, I go to the ticket checking point. Tired and hot, I don't even attempt Italian. I ask a man dressed in a smart navy blue suit for help.

He follows me to the ticket machine, inserts a few brown two and one cent pieces then adds my one euro coin. The machine clicks into action and out pops a ticket and the right change.

'Ewe mast buy a tee-ket at the *tabaccaio*,' the man says with a bemused smile, referring to the tobacconist shops that are identifiable on the street by a small square sign in blue or black with a white 'T'. 'Thees machine is beelt only for the Romans.'

I look at him indignantly. What's that supposed to mean? That the locals are the only ones stupid enough to stockpile brown coins for everyday Metro use, or that, using some form of trickery, they scrunch their noses and command the machines to do as they please?

Thwacking the odd commuter with my hefty pack, I alight at Colosseo and exit into soft, afternoon sunlight. There, smack bang in front of me, is the mighty building itself. I once read you can tell who the locals are on a bus in Rome simply by noting those who don't look up and gawk at the Colosseum. I can't imagine ever being impervious to the immensity of the grit-grey, half-crumbled facade.

Crossing the road to get to the bus stop, I peer across to the entrance gates. A handful of men dressed in gladiator costumes mill among a clutch of tourists, trying to convince them to part with a few euros for a photo opportunity. In fake body armour and carrying swords, perspiration lines their faces as they plug their trade. The poor buggers must be so hot. Go, Russells, go.

I'm tempted to have a closer look but I'm sweating madly. There'll be plenty of time to suss out my neighbourhood monuments later. I jump on the number 85 bus and count three stops before hopping off. There, alone at the bus stop, is a willowy girl with enormous brown eyes and long, chestnut hair.

'Penelope? Welcome!' She calls.

Patrizia kisses me on both cheeks and gives me a quick run-down on my immediate location. The cobbled street I am standing in is via di San Giovanni in Laterano, my new street. In front of us are huge, wooden entrance doors, painted a cheery green, which lead to the palazzo, or apartment block, where Stefano lives. Standing with my back to the doors, I can see the Colosseum in the distance to my left. To my right the street continues to Piazza di San Giovanni in Laterano, home to the first Christian basilica built in Rome and the city's cathedral.

Patrizia leads me inside the palazzo and we skirt a dismal grey courtyard and walk up three flights of stairs. My back groans and a bead of sweat works its way down my spine and between my butt cheeks. The paint on the walls is peeling and stained and the floor tiles are cracked or missing. Despite the dilapidated state of the palazzo I'm not worried. In Italy, I've found beautiful apartments are often hidden behind ugly, dirty facades.

At the top, Patrizia pushes a key into a brown door with a tatty sign instructing visitors to '*bussare fortemente*', which literally means 'knock strongly'. Inside, the apartment is silent and full of shadows. Natural light is scarce in the small entrance room, where two regal wooden chairs upholstered in mint-green velvet compete for space with a modern blue divan and small TV. Nearby a table covered in orange Indian cloth has an architect's lamp bent awkwardly to illuminate a series of spray-painted designs on canvases that tilt from nails on the walls. A corridor leads into the gloom beyond.

A vertically challenged man with wavy blond hair, blue eyes and bushy eyebrows appears from a doorway and kisses me on both cheeks. Stefano, I discover, is actually Stefan – a Frenchman living in Rome. Wearing a crisp white linen shirt and trendy jeans, he offers me a toothy grin and shows me to his room. I dump my bags with relief and look around me. The room is about three metres by four with a black plastic desk pushed against the far left wall. To the right of the desk, a tall window with two shutters lets in barely adequate light and offers views directly across the palazzo into the apartment windows opposite. Esme Watson would have a field day. A loft bed big enough for two slim people is tucked against the back wall that divides the room from the corridor.

Perhaps smelling my fatigue, Stefan gives me a towel and shows me where the bathroom is before giving me a thirty-second rundown on my flatmates: Nina, a German girl, and two Italian girls, Alberta and Tiziana.

'They are away at the moment because it gets so hot in Rome in August everyone goes on holidays,' Stefan explains with a laugh, not realising how disappointed I am at the prospect of living in an empty house in a ghost town for the next few weeks.

Stefan excuses himself, saying he has to go to a meeting. Patrizia invites me to dinner and tells me Stefan will pick me up later before the front door slams behind them.

I grab my towel and go to the bathroom. Colourful blue and white tiles lead to a bath that looks like it has never been used. I have a quick shower. The hose writhes with hostility as I try to adjust the water pressure to find the right temperature. Drought restrictions aside, I'm an Australian used to good, strong showers. Having a *doccia* in Italy is, while at first a novelty, always disappointing.

Drying off, I notice the colourful graphic designs ripped from magazines patched about the bathroom walls and even on top of the washing machine, giving the house a student feel. A large poster catches my eye near the basin mirror. A tender but racy cinematic scene, it features two beautiful women kissing passionately.

Walking along the corridor back to my room, I shriek as my feet tread on something that moves. Looking down, I see two rectangular slabs of timber positioned carefully over uneven sections of the floor where some tiles are missing. The trick is to step on the centre of the boards otherwise they flip up then slam down with a bang.

Refreshed and dressed, I check out the poky kitchen, sandwiched between my room and the bathroom. Above the tiny table and two chairs there is a noticeboard with a photo of two girls smiling merrily. I wonder if either of them could be Nina, Alberta or Tiziana. Stacked on a shelf are German brands of herbal tea which blend with the lingering scent of coffee beans and confectionery I can't find. The wire rack fastened to the wall above the beautiful old marble kitchen sink is loaded with clean plates and pans. I am yet to set foot in an Italian kitchen with a dishwashing machine. Most kitchens have a rack above the sink, mounted openly or hidden behind a bottomless cupboard. Stacked, washed items drip-dry within minutes, removing the need for a tea towel.

A bottle of Martini *Rosso* sits on top of the wall fridge alongside a half-finished bottle of *vin santo,* a cheap but delicious dessert wine I became fond of in Perugia. A road map of Italy is stuck to the kitchen door behind which shelves sag, laden down with food of all descriptions. I'm trying to work out what is missing when it hits me: the oven. Instead, there is just a vintage camping-style gadget with two gas burners.

I make an espresso using what is on offer and turn to the square, marble sink to wash my cup. I turn on one tap, then the other, but there is no hot water. I am starting to feel like I'm on the set of *Withnail and I*. Everything seems worn, torn or broken.

I decide to go for a wander, tucking my guidebook out of sight in my handbag to pull out only when required. I may be a wide-eyed tourist but I don't want to look like one. Leaving the palazzo entrance, I turn left and see the Colosseum looming. My blood rushes and I wonder how long it will take before I stop grinning at the smallest new thing. I walk to Piazza Venezia, dominated by the Vittoriano. Glaringly white against the surrounding grey, brown and pollution-stained facades, the marble building honouring the first king of united Italy, Vittorio Emanuele II, looks like a cross between an old typewriter and a wedding cake. It's ostentatiously ugly but its size is somehow impressive. The swallows circling in the air give it a Gotham City feel.

Reading my guidebook in the heat, I suddenly feel overwhelmed. Ye olde this. Ye ancient that. How many BCs and how much blinding beauty can you cram into one city?

I am watching the traffic whir around me when I see a small, black dot approaching from the distance. As it gets closer, I make out what looks to be an old woman shrouded in a head veil and gypsy clothes. Her back is bent so far forward that I cannot see her face; it is parallel to her knees if not threatening to touch her feet, which drag inwardly in tatty, dirty sneakers. In one hand the woman holds a battered cane to support herself, in the other an aluminium cup in which she shakes coins.

The huge piazza buzzes with motorbikes and the conversations of people passing by. I am hearing variations of the verb *mangiare*, to eat, and the word *cena*, dinner, every two minutes. When not eating, Italians always seem to be discussing their next meal. I try to decipher foreign street signs and stare at the building opposite, where Mussolini once resided and preached to the masses from the balcony.

I am thinking about leaving when I see another hunchbacked woman shuffle past. Hang about. Either the first hunchback I saw has had a wardrobe change or there's a homeless family of sisters with degenerative back problems who live nearby. Or, this is a big, fat sham. Resisting the urge to reach out and tickle the gypsy woman's armpit to see if she can stand, I drop a euro in her tin and hear a slurred *grazie* from somewhere beneath the rags. Even if she is a fraud she'll need extra retirement funds for back operations.

Stefan arrives on a *motorino* to take me to Patrizia's, leaping off to give me a spare helmet. He waits until I have one hand on the handle at the back of the seat and the other arm around his waist, which is appropriately skinny for a struggling actor, before he kickstarts the engine.

Whizzing out of the centre along suburban streets and in and out of traffic, Stefan toots the horn every now and then in annoyance as we stop and start at traffic lights. If they haven't guessed already, it won't take long for the locals to spot the Priscilla in their midst. I can barely contain squeals of delight. I try to wipe the frozen smile from my face – at least so insects can't fly into my mouth – and be nonchalant, but I can't. How on earth do the locals manage to ride their *motorini* among layers of historic ruins, beautiful *palazzi* and monuments without pinching themselves? If I hang around long enough I want to buy a Vespa, preferably one of the gorgeous vintage Piaggio ones.

We enter a nondescript apartment building and hop into a tiny lift that takes us to Patrizia's flat, on the seventh and top floor. Her studio apartment is cluttered with pieces collected from her life and travels, including wooden carvings from Africa, where her father lives, and vintage cinematic posters hung alongside memorabilia of theatre productions she has starred in. A tasteful stretch of fabric separates the spacious lounge room from an alcove containing a double bed and a rack of Sofia Coppola-style clothes.

Patrizia stands in the small galley kitchen, crammed with pots and pans and knives. Her upper lip is beaded with sweat as she opens the oven to check something that I can't see from where I am standing but smells delicious.

'I'm making a baked pasta my *nonna* used to make,' she says almost apologetically, as if she doesn't believe she can recreate the dish as well as her gran did. 'It's made with *uovo, carne e pomodori.*' Eggs, meat and tomatoes.

Grabbing a half-consumed salami stick, a bowl of fat brown olives and a basket of bread chunks, Patrizia steers us out to the apartment's drawcard – a huge terrace with Moroccan cushions on the floor, a table and a hammock to lap up the city skyline views and any cool breeze available.

She then disappears to have a shower, leaving Stefan and me to chat about their work. Patrizia is currently in rehearsals for a small production that she'll perform in a suburban theatre a month after they return from holiday. Stefan is in the middle of teaching in a theatre workshop to save cash while he sniffs around for roles in upcoming productions.

The doorbell rings and Stefan opens the door to greet Patrizia's friends. Actors aged in their late twenties and early thirties, Marco, Valentino and Rinaldo cut dashing figures in perfectly dishevelled designer clothes. Italian women can be mighty stylish, but I reckon the men give them a serious run for their money. If you stand in any average street in Rome for twenty minutes, the chances are eighty-five per cent of the men you see pay great attention to their wardrobe, regardless of their personal style, which varies from conservative business dress to loud designer outfits to motorbike cool. In Milan, Italy's fashion capital, the obsession with personal grooming increases three-fold.

It's commonplace for an Italian man to check his reflection in the mirror of his *motorino*, or stop outside a shop window to adjust his shirt or check his hair, without a skerrick of modesty. If an Australian man did the same, depending on his whereabouts, he could be called anything from a poof to a pansy. Italian men are openly affectionate towards one another, whether they are heterosexual, metrosexual or homosexual. Most days I see men walking arm in arm or kissing each other on both cheeks to say hello or goodbye. The openness of affection is endearing, but it makes sussing out if someone is on the market or not pretty difficult.

With a deep tan and emerald-green eyes so stunning they almost seem accentuated by eyeliner, Marco, the friend of my friend in Sydney who helped me find Stefan's room, welcomes me warmly with a kiss on each cheek.

'*Perché sei venuta a Roma?*' He asks with interest why I have come to Rome.

'*Vorrei un vacanza. Vorrei lavare.*'

The small group around me bursts into laughter and Marco explains my error in English. Instead of saying I have come to Italy to work, I said I want to wash.

'You are tired – we can speak in English,' says Marco.

Dressed in beautiful Indian-style wrap pants and a simple singlet top, Patrizia emerges to greet her guests and make sure we all have a glass of wine. She disappears to return with a huge terracotta pot of the baked pasta, placing it next to the bread, olives and salami.

Looking at the table, I can't help but think how Italians seem to make entertaining look so easy. True, Aussies have the ease of the outdoor barbie complete with beer cans in stubby holders, but generally dinner parties are more tedious affairs planned in detail.

Uncle Geoffrey seems to be an anomaly. Italian women are the backbone of family kitchens, having learnt their exceptional skills from childhood, watching their *mamma* or *nonna* whip up simple meals using fresh ingredients bought at the markets. I wish now I had accompanied Maria to the market in Perugia and watched her prepare some dishes.

The pasta bake is so delicious I want more, but with four blokes around I am too late for seconds. Luckily, Patrizia has whipped up a chocolate *torta*, which she serves warm from the oven with a dollop of *panna*, or cream, on top.

Full and happy, I struggle to understand the rapid conversations going on around me. Short bursts of English are provided for my benefit. I'm overwhelmed and still beside myself about being in Rome, but it's been a long day. I can barely keep my eyelids open.

Finally, the three *ragazzi*, lads, stand up to leave and Rinaldo, a fast-talking, olive-skinned Milanese with an Americanised English accent, offers me a lift home. I'm suddenly wide awake with the prospect of a *motorino* ride, assuming he hasn't got a car.

Downstairs, Rinaldo stoops down to unchain the back wheel of his bike before he unlocks and opens the bike seat to hand me a black motorbike helmet. Sticking up from the top are two furry triangles, shaped like cat's ears. I double over laughing. It's so Italian – showy yet somehow stylish at the same time.

Despite their fashion-conscious bent, I can't imagine even the most effeminate heterosexual Italian having such a helmet. If I wasn't convinced Rinaldo was gay before, I am almost certain now.

'It is cute, no?' says Rinaldo. 'About a year ago it was a trend, but it's still *divertente*, amusing.'

I put on the helmet and swing up onto the backseat behind him. Soon we are zipping down the tree-lined streets, the wind refreshing against our faces. We whir around Piazza Venezia, bouncing on the rough cobbled stone road. My bottom hurts but I'm too content to care. I would gladly endure pain for more wheeled pleasure, but I'm not sure how many more joy rides my heart can bear in one day.

The Vittoriano swings into view. At night it's less gaudy, the white marble softly lit by floodlights. Perched atop the tiered stairs, two elaborately dressed soldiers with rifles slung over their shoulders guard the tomb of the Unknown Soldier.

With a final, gutsy rev of the throttle, Rinaldo propels us along the long, straight stretch of via dei Fori Imperiali. I have no idea of the significance of each of the crumbling temples and buildings that formed the political and cultural centre of Rome centuries ago. Illuminated exquisitely, I vow to return during the day to do a tour.

The highlight of the ride home lies dead ahead. I crick my neck to the side to take in the Colosseum in its full glory. Devoid of the usual daytime bedlam of tourists, gladiators and illegal immigrants selling weird beaded hats and fake designer handbags, it's so classy. Nude and proud, it's lit up like a birthday cake in a darkened room.

Reality check number 325: it's stupendously beautiful, it's almost two thousand years old and it's on my doorstep.

I guide Rinaldo to stop at the green door of my palazzo and hop off the bike, legs shaking from muscle contraction and excitement. He kisses me on both cheeks and tears off into the night.

Working girl

I need a job and there's no time to waste. First, because I'd rather save the thin wedge in my bank account for a holiday or as an emergency exit fund. Second, because I am busting to fraternise with the locals and try to use the language I adore hearing but cannot piece together. Third, because I want to keep myself as busy as possible so I don't have time to stew on the obvious: for the first time in a long time I have no real game plan.

I feel a bit like I did when two of my best gal pals and I went out for a pre-Christmas knees-up a few years ago. Donning slinky dresses, we decided wearing undies would be a crime against fashion. Stepping out into the night, I felt adventurously smug for being so risqué – but I spent much of the evening petrified a random sneeze or breeze would bring me undone.

Just before I left Sydney, a work acquaintance at *Wallpaper** magazine gave me some contacts in Milan, the style and jobs capital of Italy, where many major local and international fashion houses, media and PR companies are based. During my stint in Perugia, I optimistically fired off emails with my CV attached, but I received only polite refusals. There was no work on offer, but even if there was I posed a problem: I don't have work documents – just a visa with a rapidly approaching expiry date.

The truth is, I was kind of relieved. I sent the emails because I felt like I had to find a 'real' job, a position that looks good on paper and is loaded with responsibility. I have to keep reminding myself I didn't come to Italy to jump immediately back onto the career path.

I want to give myself a break – easier said than done. Not unlike my father, from whom I take the good, the bad and the downright ugly, I need to feel like I am achieving something, no matter how big or small. Compounding this instinct is the difficulty of abandoning a strong work ethic instilled by my parents, who have run small businesses all their lives.

Throughout high school I waitressed in the family café, so I'm used to carrying plates – albeit clumsily – and making coffee. The health sanitation card should allow me to pick up work in a bar or café. I reckon a waitressing job will ease me into the language and help me settle into my new environment. I like the idea of having a job I can take or leave. And who knows, Nicolas Cage might pass one day and decide he wants an upgrade.

My dad always says if you want work you can find it. On my second day in Roma I am determined to do just that. I dress in Melbourne black and leave the house.

First things first. Coffee. I miss Piero and Sanja from Bar Papaia. I want to find a good bar where I can become a local again. I head down via di San Giovanni in Laterano, towards the Colosseum. I pass one bar but the lecherous look of the barista encourages me to keep going. On the next corner is Bar Helio. At the cash register is a young girl with too much make-up but a pretty, gentle face. Two bow-tied baristas churn out orders of the day. The bar is clean with a warm buzz about it. I roll my eyes discreetly as a cappuccino is placed before me. Sitting on the froth is a heart made of cocoa. On my first day in Rome I thought the gesture was romantic, now I just want to wallop the barista. Almost all of the cappuccinos I have ordered in Italy have appeared with one or – more impressively – two interlaced hearts on top. Bar Papaia was the only place where I didn't get schmoozed – because I became a regular, and because Sanja and Piero aren't tuxedoed cornballs. If Bar Helio becomes my local, I wonder how long it will take before they abandon froth niceties.

Tapping the cash register with blood red fingernails, the young woman gives me my receipt with a smile.

'*Fa caldo oggi*,' she says, making pleasantries about the fact the weather is hot today.

I nod, working hard to stop myself from scowling.

I am fed up with not being able to string a sentence together. Playing the stupid foreigner and getting by on charm was fun at first, but now I desperately want to be able to engage with people. Frustratingly, I can't make jokes, let alone throw out the odd aphorism. I want to be witty in Italian but I can't even order meat, *carne*, without the waiter thinking I'm craving roasted dog, *cane*.

I head on foot towards the historic centre to ask for work at some of more famous bars or cafés in Rome listed in my guidebook. I figure they'll need English-speaking staff for the summer. But the season is already half over and it's only two weeks until *Ferragosto*, the major public holiday on August 15 when, according to Stefan, the last remaining Romans in town close up shop and go on holidays. Maybe I've left it too late.

Seemingly on ice for the last three months in Australia, my heart suddenly starts pounding at the thought of having to communicate. I push my fear aside and head to Bar della Pace, just off Piazza Navona. Why on earth did I decide to wear black, a magnet for the sun? At 10.30 am the cobblestones are baking.

My sweaty feet slip around in my sandals and gather the dust that layers Rome like icing sugar.

Though the thick vine covering most of Bar della Pace is brown and withered under the belting rays of sun, I still catch my breath. Grimy but ornately beautiful, the age-worn building begs to be photographed. Inside, the unlit bar is steeped in rich timber and bottles of booze. Nothing and no one stirs. Outside, two old men sit at one of the modern aluminium tables, chatting loudly and waving their arms at each other.

'*C'è il capo?*' I ask for the boss, having checked my dictionary for the word.

A jumble of words come out and I hear the word *pomeriggio,* or afternoon, and assume I have to return then. An hour has passed since I left home and two blisters have risen stubbornly on my feet.

I backtrack to Campo de' Fiori, bustling with the daily market selling flowers and fresh fruit and vegetables, but all of the bars I am looking for are shut. At every turn something colourful catches my eye and the stall-holders' expressive banter cheers me up. Crossing the Tiber, I get lost in the myriad of streets in Trastevere, a *quartiere* Patrizia recommended I should visit because it is full of cute wine bars and restaurants. I wander along the narrow streets, staring into bakeries, *pizzerie* and *pasticcerie* and admiring the elegant windows of book, art and furniture shops.

A small, rustic trattoria catches my eye so I walk inside. At a long table, eight men sit sucking spaghetti from flat, white bowls. Two wear pristine white caps and chef's uniforms, while the others are in waiter's attire. At 11.45 am, the staff have lunch early, before the rush of tourists from noon. Italians don't go to lunch until one o'clock at the earliest and amble into a restaurant for dinner at 10.30 pm as if it's the most natural thing in the world. Given shops open for business until 7.30 pm having an *aperitivo* in the early evening takes priority before dining much later.

'*Cerco…per lavorare*. I search to work.' I am almost stuttering, intimidated by the group's collective testosterone.

A deep voice answers from somewhere at the table. The '*non*' is enough for me to get the message, loud and clear. I retreat quickly, blushing, and hear riotous laughter before I reach the door. Tears spring in my eyes. I'm hot, a little lost and the skin has been ripped off my feet in a two-hour walkabout. I would throw a tanty if I had an appreciative audience.

On my final stretch of Trastevere I spy a bland restaurant with an English menu mounted prominently out the front to trap passing tourists. Inside, a pale-skinned girl with crooked teeth and a beautiful rosebud mouth sweeps the terracotta floor. I ask for *il capo* and a strapping man called Marco appears.

Down-trodden, I stumble for words.

'*Sono cercare per lavorare, ho studiato Italiano per sei settimane a Perugia, parlo abbastanza*. I am search for work. I studied Italian in Perugia. I speak enough.'

'*Quanti anni hai?*' Marco asks my age.

I stifle my annoyance. I've seen men waitering around Rome who look like they should be in nursing homes.

'Twenty-eight,' I say in English, forgetting the number in Italian.

From what I can gather, Marco tells me I can come on Saturday. Seeing my confusion, he writes down the conditions: the pay is 31 euros, about 60 dollars, for a shift from 5 pm to 1 am.

Walking out the door, I control an urge to hug an unsuspecting passer-by, or the nearest tree. I've done what I set out to do – I have a job. Then mild depression hits. Why the hell am I getting excited about being paid peanuts as a waitress? With each minute, the charm of being in Italy is wearing off, and the reality of life bearing down. I can't get a job for which I am qualified because

I can't string more than four words together and my bank balance is as scrawny as Paris Hilton. But I can't give up. I have to live the dream I have been talking about for so long.

By the time I get home, my feet are rubbed raw on top and black underneath. It may be *bellissima*, but Rome has to be one of the filthiest cities in the world. Walking along the street, I see people spit and throw cigarettes and even rubbish with scant regard for their fellow citizens. The Romans seem oblivious to the history around them. I guess after the rise and fall of countless empires before them they just take it as a given that their so-called Eternal City will remain just that. I don't see any recycling bins anywhere. Reading the local papers, I learn that Italy dumps two-thirds of its rubbish in the streets and has the worst rate of recycling and incinerating waste product in Europe. And when it comes to smog, living an average day in Rome means I inhale the equivalent of seven cigarettes.

Inside the flat, I hear voices and my spirits soar. Company, at last! In the kitchen is Nina, an attractive young German girl with long spiralling blonde curls and pretty blue eyes. She's talking to her boyfriend, a quiet German lad who is staying in the house for the weekend.

Warm '*Ciaos*' aside, I am almost drooling in my desire to socialise. I blurt out the first thing that comes into my head.

'*Ho scopato un lavoro!*'

Nina's face crunches in amusement as she explains in good English that I've confused the past tense of two verbs that are similar in sound but very different in meaning. Rather than saying 'I found a job' I instead announced proudly that 'I fucked a job'.

'Don't worry,' she says with understanding. 'My Italian is terrible.'

Dressed in vintage and op shop gear I wish was in my own wardrobe, Nina chatters away breezily and I learn she's twenty-four, grew up near Munich and she has lived in Rome for three years, working as a graphic designer.

Ten minutes later I am heading out the door because I have *un appuntamento.* In English, the word appointment usually signals a level of seriousness – an appointment to see the doctor, solicitor or shrink. In Italy the word is used much more casually, for meeting people at the pub or the cinema.

My *appuntamento* is with Massimo, the owner of a small jewellery shop near the Spanish Steps. Three years ago I bought a beautiful brooch at the store in via Frattina – before he had taken over the management. Passing through Rome on my way to Perugia, I somehow managed to find the store again and struck up a friendship with Massimo, a French-raised Roman who runs the business with his gorgeous French girlfriend, Celine. I promised I would contact him should I return to Rome.

At three o'clock, Massimo greets me with a warm smile as I walk into the store and I remember why, apart from the fact that he's sharp as a button and quick with a joke, I am attracted to him. He's tall with wavy hair and deep-set brown eyes. He has beautiful clear, white skin, rosy cheeks and a bear-like figure – strong with extra padding that he wears well.

Positioned awkwardly, the shop is half-hidden down a corridor, and business is slow.

'I haven't had a single customer all day,' says Massimo glumly, speaking a mix of Italian and English to make himself understood. However embarrassed I feel, I bumble on in Italian, because if I don't practise with someone I will commit a felony.

He locks up the shop and we go to have an *aperitivo* in a bar opposite his shop. We stand and chat about life, Massimo lamenting the fact the business is going badly.

'*Ma…che vuoi fare?* But what do you want to do?' I ask.

'*Mi piacerebbe andare e fare il vino in Toscana.* To live and make wine in Tuscany,' he says, a dreamy look washing over his youthful face.

In an instant I am in Tuscany. While Massimo is out in the fields checking the grapes, I am busy being superwoman, working in my dream job and playing with our two beautiful young children, who have their father's unruly hair and milky complexion. Massimo returns from the fields and gives me a tender embrace before we enjoy a delicious spaghetti carbonara, which I make according to Maria's recipe, prompting my hunky beau to ask if I was not Italian in another life. Massimo and I sing the children to sleep with lullabies and have fabulous sex before falling asleep on white, cotton sheets a little crunchy from having been sun-dried in Tuscan fields.

I snap back to reality and look at Massimo, studying the ice in his Campari soda. Once again I have found the perfect man too late. He's totally in love with Celine. He just enjoys a healthy flirt every now and then. We're all human.

I reluctantly take off my cool summer dress and stick on black trousers and a white, sleeveless buttoned shirt I bought at Benetton for my new career as a plate-fetching penguin at Carlomente restaurant. At 5 pm I catch the number 3 tram from Colosseo to Trastevere and throw back a coffee at a bar before I walk into the restaurant.

Marco greets me before telling me in English to go and help clean the floors of the bathrooms. Downstairs I find Monica, the girl with the uneven teeth and beautiful mouth and, I discover as she leans over a mop, a gorgeous Celtic tattoo on her lower back.

Upstairs, tourists are arriving as early as 6.30 pm for dinner. I gulp down a small plate of risotto the chef dishes out to staff before I am taken under the wing of two Pamela Anderson clones,

Flavia and Barbara. The former has Pammy's signature barbed wire tattoo around her upper arm, fake emerald green contact lenses, peroxide blonde hair and tits that would do her proud. Polish-born Barbara is not as naturally pretty as Flavia but she's trying. Her hair is similarly long and blonde and she wears mascara thicker than Boy George to highlight her pale blue eyes. Both are whippet-thin and wear tight black pants.

A baby-faced upstart called Matteo sits *alla cassa*, calculating dinner bills and bossing staff about, while Marco walks around with a bouncer's cocky air before disappearing to chain-smoke in the office. Just when I think I have met everyone, a small man appears beside me. With a thin moustache, he reminds me of Mañuel, the bumbling waiter in 'Fawlty Towers', with Coke-bottle glasses.

'*Sono Salvatore*,' he says, offering his hand. I smile back at him and introduce myself as he adjusts his black bowtie.

The staff splits into zones – inside and outside – and, as the dinner onslaught begins, I find myself running around like a headless chicken: giving out menus, cutting bread and putting it in baskets for delivery, and clearing plates. It's hardly plastic surgery, but it's amusing because it's new.

I can't understand the banter between staff and the tables of Italians around me, but I hear conversation bites of some of the English-speaking clients, mainly Yanks and Poms. Too busy to be chatty in English, I take advantage of my dark tresses and pretend I am Italian when some tourists ask me glaringly obvious questions in English.

'*Scusi*, where is Piazza Navona?' asks a Pom whose accent is so proper I wouldn't be surprised if he had a silver spoon wedged in his larynx.

Mumbling '*Non capisco*', I scurry off. Notwithstanding the fact maps were invented to be observed and used, Piazza Navona –

long, narrow and oval – is almost as easy to peg as the Vatican on a map of Rome. Sometimes I wonder why people leave the safety of their own homes.

The night is a balmy twenty-nine degrees and the kitchen is an explosion of sweat, boiling water and sizzling pans. Plates fly in every direction, loaded with sloppily arranged food – a quick tourist buck is the main game – but brimming with colour. *Bruschetta* made with brilliant red tomatoes and basil, *spaghetti al ragù* with a bolognese sauce and, my favourite, *saltimbocca,* a tenderised layer of veal with a slice of prosciutto, melted *parmigiano* cheese and a sage leaf on top. The verb '*saltare*' means 'to jump' and the word *bocca* means mouth. *Saltimbocca* literally means 'to jump in the mouth', indicating the flavour explosion. Even if it's torturous to get my tongue around, I am becoming increasingly besotted with the lyrical, evocative Italian language.

I run around and try to help without getting in anyone's way. Soon my blistered feet are aching, and the bandaids slip from side to side. The fact I am wearing my faithful, comfy Birkenstock sandals does nothing to ease my discomfort.

The kitchen staff – two Bangladeshi dishwashers and a Polish chef who looks as approachable as Mike Tyson – give me the odd look of interest as they knuckle down to cope with the steady stream of orders. They look like they've already had a quiet wager as to how long the new kid is going to last.

Three hours fly past and my concentration begins to wane. I have hypoglycaemic tendencies and my sugar levels have dropped to a precarious level. I am irritable and need to grab something, *anything*, to eat but I don't have time and, more than anything, I'm too scared to ask, for fear they think I am slacking off.

Taking advantage of a two-minute lull, Salvatore decides to shoot the breeze.

'*Non parli bene l'Italiano, lo sai?* You don't speak Italian well, do you?' he says, using words I can, ironically, understand – because I have memorised, by way of apology, the phrase '*non parlo bene*', or, 'I don't speak (Italian) well'.

Not only is Salvatore annoying, he's bloody Einstein.

'*Hai un cuore?* Have you a heart?' I retort in a flash of frustrated anger.

Nearby, Monica and Flavia screech with laughter.

'*Brava!*' says Monica, flashing me a toothy grin as Salvatore, blushing slightly, looks at me with an expression of admiration and bewilderment.

Two minutes later we are both running near each other when he screams something at me.

'*Scusa?*' I yell back at him, indicating I have not understood. Conversation from the tables around me and the scent of food I want to eat rattles me even further.

'*Due* cheeps…CHEEEPS!' he yells again in frustration, waving his hands wildly.

Finally the penny drops. He doesn't want to do the chicken dance, he just wants chips. Hot chips. I race to the kitchen and order them. Later I try to demonstrate the difference in pronunciation between chips and cheeps to Salvatore but I just get more confused. In Italian, 'i' is pronounced like 'ee' in English, while the Italian 'e' sounds like 'air'.

When no one seems to be looking in the kitchen, I grab a chunk of bread and stuff it in my mouth hungrily. It's not the most satisfying thing, but it fills a hole. By midnight I have graduated to making coffee and serving desserts – profiteroles covered in lemon or chocolate sauce, *tiramisù* and other gooey, unidentifiable objects. When I can get away with it, I rub my finger against the blade of the knife to get a sugar hit. My hunger pains have reached cannibalistic proportions – they would eat themselves if they could.

At one o'clock the last table is on their final round of grappa and we finally get to sit down. I wolf down the plate of spaghetti with a simple tomato sauce put in front of me as the Pamelas pick at their plates then suck back Marlboro Lights and chat about things I can't even bother pretending to understand. Salvatore seems to have disappeared. To my right Monica divides up the tips received during the night. It comes to just under 10 euros each, between five.

I go and knock on Marco's door to get my pay for the shift. He seems to be doing nothing else but staring at a piece of paper with the roster on it.

'Can you come tomorrow?' he says in English.

I nod and take the money, gratefully accepting a lift home from Monica, who lives near the Colosseum.

'You went fine,' she says, steering her tiny Smart car like a shopping trolley.

I'm too tired to respond. At home, I can barely lift my legs to scale the ladder up to my loft bed.

My morning session at a huge Internet café at Piazza Barberini brings good news.

There is an email from one of the head honchos of *Italy Daily*, an English-language newspaper with Italian news, that forms an insert in *Corriere della Sera,* the biggest broadsheet in Italy. A week ago, I emailed him my CV at random, having seen his email address in the paper. I informed him I was living in Rome and, though my Italian was poor, I was keen to do some writing for *Italy Daily*.

As a test of my skills, I suspect, he has asked me to do a follow-up story on an article that appeared in *The Washington Post*, about alleged misconduct by costumed *gladiatori* who circle the Colosseum asking tourists to part with a few euros or more for a photo opportunity. The Rome municipal council has been besieged with complaints from tourists who claim that the gladiators are using unfair tactics to offer their services, such as saying a photo will cost five euros but when the photo has been taken claiming it costs that amount *per person.* Some tourists say rogue gladiators have intimidated them with their menacingly long, albeit plastic, swords.

It's hardly Watergate, but who cares – the *Corriere della Sera* wants the yarn. I sit at my desk at home with my dictionary and prepare lots of questions in what I hope to be comprehensible Italian. I figure it's better to ask too much than too little when I can't grasp every word of the answer. I grab my journalist's tape recorder and run out the door, carried by adrenalin. I'm ready to knock on doors and ask questions until I have the whole truth and nothing but the truth.

The sun is already beating strongly as I reach the end of my street and cross over to the Colosseum. I find a group of three gladiators, waiting patiently in the shade for hapless tourists to approach. One of the trio looks like an Italian Paul Hogan. With a wiry build, his piercing blue eyes flash like diamonds from a face weathered by too many cigarettes and his outdoor craft. He smokes and chats to his companions in typical, animated Italian fashion.

I take a big breath and march over before I have time to change my mind.

'Excuse me, I am a journalist – can I talk to you for a minute?'

Gladiator Hogan looks at me with interest and I am reminded how Italians – both men and women – have perfected the art of sizing each other up. If I want to check someone out who interests me, I try to do it discreetly, when they are not looking. Italians, on the other hand, make no bones about the fact they are giving you the once over. Starting with my feet, Gladiator Hogan runs his eyes up my body, lingering on my cleavage before meeting my eyes. I feel like I have been strip-searched.

'*C'è un articolo nel* Washington Post. *Ha detto che avete fatto delle cose male ai turisti.* There is a story in the *Washington Post.* It said that you did bad things to tourists.'

Oh dear. In my excitement to be a hack again, I forgot that I can't pose a grammatically correct question in Italian. How can I expect to be taken seriously?

At the mention of the *Washington Post* story, the three men start talking angrily. I can't understand much, but the words *'non è vero'* – or, it's not true – stand out.

Little by little, I grab a few sentences, already discarding my tape recorder because my level of comprehension is so bad I don't think even re-listening to the tape will help. Gladiator Hogan steers me towards a man leaning on a wall of the Colosseum nearby. He turns out to be the man quoted in the *Washington Post* article, the boss of the association representing the gladiators.

I heave an inward sigh of relief when a stream of defence comes out of his mouth. In English.

'It's not true that we are robbing people,' he says angrily, his sizeable gut indicating that he's a man with a penchant for pasta. 'We work hard and long hours to support our families. The problem is, there are bad apples. They give us all a bad name.'

We chat for a little longer before I thank the man and the gladiators for their time, promising to return with a copy of the story I am writing, if indeed it is printed. Before I leave I grab a few quotes from tourists in the area.

'They seem friendly enough but I met a guy yesterday who said he'd been threatened by them,' says Leslie, a rotund Californian licking a gelato for morning tea. 'He paid them 20 euros for one photo. He said one gladiator took the photo and wouldn't give his camera back to him until he handed over the money.'

Soon I have enough on my notepad. I walk determinedly to an Internet café, ignoring the grating pop music blaring over the speakers to file my story.

Two days later I receive an email from my contact.

Hi Penny. Thanks for the story. It came up well. We'll run it this weekend in *Italy Daily*, and it will be syndicated in *The International Herald Tribune*. Send me your bank account details. We'll pay you 50 euro for the story.

The payment is hardly a princely sum, enough to treat myself and a friend – if I had one – to dinner. But, for the first time in a long time, I am getting a good rush from work. I'm not faking anything. I'm not stressed by deadlines. And I'm having fun.

I go for a walk in the Historical Centre, smiling happily at total strangers who seem to be sharing my mood, then make my way home. As I walk past the entrance to the Colosseo Metro station I see a costumed figure standing in the station entrance. Glancing to get a better look, I see it's Gladiator Hogan. Holding a glass of beer in his hand, he sways gently from side to side, knocked occasionally by tourists and commuters using the Metro.

Mind your peas

I no longer need my travel alarm clock. Around 8 eight each
morning I am woken by the screams of the newborn baby
belonging to the Indian family whose apartment windows I see
directly across the *cortile*, courtyard. Then there's the pub located
at street level below our palazzo, which blares pub rock until 3 am.
Six days a week.

During the day I often glimpse the family: there is a handsome,
goateed young man who I assume to be the husband of the
attractive woman wearing a sari who nurses the hot pink bundle
of blood-curdling shrieks. A grandmother and another young
woman, presumably the sister of one of the married couple, are
almost always present.

Like me, the family keep their apartment windows wide-open
in summer to let in any whispers of air. It's too hot to sleep in
clothes so, before I throw my legs over the loft bed and use my
toes to find the ladder to scale down to the floor, I have to make
sure no one is looking. I don't want to give the granny a heart
attack, or the husband a cheap thrill.

When the baby cries and his wife is trying to calm her, the man
often leans on the window ledge, smoking a cigarette and looking

across at my window or the others around me. If I happen to be standing near my window and we catch each other's gaze, we exchange neighbourly smiles. When his child won't stop wailing, I wonder if the man dreams of life as he knew it before nappies and sleepless nights as much as I find myself longing for the quietness and the seemingly infinite space of my childhood at Loomberah, a hamlet on the outskirts of Tamworth, New South Wales, the country music capital of Australia. On our 40-hectare property, there wasn't a building or neighbour within cooee. Just paddock after paddock, a meandering creek, gigantic gums and fences stretching to the horizon.

Dropped off by the rattly school bus, the three Green girls would scramble over a gate and race our bikes along a bush track to reach home, where Mum would be waiting with a cuddle and, about twice a week, a freshly baked treat still warm on the inside. Tomboys in spirit and wardrobe, on weekends we packed provisions in tea towels tied to sticks, pulled on our boots and went for excursions around the property. Picking blackberries, yabbying, making mud-pies, going to pony riding school and the free thrills of country wildlife – from chooks, sheepdogs and deadly snakes to kangaroos, goannas and our pet cow, Effie – were at our doorstep. And one day I could have sworn I saw a yowie.

Soon after I finished school and left for Sydney – where Mum and Dad were born, bred and fell in love – my folks moved to Orange in the Central West. After thirty years, they're wedded to country life but, as much as I miss the bush, I crave the urban jungle and its unpredictable underbelly. Still, my nine lives as a city cat are fast being exhausted by my new Roman existence.

A typical palazzo has up to ten *piani*, or floors, and an elevator with two sets of doors. If you don't shut both sets properly, the elevator doesn't work and the building stairwell echoes with the huffy complaints of residents forced to climb to their apartments.

If you're lucky, like Nina and Tiziana, you have a bedroom window with street views. But more commonly, as with my room, you have direct views of the apartment windows opposite, across the *cortile*, or of the windows of another palazzo behind. It's a wonder *Grande Fratello*, 'Big Brother', has been such a hit when apartment life offers such rich realities.

Occasionally there is a tabloid scandal in Australia when an old person kicks the bucket at home but it takes at least a year for anyone to cotton on, perhaps because the victim had no surviving relations. In Italy, I doubt that ever happens, and not just because the elderly often live with their families. Most palazzos have a resident *portiere* who collects mail and would notice if something were amiss. If not, someone else would, because residents live in each other's pockets.

I began to understand just how much when I watched the film *La Finestra di Fronte*, *The Window Opposite*, in a beautiful Perugian theatre-cum-cinema. The film details the life of a young and unhappily married mother who spies on the spunky young man she sees each day through her kitchen window, which faces his apartment. Having a cigarette in the dark before she goes to bed, she watches in secret as her attractive neighbour goes about his life, unaware he is under surveillance. When he brings home a date, the woman observes his every move before he turns off the lights. Eventually the two end up in a damaging tryst. It's not hard to work out why the film raked it in at the box-office. The average Italian would find the plot highly credible.

I do a security check before swinging my body down to the floor. Nina is nowhere to be seen and the house is silent again, save for the sound of a man in a bathroom across the way. He clears his throat and hoicks repeatedly, reminding me of Luca in Perugia. I try to block out the noise as I swallow my cereal.

At 9.30 am, I have a new trial as a waitress at Ristorante Pasqualino Al Colosseo. Situated four blocks from home, it was the last place I visited during my marathon job hunt.

I am exhausted, having worked the night before at Carlomente and crawled into bed at 2 am then tossed to pub anthems. Yet I can't seem to say no to anything. If someone asked me to be a pole dancer I'd probably give it a whirl. Anything to avoid thinking about life's bigger questions. Like where my career is not going. Like whether being in Italy is going to cure my restless state.

Walking in the side entrance of Pasqualino it strikes me as a very traditional, family-run restaurant that is kitschly cute without trying. I stop and stare at the framed black-and-white photographs hanging on one wall. A group of people – including a young, tubby man wearing a chef's hat and an old biddy with a floral apron tied around her waist – stand in the restaurant.

I turn and look at the tables. Set with flowery blue tablecloths and decorated with wine glasses filled with serviettes and *grissini*, dried bread sticks, they remind me why I love eating out in Italy. Going to small restaurants like Pasqualino, I feel as if I'm in someone's dining room. Surrounded by the gregarious Italians, I somehow feel that I am a part of the family.

Searching for a sign of life, I walk towards the *cassa*, a small wooden booth where there is no cash register, just a locked money drawer. Fixed to the wall is a small television. Italians have a habit of putting the box on at meal times, no matter the location. It's as if they always want to feel like they are in their own homes.

I hear a noise and see the beer gut of Nicola, one of the owners, enter the premises.

'*Eccola!* Here she is,' he says, as the rest of his body arrives. He motions for me to follow him through a small door off the dining room. His bushy, wriggling eyebrows distract me when he talks. Inside is a poky cloakroom that smells of just-removed shoes.

Leaving my bag on a hook, I take a burgundy apron and team up with the head waiter, Mario, whom I find in one of the two upstairs dining rooms.

A sweet-natured Egyptian who goes by the name of Mohammed in his homeland, Mario mumbles his own version of Italian and smokes incessantly as he works. He demonstrates what my tasks are or imitates the act in question until I cotton on. I sweep floors and help him set tables, watching as he folds the serviettes and arranges them in wine glasses so they fan out like a dove's tail.

Soon I am trudging upstairs with a bucket of hot water and a mop to clean the marble floors. Mario takes me into the men's and ladies' toilets and points at the floor, hand-wash basins and porcelain toilets. It's obvious cleaning the dunny is part of the job description.

I clean the dining room floors for as long as possible before going to the bathrooms, where Mario has left some cleaning products and rags. I spray window cleaner on the mirrors and rub them clean with newspaper and I scrub the hand basins until they gleam. Then I begin the task I don't mind doing but had hoped to avoid. Inside the men's toilet cubicle, cigarette butts rest in the waste-paper bin and on the floor. The stench of urine makes me half retch. What do blokes *do* in toilets? Do they piss on the white-tiled walls and floors because they are sloshed, dud shots or, worse, just plain lazy?

Bastardi!

I hold my breath and spray as much cleaning product as I can to create a hygienic barrier. The rubber gloves I am wearing don't seem adequate. I want to wrap my entire body in clingwrap. I thank my lucky stars there is only one men's toilet.

Downstairs there are new personalities to meet. Built like a praying mantis, Ennio has an excuse of a moustache, a fine, long nose and thin lips. As Mario introduces us, he shakes my hand and gives me a wide, cheeky grin.

My eyes drop almost a full body length from Ennio to see Vittorio, a grey-haired version of the dwarf in 'Fantasy Island'. With a thick nose and lips, his hair is neatly parted to one side and slicked down. A perfectly positioned bowtie is perched on a starched white shirt. He swaps his cigarette from right to left so he can shake my hand. He looks at me with the proud smile of someone with Little Man Syndrome.

Beside him is Stella, a young Italian girl with tight, jet-black ringlets and heavy eye make-up. She chews gum constantly and wears tight, low-cut pants that accentuate her enormous booty. She smiles at me shyly. I peg her at twenty years old.

Simone is the son of Nicola. At twenty-three he is much leaner than his father, but it's not hard to see he will morph into his old man later in life. His command of English is decent, giving me hope he can be the translator-cum-negotiator I desperately need.

The kitchen is run by two Egyptians – Fabio, the head chef, and Marco his assistant. Given Italy's reputation as the culinary king, it amuses me that so many Roman restaurants have kitchens run by immigrants. Offering me a timid hello, Fabio seems sweet-natured, but Marco soon proves himself to be *un cretino*. Each time I walk into the kitchen to collect trays of prepared antipasti to put in the glass cabinet in the dining room, his eyes burn holes in my tits or bottom. He stops me whenever he can to ask questions he probably already knows the answer to by talking to his colleagues.

He asks me where I am from, cornering me as I grab a tray piled with *piselli*, peas, flavoured with *pancetta*, bacon, and another with chunks of *coniglio*, rabbit, roasted with garlic and rosemary. I finish placing dishes in the cabinet – marinated peperoni, capsicum, and *cipolle*, onions, diced and fried *zucchine*, boiled *carote* sprinkled with *prezzemolo*, parsley, *trippa*, tripe, and *fegato*, liver, cooked *alla Romana* – before it's suddenly midday and Mario is shoving a plate of spaghetti with a simple tomato sauce in my hand.

'*Mangia, mangia!*' he says, standing on foot and tucking into his own plate.

I scoff the helping on my plate then dump it in the kitchen for the dish-pig, a Sri Lankan with a strangely bloated stomach and one skittish eye.

As if on cue, the lunch rush starts. I find myself designated bread woman, cutting it and running back and forth to deliver it in baskets to new tables. I watch Mario, Vittorio, Ennio and Stella swipe plates from tables – even when the diner is munching the last mouthful, fork still in hand. In my parents' café it was *de rigueur* to wait for every person at the table to finish before clearing dishes. I feel rude, but I follow custom.

By mid-afternoon, I reckon I've mastered the *Cimbali* machine, making espressos, macchiatos and cappuccinos. But there is no pleasing Nicola, who sits at the cash register, writing bills dictated to him by the waiters. For the umpteenth time he looks at two cappuccinos I have made and glowers.

'*Guarda,*' he says, pointing at a table occupied by two Irish tourists for whom I made cappuccinos ten minutes earlier. I shake my head in frustrated miscomprehension. Nicola grabs me by the hand and frogmarches me to the women's table. Finally it dawns on me that they have not touched their cappuccinos because the milk is too hot. The women utter that they do not mind, but Nicola is still steaming.

'*Ma...*' I try to defend myself, but it's useless. Every time I go near the coffee machine Nicola watches me like a hawk.

As the last of the lunchtime diners straggle out the door, Mario sets another table with care. The kitchen staff arrive with multiple plates of *gnocchi al sugo* and within minutes everyone is stabbing the little, potatoey parcels in a thin tomato sauce and shelling out compliments to Fabio.

I am starving but I stare at my plate with dismay. If I eat pasta twice a day, I'll turn into Pavarotti. How does this unlikely crew eat the stuff twice a day – maybe even three times, if they repeat the process at dinner – and think their diet is normal, let alone interesting?

'*Grazie, ma prendo antipasti.* Thanks but I take antipasti.'

I get up from the table and go to the antipasti counter and load a new plate with *coniglio alla cacciatore* and a big mound of *piselli*, my favourite vegetable.

As I go to leave, Nicola looks up from the now deserted table, a spot of sauce resting on his chin.

'*Se ti va puoi lavorare sei giorni a settimana dalle 9.30 alle 3.30 dal Martedì alla Domenica e ti do cento venti euro.*'

Confused, I call out to Simone to check I have understood. They want me to work six hours a day, from Tuesday to Sunday, and they'll pay me 120 euros.

I ruminate on the spot. Do I look like a monkey? I've earnt ten times the amount at home. After paying rent I'll only have 80 euros – about 150 dollars – to buy food, pay bills and go out.

I give myself a reality check. I am no longer a working professional so it's obvious I am going to earn a pittance for now. Pasqualino will allow me to practise my Italian and it's close to home. I will have my afternoons off to study and I won't spend much on food, with two meals provided at the restaurant.

'Okay, *grazie*,' I respond, trying to put on a bright face.

As I am walking out the door, I see Ennio getting into a sleek, red sportscar.

'*Ti piacciono i piselli?*' he asks, looking at me mischievously. I wait for an explanation.

'The peas – you like them?' asks Marco, appearing nearby with a sneaky grin.

'*Si, si, molto!*' I exclaim, elated to speak three words in comprehension.

The two men double over laughing and leave abruptly.

At home I find Nina packing a suitcase to go to Germany for a week. Quashing my disappointment, since she's only been home for two days and I've barely seen her, I ask her what is so funny about enjoying the flavour of peas.

'Oh dear,' she says, when I explain what happened.

'In Italian slang, *pisello,* the singular form of pea, means penis.'

I laugh, but my anger mounts as Nina disappears out the front door. If I don't learn the language soon I am going to be ridiculed at every turn. I close the doors of my room and swot.

My eyes sting with tears as I read an email from my sister, Lisa, the next day, responding to the email I sent home voicing my doubts and questioning my decision to come to Rome. Absorbing every word, I can almost hear her voice. I grab a tissue to prevent a weepie in front of the sea of strangers in the Internet café.

> Don't stress too much about the what ifs, just enjoy each moment. Sydney is going to be waiting for you when you get back. Nothing has changed. Don't forget some people would kill to do what you're doing.

What? I find it hard to believe anyone would murder for the chance to clean skid marks and work like a traffic light on Parramatta Road. I force myself to write back a cheery reply, including news about my Gladiator story, then have a stern talk with myself.

In the short walk to Piazza Vittorio Emanuele II, droplets of sweat gather under my boobs, held up by a backless halter-neck frock I don every second day, because it's the coolest thing I own. I now understand why the locals go away in August. I feel like I'm a melted figure in a Dali picture and it's only 9 am.

I've read there is a huge fresh produce market halfway between my home and Termini train station. I've been in Rome for two weeks and while my lingo hasn't improved vastly, thanks to my waitressing I have more confidence and I'm determined to have more success than I did at the market in Perugia. Plus, I want to stock up on fruit and vegies to make some healthy meals. Anything but pasta.

Piazza Vittorio Emanuele II is a large rectangular space enclosing grass, trees and some ruins. Crisscrossing through the grid of streets nearby I enter what seems to be a little China Town. I pass store after Chinese store selling cheaply made clothes, sneakers and ugly lingerie. How can so many shops make a profit? Something smells decidedly fishy. Every second face I see is contorted by hardship and chaos, and noise and grime give the area an underworld pall. I will later learn the zone is the turf of a network of Chinese, Mafia-linked groups. Thrown into the mix are a series of wholesale bead and jewellery shops run by African, Indian and Sri Lankan men. Every so often an ugly Phone Centre – filled with telephone booths, old computers and blinding fluorescent lighting – blots the urban landscape.

I am beginning to wonder where the market is when I spy in the distance a stream of people carrying white plastic shopping bags, exiting from a long, factory-like building. Horns honk and men in white coats graphically stained with animal blood haul carcasses off the back of trucks. Random apples bounce off fruit crates and workers holler to be heard above truck motors and *motorini* throttling past on the dirty street.

Inside the market the sensory chaos continues. Stall after stall line the outer, rectangular market and snail gradually into the middle of the building, a pressure-cooker of humidity. I walk around the outer ring, comprised of fruit, vegetable and meat vendors. In the heat the bloody, raw meat – *vitello*, veal, *manzo*, beef, *tacchino*, turkey, *maiale*, pork, and more – appears hygienically challenged.

'*Buongiorno, bella, che prendi?* Good morning, beautiful, what will you have?'

A young man dressed in a white coat jolts me back to reality with a sleazy smile. I drop my gaze and see the sinewy, skinned carcasses of rabbits with their eyes still in the socket. I scurry off timidly, leaving him to chuckle and sharpen his tool – a big knife with a thick blade that looks as if it would cut through bone like butter.

Towards the middle of the market, the odour of fish becomes overwhelming. In the courtyard there are around ten stores selling seafood. Stacked on ice, the chunks of *salmone, tonno* and *vongole* look less than appetising. The floor is stained with bloody water and innards. I think of the Sydney Fish Markets and sigh before turning my back.

I find an attractive fruit stall with electronic scales where the prices seem decent.

'*Buongiorno, mi dica.*'

Mi dica? I stare at the old man with grey hair and spectacles in front of me with suspicion. Giving him the benefit of my serious doubt, I take a deep breath and attempt to order. The man begins filling a bag for me but soon his young assistant steps in and takes over. Grabbing a bunch of bananas, the young man fires a couple of sentences at me. I feel like I'm on the receiving end of an automatic machine which spits tennis balls. I pick out the inevitable question from the flurry. Everyone wants to know where I am from as soon as they hear my accent.

'*Hai un marito?*' The rascal wants to know if I am hitched.

'*Sì.*'

I lie to make myself feel somehow untouchable. Yet, if I ever did have an Italian husband, I bet I'd still have to wade into this male-dominated moshpit to do the shopping, because it seems Italian women are born with the responsibility of food preparation.

I circle the market again, suddenly taking notice of what is in season, more so than I would at home, merely because what you buy is what's on offer in the fields at any given time, as opposed to a product that's grown in artificial conditions and available all year. I buy radicchio, carrots, zucchini, tomatoes, lettuce, fennel and more. I grab a six-pack of eggs and throw some change into the hands of the man behind the counter.

'*Buona scelta, bella,*' he says. Here a *bella,* there a *bella.* I must remember to come to the markets when I'm having a fat day.

Hot and bothered, I leave the building. As I turn to head towards home I see an old man sitting on a dilapidated bicycle. Wearing a beret and cotton jacket despite the heat, he has mounted the stationary bike on a makeshift base on the footpath. He pedals to propel a concrete wheel, mounted on a piece of wood attached to the handles. He presses the blade of a big knife against the wheel, sharpening it with precision. As I watch, butchers run out and greet him, handing over or taking back their tools.

My contact at *Corriere della Sera* wants any story from a foreign perspective – things that any non-Italian may find remotely interesting. The old man fits the bill. A labourer who roams the city sharpening knives by hand. I can't remember the last time I saw one of those in Sydney's CBD.

I walk up to the bicycle formulating phrases in my head.

As I start talking, the old man stops pedalling and leans in so closely I can see wispy hairs growing out of his ears, nose and chin. He remains silent.

'*Sono una giornalista, scrivo per* Il Corriere della Sera – *posso parlare con te*? I am a journalist. I write for the *Corriere della Sera* – can I speak with you?'

The man grunts and looks at me suspiciously. I smile hopefully. I catch a few words of his reply. *Dopodomani* means the day after tomorrow. He will be in via Firenze in two days.

I send an email to my *Corriere* contact and write up some questions for an interview I have decided I will do even if my proposal gets rejected. I'm interested to know his story, and if my story never gets published my subject will never know. I'm convinced he doesn't speak a word of English.

Loading all my vegetables into the near-empty fridge, I decide to make the most of the afternoon light, and a rare night off work, and go for a long walk. I wander through Villa Celimontana, a sprawling park near home, and then find myself in the adjacent Terme di Caracalla ruins, where well-sneakered locals in top-name gym gear run around a dirt track. It's rare to see Italians exercising, but when they do they tend to look as if they're competitors at Olympic trials. I have done one lap of the meandering track when I notice a bride and groom having their wedding shots taken. As I get closer I have to work hard to stop myself from laughing out loud.

With her chest thrust out and gown arranged so it falls perfectly around her, the exuberant bride stands with her back to a tree and her outstretched arms pushed back to embrace the thick trunk in a *Gone With The Wind* gesture. Standing beside her, the groom poses for the camera by looking at his newly betrothed with exaggerated adoration.

Sniggering to myself, I continue on my way but curiosity gets the better of me. I do another lap to see if Romeo and Juliet are at it again. This time the bride and her meringue have straddled a felled Roman column. She leans forward to look at her hubby, who lies on his back on the ruin beside her. As I walk past, I notice she has donned a pair of designer sunglasses and, on cue for the photographer, slides them down the bridge of her nose, as if to suggest her Romeo is such a hottie he's worth a second look.

I head home, feeling highly amused but strangely empty. Seeing a bride usually fills me with a mix of romanticism and fear but today I just felt envy – not because I want to get hitched, but because I long to be part of any *festa* surrounded by good friends and food.

At home I call Uncle Geoffrey and have a quick chat before Anna gets on the line.

'Anna, what's the Italian equivalent of the saying "You can't have your cake and eat it too"? When you want something badly but you can't expect to have it all at once?'

'*Non puoi avere la botte piena e la moglie ubriaca,*' she responds with a laugh before translating: you can't have a full keg and a drunk wife.

Sunday, bloody Sunday

Wherever I go in Rome the abrasive shrill of mobile phones is omnipresent. Whether on foot or *motorino* or in the car, the locals are always engaged. Prepubescent kids brandish them as a sign of wannabe maturity. Teenagers flaunt them as fashion accessories, sliding them into the pockets of their low-slung cargo pants. Business people use them to posture with importance as they pace to and fro. Even the blue-rinse set aren't exempt – a well-dressed *nonna* passes me on the footpath, click-clacking in modest heels and chatting on the mobile she must keep on vibrate: she's as deaf as a post.

'*Pronto…pronto…Mi senti? Ci sei?…pronto* – Hello, hello…do you hear me? Are you there?…hello –'

Using one hand to hold their power tool, the locals use the other to gesticulate like sign language interpreters. But by far the funniest thing is hearing them hang up. Uttering at least five *ciaos* in quick succession, they sound like human machine guns.

I have decided to get my Australian mobile connected. It's important to be contactable should a good job opportunity arise. Having a *telefonino* will also help me fit into the local scene. I wonder if I am doing the right thing by going to the TIM (Telecom

Italia Mobile) store. Watching TV I have noticed there are various phone carriers including Omnitel, Wind, Three and Vodafone. The latter is promoted by Megan Gale, who seems to get more soundbites than the Pope and Francesco Totti, the pin-up captain of Rome's soccer team, put together. All the carriers are offering different deals I can't understand. Whatever. Just connect me for the lowest price.

I enter the phone shop and produce my passport on request. Within ten minutes I have managed to convince the store assistant to give me an easy-to-remember phone number. It's a family tradition – moving house often in childhood, as my father built or renovated then resold properties, we had a few different phone numbers. But we never had a number that didn't have the same digit in succession at least three times.

'Can't you do better than that, mate?' my dad would ask the Telecom operator every time we moved.

I put the SIM card into my mobile – then suddenly feel very uncool. Everyone around me has a phone as small as a tampon. My three-year-old mobile is the size of a super sanitary napkin. With wings.

Explaining I can charge my phone credit at any TIM store or just buy a phone credit card at any *tabaccaio*, the store assistant asks me if I want the commands of the phone in Italian or English.

'*Italiano*,' I say stubbornly, watching him smirk in amusement.

Arriving at Pasqualino, I give Simone my new number to be put in the contact book then ask him to teach me some basic Italian as we work.

'*Cos'è questo?* What is this?' he asks holding up a spoon.

'*Non mi ricordo*. I don't remember.'

'*Un cucchiaio*,' he answers.

'*Cos'è questo?* He's holding up a knife.

'*Non lo so*… I don't know.'

'*Un coltello. Cos'è questo?*' He holds up a fork.

'*Una forchetta!*' Thank God some things are obvious.

'*Brava, Penelope!*' he says, patting me on the back as if I've just discovered the lingual equivalent of the theory of relativity.

As I mop the bathroom, I question how long it's going to take for me to master the Italian language. Working to my disadvantage is my shocking memory: I have to repeat words up to three times before they stick. I find this highly annoying, given my uncanny memory for the titles and lyrics of every crap song written in the '80s.

My biggest problem, however, is the fact I can't roll the letter 'r', present in every Italian verb. I can't physically curl my tongue from side to side – that is, shape it like a fat, hollow straw. They say it's a genetically traced skill, all I know is that most of my mates can do it. I've always wished I could too, just for the sake of it. Now I desperately want the skill for practical purposes. I'm convinced it's mysteriously connected to my failure to say '*Prrrrrrego*'. Until now an insignificant member of the alphabet, 'r' has taken on behemoth proportions.

The lunch-rush starts and I stifle a laugh as Mario, with a wonky bowtie and polished shoes, stands at the front of the restaurant, trying to lure in English-speaking tourists.

'Good morning. Like some lunch? Here you eat very good, very well, sir.'

I soon discover the locals and tourists are treated very differently. I overhear Mario asking the kitchen to prepare two plates of *bruschetta* and two *secondi* – then adding that the order is for Italian diners. I guess that cooking well for Italians, in particular Romans, takes priority since their patronage keeps the restaurant afloat in leaner months. Still, I can't help but think how contradictory the Italians are.

On the one hand they make me feel so welcome because of their open-arm affection and generosity, which explains why I haven't felt really homesick. Even though I am totally alone, wherever I go I still feel like I belong.

On the other hand, I am beginning to notice the locals often treat *stranieri* in the true sense of the word – as foreigners. Some Romans assume every foreigner is a fly-by-night tourist loaded with cash. As such, they try to milk them via unscrupulous means.

For someone like me, who hopes to call Italy home for a long time, it's hard to gain true acceptance. Whenever I talk to shopkeepers or people in my neighbourhood, I try to convey the fact that I plan to live in Rome for an indefinite period. The problem is, when I tell them I am Australian they shake their heads, unable to comprehend why I would possibly want to leave a country *così bello*, so beautiful, to put up with the *casino*, mess, that is Italy.

For now, I am too green and language-ignorant to notice the cracks in the system. But as I slap another dirty plate on the kitchen sink at Pasqualino, I can't help but dwell on my own private *casino*.

It's almost September and within three weeks I'm meant to be flying home, not just because my visa is close to expiring but because I have been invited to attend the wedding of two of my dearest friends in Sydney. I would give the world to return to Australia for such a special occasion. But apart from the fact my funds are low, I'm afraid if I go home I'll lose the tiny foothold I've created in Rome. I delay my decision, vowing to resolve the situation at the end of the month.

I walk the length of via Firenze near Termini station until I find what I am looking for. The old man on the bike is stationed outside a pizzeria, pedalling madly and sharpening a small filleting knife.

'*Buonasera*,' I say, feeling proud to have used the term correctly. Before my arrival in Italy, I thought one said good evening only at night time, but now I know better: it's advisable to say *buonasera* anytime after midday. *Buongiorno* tends to be expressed only in the morning, just like a cappuccino is normally only enjoyed before midday.

The man looks at me blankly over the bridge of his antiquated spectacles and I reintroduce myself.

The man continues pedalling and looks at me with curiosity.

'*Prego.*'

I begin asking him the questions I have carefully written and rewritten on my notepad.

Trying to understand Pietro Ciccone is confusing, and I feel pesky repeating questions two or three times, but slowly I make ground. From what I can gather, he's seventy-six, he works six days a week and, in days gone, once rode from his home on Rome's outskirts to the city to work. Now he catches the Metro into town. He and his brother carry on a trade their late father taught them. He loves his job because he moves around the city and is always outside. His work requires attention and he has never injured himself. Things I can't catch I write down phonetically.

'*Grazie tante, grazie tante*,' I tell him, heading home to escape the blistering heat. One particular phrase takes me ages to decipher because of the different tenses used. *Se passasse una bella donna il mio lavoro potrebbe essere pericoloso* translates as 'if a beautiful woman passes my work could be dangerous'.

I smile to myself. From young couples I see pashing in public to old men like Pietro, Italians have a keen sense of the romantic.

I arrive early at Pasqualino on Sunday, the sixth day of my second working week, tired and irritable. I interrogate myself angrily. What are you doing working so hard? Are you trying to punish yourself for leaving a life that was perfect on paper at home? Why don't you give yourself a break?

I set a few tables before eating my pre-lunch rush pasta and watch Ennio grin at himself in a mirror to make sure he hasn't got any remnants of food between his teeth. As the first tourists arrive – a tall, lumbering German couple who look like they regularly drink their bodyweight in beer – I go to the small room at the back of the kitchen to cut some bread. The loaf is unusually crunchy and hard to cut.

Vaffanculo! I curse to myself – then smile. I am swearing in Italian. It's supposed to be a good sign of progress when you start swearing or dreaming in another language.

'Penelope!'

Simone is in the kitchen, yelling out something else to me. Distracted, I look up. The knife slips in my hand and another Italian swear word comes out of my mouth as swiftly as the blood that stains the bread and chopping board before my eyes.

'*Aiuto!*' I bleat for help and Marco is the first on the scene.

He assesses the scene and runs off, returning with a bandaid. The cut is small but it's on the tip of a finger, so blood flows freely.

'*Non c'è niente de male – tranquilla*, It's not bad – stay calm,' he says.

Marco rests his hand lingeringly on my hand but for once his sleaziness doesn't annoy me. I'm tired and a kind face is welcomed. In an instant tears are springing in my eyes. Like falling off a bike, it's not the graze that upsets me, just the shock of the accident.

I contain myself and throw myself back onto the dining floor, slicing desserts and making coffees while ignoring Nicola's displeasure at my work.

Half an hour later, Mario blasts me in front of the whole restaurant for bringing him a litre of wine, rather than the half-litre he had requested. Defeated, I run for cover, seeking solace in the upstairs bathroom. Having seen no one is dining upstairs, I emerge after a few minutes and plonk myself on a chair to try to compose myself. But try as I might to contain them, tears slide steadily down my cheeks.

As an adult, it doesn't matter who yells at me, I am suddenly transported back to childhood, standing in front of my dad, who is a gorgeous man but has an explosive temper. If I did something naughty he would fly into a rage that would last less than a minute. But his angry, shouting voice would reduce me to tears in seconds. Tonight, Mario has pulled my kid trigger.

Right now, three weeks of frustration and sleep-deprivation, of waitressing for below-award wages in an environment I don't fully understand, is gushing out. I am studying at home and trying to force myself to speak the language but nothing seems to be working. I am sick of feeling stupid at every turn. I can't work here any more. I am a liability.

Simone arrives and I spray my emotions his way. I tell him I don't think I can carry on. Raising his eyebrows, Simone remains speechless in the face of my Academy Award-winning performance, evocative of the speech Gwyneth gave when clasping her Oscar in 1999. Suddenly Fabio appears, interrupting his kitchen duties to give me a can of soft drink. Streams of sympathetic words come out of his mouth. From what I can gather, he is trying to tell me Mario has problems at home. Clutching a wad of toilet paper to pat my eyes dry, I listen to him with a rush of gratitude. Here he is consoling me, while the orders stack up downstairs. I am starting to feel like a nuisance, making such a fuss over such an insignificant event.

Offering parting words of comfort, Fabio goes back to the kitchen.

Simone clears his throat and speaks in English.

'This is one moment. Come back on Tuesday and we will see. I will not play the clown so much. I will help you learn things, how to do the antipasto and wine. It will be okay.'

I spend the next twenty minutes composing myself when I hear Nicola yell out my name. I walk sheepishly downstairs, still teary despite the fact I have resolved to come back – because I want to prove to them, to *myself*, that I can master this blasted language.

'*Penelope, ti prego. Che brutta figura – calmati.*'

Walking home I try to decipher what Nicola said, but I can't. I choke back tears of frustration again. I grab the dictionary as soon as I walk in the door. *Figura* means figure, form, shape or picture. *Fare una brutta figura* means to make a bad impression or scene.

Bloody Italians and their fixation on veiling the ugly and keeping up appearances. Still, looking at my puffy red face and bloodshot eyes, I can't help but agree with Nicola.

In less than two hours I head to Carlomente to do an extra shift, because it's too late to cancel and the extra cash and change of scenery are welcome. Arriving early, I wander Trastevere's quaint, narrow streets and sit on the steps of the fountain in the main piazza. Directly opposite me is the Basilica di Santa Maria in Trastevere, a grey church illuminated by a mosaic image made from coloured and gold tiles.

I never tire of people-watching, no matter the location. Tourists ignoring the heat soldier past with water bottles and maps, looking for the next historic location listed in their guidebook. They seem oblivious to some of the smaller subtleties of life around them, like the five old men sitting in café chairs nearby and the group of heavily-pierced, undernourished young punks standing chatting, smoking and patting emaciated, ugly dogs.

I take in the scene in the piazza and feel a small surge of joy. When I slow down and think about everything I am doing, I am fundamentally happy. Sure, I have daily doubts as to what the hell I am trying to achieve, but I had those at home. Creating a new life in Rome is turning out to be far harder than I thought, but at least it's all new. And I'm in a country I have long adored – for reasons I am still beginning to understand.

For the entire night at Carlomonte, Sylvia, a feisty flame-haired waitress I haven't met before, is on my case. If I am not cutting bread fast enough I am making mistakes with the order of desserts or dropping cutlery. After a day at Pasqualino, I'm tired and it's showing. My energy and patience are perpetually running on empty.

Suddenly one of the Pammies is by my side, looking annoyed.

'*Sono troppo grandi!*' says Barbara, shaking her head at the two plates of dessert I have just served.

Grabbing the knife from me, she slices a much leaner portion. I look from the dessert plate to her emaciated figure. *That might be enough for you, Babs, but where I come from that's a mouthful.*

Clearing a table, I spy a 10-euro note sitting near a fork. Without thinking, I put it in the pocket of my burgundy apron when no one is looking.

My mind whirs. What kind of a monster is Rome making me? I've gone from having a respectable career to stealing pears and pocketing a sizeable tip I should share with the others.

But I have already decided I will never set foot in the door of Carlomonte again. No pride is taken in the preparation or delivery of the food and tonight I saw the chef smoking in the kitchen. I may be a petty thief, but I have standards.

In my bid to saturate my brain with Italian, I leave untouched the new English books I bought when passing through Heathrow and instead sample the range of newspapers sold at the *giornalaio*. I want to know everything that is happening in Italy, but it takes me forever to read one article. One newspaper could last me a week – I'm hardly going to be abreast of current affairs.

My English boycott is foiled when I get a surprise visit from my dear Pommie friend James, who lives in London. We met two years earlier, when he was in Sydney on a working holiday, and had a brief fling. I'd just split up from a serious relationship and had decided I was going to Italy. There didn't seem to be any point in getting involved.

Later, I wondered why I'd been so adamant. He's a catch: tanned with blond hair and cheeky, twinkling blue eyes, an IT guru who loves travelling, a beer and a chat. One of those blokes you always invite to a dinner party because he's a born entertainer, and who you want your mum to meet because he's a total charmer. But I had already promised myself no bloke was going to stop my trip to Italy.

Standing at the airport arrivals gate, I'm excited but suddenly full of suspicion. Is he coming purely as a friend or does he have an agenda? Passengers file out and there he is, gorgeous as ever, grinning from ear to ear. He gives me a big hug then hands me a black bag. Inside is a Mac laptop.

'James, what *have* you done?' I am elated, but feel guilty accepting such an expensive gift.

'I'm sick of getting text-corrupted emails from Internet cafés,' he jokes. 'Seriously, someone owed me a favour. It's second-hand but it works well. Don't think about it, just use it!'

Night has fallen by the time we get home, where James dumps his bags before we go to eat at a little pizzeria a few hundred metres from my palazzo.

'You look well, what's been happening in London?' I ask, remembering why I am attracted to him and trying not to sound like I am fishing for obvious facts.

'I seem to have landed on my feet since getting back. I'm paying dirt cheap rent for a flat on the Kings Road – only one of the most exclusive addresses in London – because I know someone, and I've found a job I'm really enjoying,' he says.

'Any other news?' I can't help it.

'Well, yes. I've just started seeing someone – it's early days, but it's going really well.'

I nurse a sharp jab of disappointment. Of course I am not surprised, but I wonder what could have been between us if the timing had been different. I remind myself that one always covets the unattainable.

'That's unreal – it's really good to see you looking so happy,' I say, suddenly relieved to realise I mean every word. James has no agenda. And neither do I.

We polish off a litre of red wine and catch up on the old and the new. Belly-laughing at a joke, the obvious hits me. I haven't had a good giggle since I arrived in Rome. I mean a *really* good giggle. I came to Italy to enjoy life more, but without even realising I've turned into a maniac, working like an idiot to keep myself busy and because I want learn the language. The problem is I've been so uptight about speaking only Italian that I've cut off my nose to spite my face.

Speaking in my own language, I feel a tidal wave of unexpressed emotion barrelling through me. Before I know it tears are filling my eyes and I am up for my second Oscar nomination.

'Oh God, I'm so sorry,' I say, trying to not draw attention to our table. 'I've just realised I haven't laughed so hard for ages, and how good it is to speak. I mean, do have you any idea how frustrating it is not to be able to speak, James? Every day I try and so often I can't say the smallest thing, the tiniest thing. I just want to *communicate*.'

'Pen, you are doing what you wanted to do, but it will take time,' he says, taking my hand. 'Don't be so hard on yourself, but if it does get too hard, there's no shame in leaving.'

Sweating under the relentless August sun, the next day James and I walk for miles around the main tourist sites before seeking shelter in the cool shade provided by Villa Borghese, the massive park perched just above the Spanish Steps. We dine out late and crash together in the same bed like old friends – without fear of crossing the mid-way mark accidentally.

When his visit comes to an end, I walk him to Termini, where he will catch the train to the airport. In three days the tough shell I have built around myself to cope with every day challenges has been melted by the love, support and companionship of a dear friend. Suddenly I feel very fragile.

We hug and as James looks back from the door of the train, my face threatens to betray my anguish.

'Bye!' I manage. 'I'll come and visit you soon!'

As the train pulls away I've already turned on my heel to save face.

Aspetta!

James has long gone, Nina is still in Germany and Alberta and Tiziana, if they do indeed exist, are yet to make a cameo. If I don't get some company soon I will be found wandering the neighbourhood, trying to strike up a conversation with anyone who looks innocuous – not just old men sharpening knives. As it is the newsagent thinks I'm a nutter – when I go and buy the paper once a week I always ask him how he is, even if he can't remember my face. I'll do anything to prolong random conversation. He has no idea how crushed I feel when he's too busy to respond.

With far too much time on my hands, I spy a clump of white just above my hairline. If they're not falling out in clumps, my hairs are going white or grey. So much for the low-geared life in Italy. It must be stress. Without realising it, each day I operate on a constant wave of anxiety trying to decipher all things foreign. It's time to hit the bottle.

I walk to the supermarket and stand in front of the rack of hair products. Buying anything packaged in the Italian language is fraught with peril. In Perugia, I bought bleach instead of washing detergent. I could have sworn all the pretty diagrams were telling me it was detergent and almost felt smug at the cash register. If not for Maria's last-minute intervention, my limited wardrobe would have resembled that of ABBA in their 'Arrival' days.

Thankfully hair-dye brands have global roots. I work out which are semi-permanent products and choose a deep-brown, almost black, colour that nukes my white hairs and leaves a few ugly splotches on my hands.

Fresh out of the home beauty salon, I whack on my Birkies, a faded denim skirt and a singlet top and decide to go outside to dry my hair and catch some mid-morning sunshine before it gets too hot. Finding a bench seat on the corner of an intersection of two streets near home with a view of the Colosseum, I sit down for a game of solitary people-watching.

Everyone raves about how Italian chicks are among the most stylish in the world, and it's true around gorgeous parts of Rome, like Piazza Navona and Campo de' Fiori, I've seen women who look like they were born in the house of Chanel. But in downtown San Giovanni in Laterano today there are no Cates or Graces – just a few women with stomachs so flat and brown I'd like to maim them.

As I watch the morning crowd pass I decide the average Italian woman wears clothes a bit too tight and pop-tart trashy for my simpler tastes. So why do they make me feel daggy?

Maybe it's because they are well shod, I think, watching a slim local woman wearing nail-thin stillettoes negotiate the cobblestones like grass. I rarely wear heels, because usually the shoes in vogue are so delicate I fear my muscular frame will snap them. I also avoid them because I am dangerously clumsy. Wearing disco heels to a party a few years ago, I fell down a small step and landed at the feet of an ex I would have swallowed a witchetty grub to avoid. While alcohol was a factor, the dastardly heels were to blame. Thankfully the ex had the grace to pull me up off the floor – and save his belly laugh until I melted out of sight.

Or perhaps I feel like a crumpet because Italian women, even if they look like mutton to me, dress to look their personal best for any occasion. Standing in the supermarket, I often feel like I am in a fashion warehouse, surrounded by designer labels and Liza Minnelli make-up.

The thing is, I suddenly realise, Italian women carry off pretty much any fashion faux pas because they wear their clothes with attitude. Whether *bella* or *brutta*, they know how to carry themselves. And they always make a riveting show of their femininity.

I love frocking up for special occasions, but I'm a tomboy at heart. I feel overdressed in clothes some girls would dismiss as casual and feel dressed up in a new Bonds T-shirt. I haul out a dress to wear to a party only to shove it back in the wardrobe in favour of jeans and my Blundstone boots.

An agitated woman sits down on the edge of my bench, screeching angry words into the mouthpiece of her mobile. I steal glances at her sideways. Despite the heat, her make-up coats her bronzed complexion in perfect proportions. Light foundation, heavier eye make-up and eyebrows plucked to perfection. I have eyebrows like Brooke Shields in *The Blue Lagoon* and, beyond lipstick, am incapable of applying any form of beauty-enhancing product without making myself resemble Chucky.

I drop my gaze to look at my very casual outfit. At the very least, the appearance-conscious locals shame me into wanting to dress better – and perhaps even get chummier with my feminine side.

My hair has dried. It's too hot to stay outside. I walk home, trying to make like a local, striding with sass and self-importance. My Birkenstocks thwack the pavement. I give up.

Heeding the advice of the Romanian waitress, Maria, at Carlomente, I sit down to watch TV to improve my Italian. She told me that she learnt Italian in six months, mainly through watching the box. I try to concentrate on the words but the dialogue is way too fast.

I flick it off and return to my room to lie down when I hear the front door bang open. Nina is in Germany for a few more days. It must be one of the Italians! Company!

I race into the corridor to see a petite, curvaceous girl with mousy brown hair lugging a bag through the door. It's all I can do to stop myself from lifting her bosomy frame high in the air.

'*Ciao, sono Alberta,*' she says.

I introduce myself and we make small talk – in broken Italian and English. I don't want to tell her I can't comprehend much because I want her to express herself normally and treat me as an equal.

I soon learn Alberta is an architect who works for a small firm in the city and also lectures at university. She has just returned from her family home in Bari, the port capital of the region of Puglia, basically the heel in the boot-shape of Italy, which she shows me on the map stuck to the kitchen door. Tomorrow she is going to Morocco for a holiday.

I suddenly realise I have no idea what Stefan has told her or the household about me, so I tell her that he has lent me the room for a month and that I have found a few waitressing jobs. Alberta's face seems to cloud over at the mention of Stefan. I had forgotten that Stefan, in minimal detail, explained that he and Alberta had a live-in relationship in my current home for a couple of years until recently. He's moved out and is living with his new love, Patrizia.

Great, if she thinks I am chummy with Patrizia we may already be off to a bad start. Alberta mumbles something about life being difficult and wipes away a few random tears. We sit down at the kitchen table and share a bottle of Nastro Azurro beer and a cigarette. She apologises for being emotional.

'*Non devi dire sorry.* You don't have to say sorry,' I say.

I want to speak in English, to tell her that I know how she feels, having left Australia feeling disillusioned with men and the world in general. But now doesn't seem the right time. She seems to want to have some peace. We go to our respective rooms.

A few hours later I am in the kitchen, sweeping the floor after making a mess of my afternoon snack, when the doorbell rings. Alberta answers and I hear a man's voice. Alberta passes the kitchen door, talking to a tall man with a young face and wavy, longish hair. Standing in the corridor within sight, he seems not to have seen me.

Dressed in loose jeans and a denim jacket, he has brilliant blue eyes, pale skin and a cherubic mouth. He's rock 'n' roll gorgeous.

I'm busting to say something but embarrassment and nerves hold my tongue hostage. Introductions aside, I can't think of what I might possibly say that might be appropriate.

Finally Alberta enters the kitchen with the man, who seems about my age.

'*Ciao, sono Federico,*' he says, a shy smile lighting up his face.

Christ, he's divine. As he leaves with Alberta I notice he's carrying a guitar case.

Resisting an urge to offer to be his sherpa, I decide to take advantage of the cooler evening temperature. Grabbing a guidebook and dictionary, I decide to take a *passeggiata*. I haven't really played tourist yet. I've been too busy being the waitress with the leastest. It's time to get a feel for the city.

I amble down my street until I am standing beneath the Colosseum. I do a guidebook skim and read it was built in 72 AD. Having cold water in the house suddenly seems a whole lot more romantic. With its foundations dating back to 753 BC, Rome is blanketed in scaffolding as centuries of history are constantly under repair.

I gaze through the security bars flanking the side of the Colosseum. I don't have to close my eyes to see fearsome gladiators springing from their underground cells to fight man or animal to the death in the circular combat field. Gnashing lion teeth and great paws tear shreds from recoiling bodies. I hear 50 000 spectators baying for blood then screaming for clemency from the emperor of the day, who is too busy ogling his mistress's cleavage and avoiding a platter of food he suspects is poisoned, to properly observe the dirty duels.

Near the ticket office, three costumed gladiators enjoy a smoko, apparently fed up with their battle for the tourist buck. Gladiator Hogan is not in sight.

I stride along via dei Fori Imperiali, past the rubbled layers and crumbling columns of the Forum; once the social, economic and legal heart of ancient Rome. In another leap of imagination the marching ant-line of tourists scrambling over the ruins become senators striding about pompously, plotting wars and secretly planning to assassinate or overthrow the ruling emperor.

I walk down into the Forum but apart from a few obvious buildings struggle to identify the ruins marked in my guidebook. Frustrated, I sneak into an English tour guide's group.

'So, this temple is pretty old and kind of important, huh?' an oversized, elderly American woman says loudly after the guide has slowly explained that the Temple of Saturn, built around 497 BC, was once used as a treasury where Caesar stockpiled tonnes of gold, silver and *sestertii*, the ancient Roman currency. I bite my tongue and think of all the intelligent, nice American friends I have.

I stroll up via del Corso, a main shopping drag, and turn right into via Frattina, one of the three trendiest streets in Rome which leads to the Spanish Steps. I stop beneath the Steps and glimpse a tall Franciscan monk, his chocolate brown robes billowing in his stride, with a mobile phone in his hand. I cut through a narrow street and see an old man wearing work overalls and sitting on a wooden chair outside a strange little shop crammed with wooden puppets. I pass a *pasticceria* and, in a backroom, see a tubby man cutting biscuits from dough.

Have I spent my whole life walking around with my eyes shut, or am I in Wonderland? I can't stop grinning at all things new and captivating.

I reach Piazza Navona, the enormous long oval piazza full of Baroque facades and marble fountains designed by Bernini, the renowned architect and sculptor whose name I constantly confuse with Bellini the famous Venetian artist active in the Renaissance. Strangely, I have no trouble remembering the ingredients of a Bellini, a refreshing Italian cocktail mix of *prosecco*, peach juice and a drop of raspberry syrup.

Caricature artists and street painters with leathery faces fill the length of the piazza. Nearby, white-tuxedoed waiters hawk menus to the stream of tourists filing past the bland restaurants with gaudy tablecloths. I find the street that intersects the piazza and follow it to find Bar della Pace. I had planned to ask for work again, since the bar is now open and packed with tourists, but on my one day off I suddenly lose interest. It can wait.

Turning on my heels, I head again to Campo de' Fiori. At 6.30 pm the famous produce market has long been packed up and a stack of wine bars that remain closed during the day are doing a brisk trade. Students and street kids sit chatting and smoking around the huge, cloaked statue of Giordano Bruno, the monk burnt on the stake in the same spot in 1600 for heresy.

I spy La Vineria, reputed to be the oldest and trendiest bar in the Campo, and peer inside to admire the wood fittings and antiquated charm. I make a mental note to return and ask for work there.

I start to head home when I realise I can barely move my over-waitressed legs. I wait on Corso Vittorio Emanuele at a bus stop with services to the Colosseum. Half an hour later no bus has arrived.

Seeing a man with a bus driver's uniform nearby, I try to discover what is going on.

'*Oggi cè lo sciopero,*' he says.

I look at my dictionary. *Sciopero* means strike. I will soon learn that Italy has almost as many strikes as public holidays, and if you don't read the paper you can get stranded at the most inconvenient time.

I get dressed to go to dinner at Patrizia's flat in Trastevere. She and Stefan are about to go on holidays for a month in Africa. I'm sad they are going. Alberta leaves tomorrow for a two-week holiday. The house will be empty. Again.

My weekly trips to the market tell me figs are in season and affordable even for those on a budget. I carefully wrap ten in a serviette to protect the soft, green skin from bruising, and put them in a bag with some slices of prosciutto. At Pasqualino and most restaurants in Rome, a standard, seasonal entrée is thin slices of prosciutto served with melon or fig. The salty meat contrasts exquisitely with the subtle texture and sweetness of the fruit. Tonight I've stolen the idea.

Patrizia sweeps open her apartment door and a waft of garlic and roasting tomatoes tantalises my nostrils. We are making small talk in the kitchen with Stefan when the intercom buzzes.

'*Pronto? Si, vieni!*' Patrizia says into the speaker.

Two minutes later the doorbell rings and my host opens the door. A blur of colour rushes in the door. Gibbering like a lunatic, a bald man wearing brown Jesus sandals and a shapeless burgundy smock drawn in slightly at the waist with a rope tie approaches me. Notwithstanding his scraggly beard and thin-framed spectacles, he is the Italian version of the Dalai Lama. He carries two mobile phones and two connecting earpieces that remain stuck in his ears when he's not talking on his mobile.

'Penny, this is Francesco, the landlord of your house,' says Patrizia.

The man smiles at me and offers his hand before a stream of incomprehensible Italian spews out of his mouth. I spend the evening trying to understand the sense of the conversation between Stefan, Francesco and Patrizia. Francesco speaks like he's just inhaled five lines of cocaine. Fast and furious.

Thankfully, after a delectable rigatone pasta with tomato and garlic and basil sauce, Francesco rolls a joint as long and thick as a cigar and within a few tokes I'm happily pickled. I forget any sense of the conversation and let the words wash over me as I watch the glow of city lights from Patrizia's outdoor balcony.

Stefano interrupts my trance.

'I am not moving back to my room where you are living, so if all goes well, once you meet everyone and talk about it with them, you could stay in that house,' he says.

'Great, thanks. Well, there are two weeks left to go, so we'll see.'

It could be a good option. It's a great location and despite its temporarily empty feel, the house and its quirky defects have already grown on me.

By midnight I am almost falling asleep when Francesco offers to give me a ride home. I kiss Patrizia and Stefan goodbye, trying not to show how sad I feel that they are leaving, and jump in the elevator with Francesco. Once outside he scurries to a black Porsche parked nearby and leaps in. Giggling at the incongruity of his Buddhist robes tucked behind the wheel of one of the fastest machines in the twenty-first century, I hop in the passenger seat. We zoom home, Francesco driving at breakneck speed, which no longer frightens me. Pulling up at the green door of our palazzo, his beard bristles my cheeks as he kisses me goodbye, then he roars off.

My waitressing shift at Pasqualino has changed to night duty every alternate week. I make the most of my morning at home studying but after lunch I usually succumb to tiredness and have an hour-long siesta before I wake, shower and go to work at six.

Today, however, I can't sleep. The baby in the apartment opposite won't shut up. I swing my legs over the loft bed and feel with my feet until my toes are on the ladder and climb down to the floor. I need to sleep somewhere quieter. I stick my head into Nina's room, across the hallway, but it faces the road. Alberta's room, like mine, faces the flat with the baby.

Finally I look into the room of Tiziana, the only person I am yet to meet. Tiziana. I cannot say her name without laughing. I wonder how I might address her should we become good mates.

'Hey, Tits, you're not looking too perky today, what's up?'

'Rug up, Tits, it's a bit nippley out there today –'

'Have you seen my bra, Tits?'

Though facing the road, her room is darker than Nina's and more inviting as a sleeping den. I feel guilty invading the private space of someone I don't yet know, but I'm driven by tiredness. Like Goldilocks, I collapse on Tiziana's comfortable bed and crash out.

An hour later I wake up, my mouth as dry as chalk. I raise my head to get my bearings then look down at the pillow. There's a long, wet patch on the pretty cotton pillowcase. Whoops. I forgot that I sometimes dribble like a newborn if I have an afternoon nap. Oh well, the pillowcase will dry soon enough. Stefan said Tiziana wouldn't be home until the end of the month. I smooth over the quilt and jump in the shower.

I'm in my room twenty minutes later, reading on my bed, when I hear a banging noise and the sound of luggage being dragged along the corridor. I swing myself down the ladder onto the floor and poke my head out into the corridor.

A curvy girl about my height is standing in the kitchen doorway. Her look is foxy. Funky short skirt, beaded sandals with heels and a tight singlet. Her hair is short with cherry red streaks in the fringe. Her make-up is expertly applied to enhance deep brown eyes. I look down at my denim skirt with a broken side zipper and try to cup my chin to hide a pimple. Whether it's smog, stress or both, lately I'm getting skin blemishes only a teenager should suffer.

'Penelope? I am Tiziana.' The girl gives me a warm, wide smile.

Barely managing to stifle a giggle upon hearing her name, my head races with options as she plants two generous kisses on each of my cheeks. I have two choices: one, keep my trap shut about dribbling on her pillow and hope she doesn't see the wet stain or, two, confess and explain.

Sometimes I fervently wish I could curb my tendencies to wear my heart on my sleeve and speak my mind. But I have little time for games for the sake of making a good impression or currying favour. I prefer to shoot straight, if not blindly.

Building up the courage to confess, I first wait for Tiziana to tell me about her holiday with her family in Latina, about 50 kilometres south of Rome, according to the kitchen door road map.

In broken but decent English, she speaks of lazy days spent on the beach with her mother and brother. Warm and bubbly, she engages me in conversation, asking me about my time in the house alone. I tell her I have met Nina and Alberta briefly, and that I have found two waitressing jobs.

'But your Italian is not good and you have two jobs? *Brava!*' exclaims Tiziana, pouring two coffees for us from the small, silver espresso machine sitting on the stovetop. My heart sings. I've been feeling so unremarkable doing what I am doing but in one sentence Tits has somehow made me feel like a Nobel laureate.

'Tiziana, there is something I must tell you.'

As my innocent story unfolds, I watch in dismay as her eyes harden and narrow.

'I am really sorry I went into your room, I was just so tired. I didn't want to invade your privacy,' I say lamely, thinking of the day I kicked a hole in my sister's door because she wouldn't let me in after she found me devouring the pages of her diary. Okay, so I did cast an eye over Tiziana's room but I haven't been foraging through her belongings like a *News of the World* hack.

By the time I reach the point of telling Tiziana about the wet patch her lips look like a cat's bottom. It doesn't help that I am using basic English to try to better explain the problem. I can't make jokes to try and make light of the situation.

I listen in horror to my own voice, stumbling on.

'I forgot that when I sleep I sometimes dribble,' I say, laughing nervously.

'What is dribble?' she asks.

I don't have my dictionary and now isn't the time to climb up to my loft bed and get it.

'It is when you sleep and, um, saliva, do you know what saliva is? No? Um, you know when a baby –'

Tiziana watches, incredulous, as I play charades, trying to impersonate a baby who dribbles. She looks shitty, but she has at the very least understood I have the lingual skills of a three-year-old and I have been snoozing on her bed. I'm still not sure she understands the word dribble.

'No problem,' she says briskly, pushing her chair back and standing up in the kitchen.

'I must sleep now, I am tired.'

I retreat into my room and close my door, burdened with guilt. Surely I did the right thing? I am convinced she would have sprung me if I hadn't told her. I imagine her in her room, looking at the wet patch with disdain.

An hour later I dress for work. But before I go I want to make one last effort to smooth things over with Tiziana – even if there is nothing to add and I could make the situation worse by harping on about it. I want her to know I'm sincere.

I walk to her room and knock on the door. I can hear music playing softly. There is no answer. I knock harder.

'*Sì?*' A voice sings out.

'Tiziana, can I talk to you for a minute?' There is no response so I start to push the door open a little. She can't have heard me.

'*ASPETTA!*'

Tiziana's voice shrieks out with such force that instinct tells me I've done something wrong. I pull the door back hurriedly towards me and hover helplessly outside in the corridor, not understanding what she has told me and having no clue what to do.

Suddenly the door flings open and Tiziana appears, flushed and breathless. She's dressed in a blue satin nightgown. Her face flashes in annoyance at the sight of me. Again. At least I'm not dribbling.

'Um, I know I've told you before, but I just wanted to say I am sorry again for sleeping on your bed, I was tired and –'

Tiziana listens but appears distracted. I hear a mobile phone sound in the room behind her. I am about to tell her to respond when a man's voice intercepts the call.

'My boyfriend, Enzo, is here,' says Tiziana, peering down to make sure her boobs aren't escaping, her face as red as mine feels. 'We are...resting. Don't worry about it. It's okay.'

Tiziana backs carefully into her room, as if escaping a hostage drama situation, and shuts the door. I stand stupidly, wanting to lift up a marble floor slab and bury myself. I hear laughter coming from inside the room. I can imagine now the conversation between Tizi and Enzo, who were obviously going for it hammer-and-tongs when I knocked.

'She's Australian, poor pet. Doesn't understand a word.'

I go to my room and grab my dictionary. The verb *aspettare* means 'to wait'. I gather Tiziana was using the imperative form.

I grab my house keys and skulk out the door before there is any chance of bumping into anyone in the corridors and disgracing myself again. My memory is rotten, but I won't forget the word '*aspetta*' in a hurry.

I just hope Tits is woman enough to forgive me.

Una clandestina

All roads may lead to Rome but how to advance, now that I'm finally here? Spurred into action, I call the Australian Embassy and make an appointment to see the ambassador. I plan to tell him I'm a journalist writing the odd story in English for the *Corriere della Sera* and that I want to be put on the embassy contact list and informed of events happening about town.

The truth is my visa is due to run out in two weeks. I'm madly hoping an embassy job might be up for grabs, which might help me get a work visa. I've got good work contacts, plus writing and PR experience – but let's face it, I'll make coffee all day if I have to. It would be like being a CEO compared to my current gig.

Tiziana has left the house again to go on holidays in Sardinia with her mother. Nina and Alberta are still away. Thankfully one of my greatest friends, Coff, is flying in from London for a four-day visit. I'm looking forward to company, not to mention that of a close gal pal.

Organising two days off from Pasqualino to play host, I walk to Termini to meet her. The train pulls in and there she is, dressed in black pants and top with lashings of pink accessories and dragging more luggage than the Royal family.

'I knew you'd have this much gear,' I tease, as we walk to the Metro to catch a ride home.

'I've been to a wedding in London,' she protests, before breaking into her hearty laugh.

I know I'm being foolish, but I feel nervous taking Coff to my frightfully rustic home. Her life seems so adult compared to mine. She earns a great wage and has a modern house brimming with trendy appliances and luxuries – like a second bedroom. She'll be sleeping in my room on the futon bed I asked Alberta permission to borrow before she left for Morocco. And how do I explain that there's no hot water in the kitchen, not to mention an oven? Oh well, she'll just have to lump it. She may be the girliest friend I have, but Coff's no princess. She drinks like a truckie and barracks so fanatically for Collingwood it is only a very brave friend who accompanies her to the MCG for a home game.

We drag her bags home and spend the early evening catching up on all the gossip. The last time we saw each other was five months ago in Melbourne, working together to help co-ordinate publicity for the city's annual fashion festival.

Seeing Coff inevitably makes me reflect on the decisions I have made. She is going home to begin a fantastic new job for a chic boutique publicity firm in Melbourne. I am cleaning toilets in a restaurant for less than five dollars an hour.

'Pen, you've only just arrived, give yourself a break,' Coff says when I air my concerns.

I want to take her out to all the hip places – if only I knew where they were. I've been working nights and, besides, I haven't felt courageous enough to go out clubbing on my own to places that generally skirt the city, where public transport and taxis are harder to find.

I've heard, however, that the inner-city suburb of Testaccio is *the* place to go, so we get ready to hit the town. For dinner we head to a cosy little trattoria around the corner from home, where I once ate with actor Stefan. On that occasion, he translated the daily offerings rattled off by our waiter at high speed. Tonight, the minute we sit down, we are handed menus in English. Watching the waiter go to a table of Italians nearby and take their order without the assistance of a menu, I stifle annoyance before telling myself not to be so ridiculous. I can't understand what the hell he's saying, so it's obvious I need a menu. I just hate being treated as a tourist when I live around the corner.

Coff and I have an antipasto of roasted, breadcrumb-coated vegetables and two hearty plates of pasta, washed down with a bottle of red wine. We roll out the door in grand form.

I thought it might be nice to stroll to Testaccio on foot. Half an hour later we are hot and sweaty when we arrive in the general area, which seems strangely quiet. We ask for directions three times before we finally stumble on a clump of bars and clubs grouped in a dirt area resembling a disused parking lot.

Gay Village is a huge club that has several long queues at the entrance. Standing in line are twenty-something trailer-trash girls, wearing slutty jeans with wide, white belts and sequinned, off-the-shoulder tops beneath which they wear the latest trend – bras with transparent straps. The bras make me laugh, because they are worn as an obvious fashion statement not as the invisible aid they were perhaps originally designed to be.

The scent of perfume is overbearing. Coff and I eyeball each other with masked amusement, taking in the drama of the queues and acting nonchalantly cool. I have forgotten how try-hard the nightclub scene is. Dressed in jeans and a simple singlet top, I feel as sexy as Camilla Parker Bowles.

At the front of our queue we are told it's 15 euros to enter. We look at each other and read each other's mind, instinctively knowing that we don't want to pay almost 30 dollars to get into a club that has the ambience of a supermarket. We turn on our heels and continue along the dirt road.

From nowhere, a tall African man appears and starts laying compliments on Coff, who is pleasant until he won't stop harassing her.

'*Vaffanculo*,' I say.

The man sticks his face close to mine, hissing furiously and telling me it's none of my business. I grab Coff's arm and we escape to the nearest club we can find, paying a smaller entrance fee and leaving the man ranting to the bouncers at the iron door.

I don't know what I expected, but after the minimalist-cool decor Australian clubbing experience I feel like I'm at the Royal Easter Show. It's an open-air club and dust rises from the dirt dance floor that is being stirred up by the heaving crowd. Breaking off to the right and walking past two palm trees we stand at the bar, a makeshift affair with bottles of alcohol haphazardly stacked together. Our vodka sodas arrive tepid and made with lemon squash because although it's above thirty degrees the club has apparently run out of ice. And soda. Laughing at the inconvenience, we head to the dance floor, which takes up most of the cramped space.

Forgettable techno music pumps and I stare at the crowd around me. Flesh flashes from people who look at least ten years my junior, dancing like their lives depended on it. A young couple sway in time, the slick-haired guy spooning the girl from behind and rubbing his hands all over her belly, amid the blur of limbs and body parts which jerk and roll to the hip-hop beat. But it's the African dancers who cut up the dance floor, moving effortlessly to the music, their muscled physiques glistening with sweat and fake gold and silver neck chains. I'm not drunk enough to lose my inhibitions. I skol my warm vodka and bury myself in the crowd.

Suddenly I spy Coff eyeing me desperately for attention. She is being circled by a Sean Coombs lookalike who is getting seriously jiggy with it, thrusting his pelvis, barely covered by low-slung jeans, in her direction. I casually dance over to her and help her try to maintain some distance.

Within an hour we've grown so tired of unwanted male attention that we leave the club, well over the manic scene inside. It's 2.30 am and we're already stuffed. We walk home arm-in-arm, cackling like old biddies at a CWA meeting, reminiscing about glam events we attended in Sydney, from film premieres to product launches, drinking like fish and disgracing ourselves in some fashion.

Occasional as they were, I realise now I definitely took all the perks for granted.

The day of my appointment with the Australian Ambassador dawns. Coff goes off to melt her credit cards and I decide to walk to the embassy for a bit of exercise. Big mistake. By the time I arrive I am sweaty and probably stinky. Seeing the Australian flag for the first time in five months boosts my spirits.

Past the security at reception I take the lift upstairs and wait a short time before being shown into the ambassador's office. A small man with snowy hair and glasses, the ambassador is an amicable bloke I can imagine roasting a snag with at a barbecue. I had expected him to speak with more pomp and ceremony. Nevertheless, it doesn't seem appropriate to grill the ambo about how I can extend my almost expired visa, and I feel myself losing my nerve. After giving my journalist spiel, I skirt around the subject until I more or less establish that there's nothing up for grabs. We chat for half an hour or so about life in general, my legs sticking to the divan I have sunken into opposite the chair he is sitting in. I shake his hand and walk out the door, wondering if he thinks I'm as directionless as I feel.

Coff and I hook up to go to Trastevere in search of a homey trattoria for dinner on her last night in Rome. I am throwing money around like a Monopoly contestant but who knows when will be the next time I have a dear friend in town. I pretend I am spending Aussie bucks and avoid checking my bank balance.

Negotiating some backstreets to avoid walking past Carlomente, we search the maze of cobbled streets in Trastevere in search of the perfect ristorante. Every place seems to have a tourist menu. I am determined to find somewhere low-key where the locals chow down.

I signal to Coff, spying a narrow, timber-lined trattoria full of Italians without a tourist menu plastered outside. We enter to find a restaurant vibrating with commotion and fun. Italians sitting higgledy-piggledy at old wooden tables yell out to waiters who whir out of the kitchen juggling plates of antipasto, pasta and meat they deliver without airs and graces.

A stocky man with Jimmy Somerville's peroxided hair and camp disposition approaches us and says something we can't understand. The crowd laughs as he ushers us to a table, where a couple, their young daughter and a grandmother are sitting, and hands us a menu in Italian. The prices seem average, the food simple but delicious. The waiter returns and takes our order, including a dirt-cheap bottle of red.

We've barely started on our prosciutto antipasto when a voice blares out from a microphone somewhere. I swivel my body around to see Jimmy Somerville on stage, alongside a man with a guitar. Jimmy starts to sing in Italian as everyone starts clapping around us. The small girl beside Coff screeches in excitement and the *nonna* smiles patiently. Jimmy seems to be singing folk songs which range from the ribald to downright vulgar, judging by the uproarious laughter around us.

Jimmy walks off stage and sings as he walks around the tables, every now and then using his hands to gesticulate rudely at his crotch or chest or bottom, to the amusement of the crowd. Soon on our second bottle of red, Coff and I laugh along, in good humour despite the fact we can't comprehend a word – not just because we are half tanked, but because the lyrics of the songs seem to be in Roman dialect or slang, as far as I can guess.

'What is your name?' Jimmy appears beside our table suddenly and stares at me.

'Penelope,' I blush wildly, '*e* Michelle.' I point at Coff.

Making his way back to the stage, Jimmy continues to sing cheerily and a few minutes later I hear my name and Coff's being repeated. The crowd screams with laughter. The joke is on us but we don't get it. As amusing as the scene is, the folk ditties are beginning to wear thin. We can't get the gags, only giggle at the crowd, which is getting increasingly raucous.

I plaster a smile on my face while trying to grab Jimmy's attention to call for the bill. He whacks it on the table and Coff and I stare in horror. It's 80 euros, 140 dollars, for what was, while tasty enough, a very simple Italian meal. Unbeknown to us, the restaurant charges an 18-euro cover charge per person for the 'entertainment'. We've been had.

We cough up the dough and leave slightly dejected, trying to avoid the attention of Jimmy, lest he make another one-liner at the expense of two ignorant tourists.

Bidding Coff a teary farewell at Termini station, I go to my shift at Pasqualino and try to keep my chin up.

Pushing open the front door that afternoon, I hear the sound of voices. As if knowing I might be feeling flat, my three flatmates have all returned home. Better still, Nina has organised a dinner for at least ten. Socialising! Conversation! I can hardly contain my joy.

Nina arranges the kitchen table alongside another in her room, which is at least three times the size of the tiny kitchen. She sets the tables with candles, serviettes, cutlery and plates, creating a cosy if not hippy dining space.

Soon the *citofono*, door intercom, is buzzing and everyone has arrived and is seated around the table for dinner: a gigantic bowl of spaghetti with *vongole*, a never-ending salad and chunks of bread.

Apart from our household and Nina's boyfriend, there is Francesco, Tiziana's brother; Andrea, Nina's German friend; Simona, an Italian pal of Tiziana's; Francesco, our landlord; and two of Alberta's mates, Raffaello and Sascha.

During dinner, I find my eyes drawn to Raffaello. He's not conventionally handsome but his unusual features intrigue me: dark, wild, curly hair, beautiful eyes with irises so dark they seem to blend into the pupils and long, camel-like eyelashes. He's wearing a T-shirt that exposes slim but wiry arms. He doesn't speak much, which only adds to his mystery.

I corner Nina in the kitchen and ask as casually as possible for information about him.

'He's an artist, and he also plays the drums in Cactus, the punk band that Federico plays guitar in,' she tells me.

Tragic. I've got a crush on Federico and also think one of his best mates is a babe. I should write a letter to *Cosmopolitan* asking for advice.

'Raffaello's girlfriend is Sascha, but I'm not sure they're that happy.'

Fine. If Raffaello is with someone else that narrows down the playing field. I wonder where Federico disappeared to. Somehow I have to work out a way to meet him.

I'm struggling to read *Pinocchio*, given to me by Nina as a study tool, when my mobile rings. It's Alessia, a Sicilian friend I made during my trip to Italy in 2000. She invites me to dinner at the home she shares with her fiancé, Andrea, in Rome's north.

The area they live in is a suburban wasteland of grey apartment blocks and ugly concrete shop fronts. It makes me feel lucky to be living in Rome's historical centre. I might be living well beyond my means near the Colosseum but I wouldn't have it any other way. I'll be happy as long as I can afford to eat and socialise a bit – which will hopefully be easier now I have flatmates.

Alessia and Andrea, whom I have not seen for three years, nonetheless greet me with familial warmth. Two minutes later another man, Carlo, arrives. Slightly taller than me with a nice build, he has a goatee below a gorgeous full mouth. He also has one straying eye. Talking to him I don't know where to look. As if to compensate, he speaks in slow Italian so I can understand more than usual.

A born entertainer, Carlo soon has everyone at the table – including two other friends of Andrea – in stitches. Everyone at the table is Sicilian and some dialect is creeping in – I feel like I'm in a family scene from *The Godfather*.

Carlo is a production assistant for a small company that makes music video clips for occasionally famous but usually run-of-the-mill Italian bands. Most of the guys I have ever been out with either work in the music business, hang out with people who do, or simply have an endless passion for music. I grew up listening to Dad's vinyls and singing alongside him on a guitar. I am drawn to musical types.

Over dinner Carlo flirts using his reasonably good command of English. I try to flirt in bad Italian for effect, drunk from imbibing red wine like water, noting with dismay that Alessia remains composed and sober. The way Carlo speaks and waves his arms about makes me laugh and relax. Humour is so sexy.

He offers me a lift home, and I know what's going to happen before I even get in the car. He pulls the car over in my street and walks me to the front door and before I can say *baci* he's kissing me. And damn, he's good. He gives my nose an Eskimo rub with his afterwards. I'm a sucker for sweet gestures.

I climb up to my loft bed as carefully as one can when half-cut and collapse on my belly, singing to myself happily. Blame that last *grappa*, but I'm soaring. An innocent snog has made me feel infinitely better than I have for weeks.

I finish work at Pasqualino on Sunday afternoon and go home to chill out for a few hours before I get dressed. I have accepted a dinner invitation from Carlo, who buzzes the intercom just after 8.30 pm.

As I walk out of our palazzo I bump into Federico and Raffaello walking out of Soul Food, the vinyl record store below our house. They are both dressed in scruffy jeans, punk T-shirts and Converse boots. Seeing Federico makes my stomach flip. I choke out a *ciao* and walk further up the street to where I see Carlo standing beside his car. Suddenly, it's raining men.

Carlo smokes as fast as he drives his battered two-door bug. We arrive at a grey palazzo and Carlo leads me down a flight of stairs and opens a door. Inside, the small one-bedroom, basement apartment is dark and dank, but framed pictures and musical posters give it a homey feel. As he gives me a brief tour, he apologises for his house but explains the rent is cheap because it's the basement and, besides, he works so much he's almost never home. Sitting in the small kitchen, crammed with empty wine bottles and a few unsightly trinkets, I curse myself for thinking interior design can make or break a relationship. But let's face it, physical appearance and individual taste play a role in the attraction between sexes.

Carlo pulls some *parmigiano* from a fridge that is bare but for big vats of tomato sauce his mother, who lives in Siracusa in Sicily, made him. Putting on a CD he tells me is sung in Sicilian dialect, he slices up some salami and bread to have as an appetiser then joke-dances and hums to the music as he prepares a tomato sauce loaded with chilli. Served with spaghetti, it's simple but moreish.

Speaking in slow Italian, at my request, Carlo tells me a little about typical Sicilian foods – such as *cannoli*, the crunchy pastry cones filled with ricotta, which I became addicted to during my time in Sicily – and his love for the spicier flavours of his homeland, which he describes as another country. His eyes glaze with pride as he talks of his heritage. I can understand about 40 per cent of what he is saying – but I say '*sì*' a lot convincingly.

We polish off a bottle of red wine and before I know it Carlo is pulling me into his bedroom. Kissing me, his breath smells slightly of cigarettes. And then a strange thing happens. It's four months since I've had a shag but I can't get excited about the prospect of getting one right here, right now. Tired and drunk, I just want to be cuddled like a child. What is wrong with me? Would it be different if it were someone else? How do I explain myself to this hot-blooded, well-hung Sicilian?

Sensing I'm not there in every sense of the word, Carlo eventually gets the message and snuggles up beside me. I am exhausted yet I cannot sleep for analysing the situation I am in – lying in bed with a man I have only met once, in the basement of a palazzo that looks like every other in Rome. I have no idea where I am and I can't explain myself eloquently or articulate my true feelings. I really like Carlo, but while I don't know him that well, nor can expect to easily given the language barrier, instinct tells me I want to be his mate, not his lover.

'Carlo, I'm sorry – I can't sleep. Can I go home?'

It's just past 4 am when Carlo, eyes drooping from tiredness, drops me off at my door. Walking up the stairs I swear I can hear him cursing women worldwide on his drive home.

Monday, my only day off. I wake early and march to the *Questura* office, where *Permesso di Soggiorno* applications are processed, in via Genova, a short walk from home. At the gates is a policeman with a gun near his pocket who doesn't look pleased to see me or anyone. When he asks me what I am doing, I mumble something about trying to get a *Permesso*. He points through the doorway to an office that backs onto an ugly courtyard.

I walk in to be confronted by stale air loaded with impatience, frustration, poverty and misery. There are African women with babies, middle-aged Polish women with gold-capped teeth and a mixture of Albanians, Egyptians, Moroccans, Indians, Russians – just about every nationality imaginable. I seem to be the only WASP in the bare, grimy room. I grab a number from a ticketing machine and join the throng waiting for their numbers to flash in red on an electronic billboard. Everyone holds a *Permesso* application form in his or her hand, along with passport photographs. Babies cry, adults clear phlegm from their throats and the scent of overheated people increases with the temperature outside.

I approach an information desk where a man and a woman are fielding questions. I wait my turn before thrusting my passport into the woman's hand, explaining that my study visa is stamped to expire in October and I want to know what I can do to extend it.

The woman looks at my visa and shakes her head.

'The visa is only for 160 days from when it was validated, in April. It has already expired,' she says.

I struggle to contain my shock. The stamp on my visa had a date of October 31. Since I had renounced my study visa in

Perugia, I thought I could argue it had not been activated and thus lasted until the end of October. Apparently not.

I ask if I can renew my just-expired *Permesso* by re-applying for a tourist visa. She shakes her head firmly.

'No, your passport shows you have not left the country. You have overstayed the ninety-day tourist visa period. You must leave the country and wait three months before coming back.'

My heart thuds. I *am* an illegal alien. I look at her with sudden fear. Is this the part where she calls that surly guard on me?

Explaining that my Australian uncle is married to an Italian, I ask if I can get a family visa of some description.

'It may be possible but you must check if your uncle has Italian residency and you must ask the Australian Embassy,' she says.

I roll my eyes in frustration. The embassy and the *Questura* play a cat-and-mouse game, referring enquiries back and forth. I know immigration laws are under constant upheaval, but it's confusing. Vowing to call Geoffrey, I thank the woman for her assistance and disappear into the crowd, tossing my ticket in a bin and ignoring the guard, who has not moved from the gate.

As I walk home, I try to rationalise the situation. I've met a few foreigners who have been living and working in Italy for up to ten years without the required *Permesso*, who say that they've never had any problems. And if they did, they always found a way around it through contacts in the right places.

But what if I want to do any freelance stories as a journalist that involve leaving the country – and going through passport control? Maybe I'll be lucky and never get pulled up. But they might nab me first go.

Work ambitions aside, deep down I think that having a *Permesso* will help me feel more settled. I don't want to be *una clandestina*, an illegal immigrant. If I end up in hospital I believe Italy and Australia have a mutual agreement of covering medical costs. But will my missing paperwork cause suspicion, or do I just speak English and feign ignorance? Touch wood I'll stay healthy.

The insecurity I face is grossly insignificant compared to the deep despair experienced by the scores of malnourished, impoverished people I saw in the *Questura* waiting room, not to mention the hundreds of illegal immigrants, largely from Africa, who sneak into southern Italy in the dead of night. But for a moment I can imagine a microscopic fraction of their despair.

Calling Geoffrey's home, I speak to Anna to ask her for help. Promising to contact the authorities in Tuscany in relation to the family visa situation, she calls a few days later.

'Geoffrey is not an Italian citizen, Penny, and the people here tell me the family visa is reserved for immediate family members,' she says.

'Oh well, I'll just have to marry an Italian or stay here until I get booted out,' I joke lamely, trying to hide my anxiety.

'Don't worry, Penny, it will be okay – just extend your tourist visa.'

I can't bring myself to tell Anna it doesn't seem that simple.

Later at work, Simone corners me as I am chopping bread in the small room behind the kitchen. He knows all about my visa dilemma.

Speaking in slow English, he explains that Italian authorities have just announced an amnesty in which illegal immigrants (those without a *Permesso di Soggiorno*, like me) are allowed to apply for a visa – as long as they have a sponsor. There are two types of visas – one for domestic helpers that lasts three months but can be easily extended, which costs 345 euros; and a twelve-month work visa for 800 euros that is open to anyone in any profession. If I understand correctly, the employer normally pays the cost of the visa, but many illegal immigrants are paying anyone to sign them into jobs that may not even exist.

'My father said he may be able to help you get a work visa – but you will have to pay,' says Simone, looking a little embarrassed. 'I have to go and talk to some people. I'll let you know what is happening as soon as I can.'

Heading home after work, my mind spins with excitement. I've only been in Rome a month and though the initial weeks have been hard, I'm starting to feel more settled, thanks to the fact my house now has other occupants.

If I fork out 1500 dollars for the visa I will use up the last of my savings. But it will be money well spent for peace of mind and freedom of movement.

At home I chatter to Nina, who is on her way out the door to a party I can't muster the energy to face, then write myself a note before I go to bed.

Call British Airways. Postpone ticket.

An Italian stallion

Late September. The blistering summer heat begins to subside, and without any pomp, I am accepted as the latest addition to the household. I feel detached from my Australian life, the emails to family and friends lessening as I immerse myself into life *alla Romana*.

I find it hard to articulate to anyone at home what I am doing, because I'm not quite sure myself. Life has slipped into a routine of waitressing and studying. I try not to navel-gaze too much because I can't pinpoint what is keeping me in Italy, apart from simple joys: mixing with the often abruptly in-your-face but always entertaining locals; the staggering beauty – historical and aesthetic – of Roma.

My contact at the *Corriere della Sera* emails to tell me that my story on the old knife-sharpener will not run in *Italy Daily*, because it has folded. It will, however, run on Sunday in the *Corriere*. I can still file pieces to him because the *Corriere* will run a small weekly English column with a Rome perspective. I suspect a high percentage of the Italian readership will devour the new column.

Every time I open my mouth to practise Italian I face a battle with an educated local who wants to practise their English. Talking in English, or at least dropping key words into conversation and wearing fashion with English slogans, is big in Italy, a sign of being well-educated and *intelligente*. At first I got offended when Italians insisted on speaking English with me. Was my accent that bad they couldn't even encourage my efforts? Then I accepted the obvious. I'm not the only one trying to be bilingual. Now, depending on my mood, I either stubbornly persist in Italian or speak in my native tongue, to their delight. If they're annoying, I'll sometimes speak English so fast they don't know what's hit them.

On Sunday, I march down to the newsagent to bleat my *buongiorno* and get a copy of the *Corriere*. My story is buried on the *Opinioni* page in the Rome city insert, but I am still elated. It's one small step forward in the direction I want to take. I buy two extra copies to send to my parents and my grandfather, who I know will get a thrill to see my name and read about a true Roman around his vintage.

Cleaning the loos that day doesn't depress me as much as usual. In fact, the more time I spend at Pasqualino the more enjoyable it becomes, thanks to the tragically comic cast of characters.

Vittorio, the dwarf-sized Sicilian, likes nothing more than when a female tourist stains her top with pasta sauce. He dashes to get the stain remover, which he insists on applying personally on the woman's shirt, easing his hands as close to her chest as possible, his eyes widening with glee.

Ennio's trick is dropping a white napkin anywhere in the vicinity of a woman wearing a skirt and peering up as he retrieves the napkin from ground level. When there are no women around, he makes a point of practising in front of me to see if it amuses me. Watching him, I wonder if he and Vittorio, both married, have ever had sex lives.

Mario, I have discovered, has a problem with the drink. When diners leave a quarter of a carafe full of house wine we put it above the sink to refill for new orders, but often I catch him skolling the remains of whatever he can get his hands on. He is either a ray of sunshine or an ominous thundercloud. I turn a blind eye and try to stay out of his way.

Chef Marco continues his aggressive campaign to woo me, despite the fact his girlfriend comes in to see him regularly, rendering him a puppy. Head chef Fabio, still my favourite, watches the mayhem around him and stays calm, whipping up dish after dish and occasionally giving me bags of fruit to take home.

Within weeks some faces have become familiar: a lawyer who dines alone as he reads a John Grisham novel, a balding pensioner who always has minestrone and *penne arabbiata* and asks for two helpings of bread she leaves half-chewed and scattered across the table, a businessman who brings in a different woman for lunch every second day and tries to speak English with me to impress her, two gladiators from the Colosseum who rip off their plastic chest shields and put down their swords to demolish pasta, *vino* and *grappa*. No wonder the tourists are complaining.

Two Irish priests are also regulars, squeezing their corpulent body masses behind a small table in a corner then ordering dish after dish and leaving a sizeable tip. One chaotic evening I find myself at the priests' table, opening a vintage bottle of Chianti. Usually my more experienced colleagues perform the task, but we are short-staffed. With their full cheeks already flushed from a pre-dinner glass of *prosecco*, the priests ogle the bottle with unbridled anticipation. I have opened countless bottles of wine before, but, to my dismay, the moment I have to pop a cork in a more formal setting – before clients who are paying good money for professional service – I freeze and panic. Tonight my worst fears are realised when the cork in the prized Chianti stubbornly resists my tugging. Flustered, I subtly try to use brute force but the move backfires.

The table jerks and I watch in horror as a glass of *prosecco* tips over, splashing the beautifully pressed robes of one of God's children.

Apologising in a state of mortification, I hightail it to the kitchen and find Vittorio, who returns with me to the priests, who graciously accept my apologies and watch Vittorio carefully ease the cork out of the bottle. From that moment, Vittorio asks me to open bottles of wine at every new table he serves in a deliberate and thoughtful gesture to build my shattered confidence. Slowly, my view of waitressing as a casual gig to help me learn Italian and cover my rent is being challenged. At Pasqualino, I love hovering in the kitchen, watching the preparation of Roman cuisine. I enjoy the social interaction with staff and clients, however limited, and I am keen to learn much more about Italian wine. Waitressing in my parents' café aside, I never would have imagined doing such work again. If I returned to Sydney tomorrow would I still get the same enjoyment? Or is this just a part of the novelty of surviving in an exotic new city?

One of the fixtures at Pasqualino is The President. Each night the short, slight man with tanned skin, snow-white hair and smoky blue eyes shuffles in and takes a table on his own. From what I can work out, his nickname is derived from the fact he was once one of the top brass in Rome's soccer team. Now aged anywhere between fifty and sixty, he has a freelance office gig and loves a drink and industrial-strength cigarettes. He is kind to me, and speaks a little English now and then. Each week he gives a 10-euro tip to one of the waitering team, making me think he's loaded, especially since he dines at Pasqualino five days a week. Usually he comes in around eleven o'clock, eats like a bird then plays cards with Nicola until the restaurant closes.

When I'm not at Pasqualino I try to study at home as much as possible but it's useless if I don't put it into practice. Angling to be included in more household activities, I go out for a drink one night with Alberta, who has made plans to meet Federico and Raffaello at The Druid's Den. Alberta, like Tizi and Nina, seems to work manic hours, though she usually manages to make it home for lunch. Quiet but friendly, she is the least transparent of my three flatmates.

We enter the small Irish pub, layered with timber and choking with cigarette smoke, and sit down at one of the low tables. It's a struggle to hear over the chatter and blaring English television, but I get the message that the trio are talking about relationships. Smoking and speaking quickly, they laugh constantly at things I can't grasp. I smile and try not to let my frustration show. I throw in the odd convincing *sì* and steal glances at the men at the table. Raffaello seems to be despondent due to relationship blues. With a poker face, Federico rolls Golden Virginia cigarettes, which only amps his rock star aura. Walking outside it's a relief to get fresh air. Federico and I amble behind Raffaello and Alberta. He asks me for my number. I give it to him, struggling to pronounce the number *tre*, three, in succession three times. Hating that pesky 'r'.

Two days later my phone rings and my heart pounds. The name FEDERICO flashes.

'*Ciao, Penelope. Dai, prendiamo un caffè!* Come on, let's have a coffee!'

Talking to Federico one-on-one without the help of any friend-cum-translator is difficult – his English is almost non-existent. I stumble over my limited vocabulary, trying hard not to be embarrassed. I want to give off a cool, in-control attitude, but I feel like a kindy kid. The more I look at him, the more I am attracted to him. He has a gentle manner and when he smiles his eyes light up with a cheeky sexiness.

I'm discovering I have to trust my gut instinct when socialising, because I lack the communication skills to size people up. Meeting friends of my flatmates I am pretty sure the acquaintance is worth knowing. Meeting people outside the house, unconnected to anyone I know, can be confronting.

Federico works as an office manager in a hotel administered by the Catholic Church. He works 1.30 pm to 7.30 pm six days a week and has a job that is *tempo indeterminato* – for as long as he doesn't throw it in he is guaranteed the job for life. He can afford to take holidays regularly because he lives at home with his parents, who have separated but remain under the one roof because it's easier for both of them financially. He shares a room with his younger brother.

'*Ma il letto è singolo?* But the bed is single?' I struggle to comprehend that Federico, at thirty-two, shares a room with his slightly younger brother, let alone that the pair sleep in single beds.

'*Sì*,' he responds, not looking at all perturbed.

I left home at seventeen. Lovers aside, I can't contemplate sharing a room with anyone now, including family members. At his age, how can Federico think it's normal to sleep in a room with his brother and live rent-free for years with no real sense of independence? More to the point, if he's going out with an Italian girl living at home too, how does he ever expect to get laid? He must spend a lot of time in the shower.

A few days and many SMS text messages between Federico and I pass before we meet again. He offers to drive me around town to help me search for a wedding gift for Evie and Andrew, two close friends whose nuptials are in September in Adelaide. I have already called them to say I won't be attending.

'It's hard to explain, but I'm only just starting to find my feet…I'm scared if I come home I will find everything so easy I'll lose my desire to come back to Italy,' I tell Andrew before repeating the same thing to Evie and shedding a few tears of disappointment down the telephone line.

As we trawl around the shops, I look at Federico beside me with growing affection. He's so patient and sweet. And spunky, ambling along beside me wearing scruffy jeans with his guitar case slung over one shoulder.

Parking outside my apartment building, Federico pulls something out from behind his car seat. He hands me a brown paper bag. Inside is a copy of *The Little Prince* in Italian. I leaf over the first page and see a note he has scribbled inside. *For Miss 'Senti Senti'......Fede!*

I laugh out loud. It's a reference to the fact I often use the word *senti*, an imperative word that effectively means 'listen to me'. It's something I've picked up from tuning in to others around me. Once I have used the word to command the attention of the person I am talking to, however, I usually can't follow it up with a lone, grammatically correct sentence.

I take the gift, smiling with a burst of affection and gratitude. Plucking up some courage, I lean over and plant a soft kiss on his rosebud mouth. I'm growing tired of our double-cheek kisses. I get enough of those from strangers. Federico appears surprised then smiles bashfully. I leap out of the car with a quick *ciao*.

The following week I invite Federico, Raffaello and Sascha, his American girlfriend, to have dinner with Nina, Tiziana and me. Alberta has made other plans.

After dinner, Federico takes us all to see a band. Inside the dim, smoky venue we go down a set of stairs to an even darker basement area. The support act, two performers wearing pagan smocks and face masks, is already on stage. The man blows a wind instrument while the woman wails like a cat on heat. Sitting on the concrete floor leaning against Federico, I watch Raffaello and Sascha in front of us, sitting apart and showing no signs of affection. I look at Raffaello again and stifle a strange sensation. He seems so sullen sometimes I want to know what is behind all his angst. Old habits die hard. As the headlining act – a classy, all-girl punk garage group called Motorama – cranks through a set I look at Federico, enjoyment etched on his face, and remind myself uncomplicated is good.

Federico and I leave the pub and drop the others home before we get to my apartment.

I tell Federico he can stay as we pull up at the door. It's not a good look to climb naked up the ladder to my loft bed, so while he is in the bathroom I haul on a pair of knickers and a singlet top reluctantly – it's a humid night. Federico appears at the top of the ladder in a T-shirt and, I'm relieved to see, boxers. Why Y-fronts are allowed to go on sale I'll never know. Soon we're lying in my bed; smaller than a double, it's a snug fit for two.

It's funny how a kiss can make or break a future relationship within minutes. At times, Federico is like a child learning how to swim: too scared to lift their head and breathe while their head is submerged. Who knows, maybe it's my fault. In any case, it's still tenderly sweet.

Happily, he is a dynamo in the shagging department. We giggle at a few awkward moments, trying to work out what tickles our respective fancies between the sheets. Come to think of it, I don't even know how to say 'sheet' in Italian.

Falling asleep spooning, I feel warm, snug and smug. I'd forgotten the joy of having someone's body wrapped around mine. Forget prostitution, why can't people be satisfied with the humble hug? It's a niche business just waiting to happen. 'Quality spooners for hire', 'No body too big or cuddly', 'Reap psychological benefit in seconds – free trial spoon!'

I wake in the morning while it's still dark, to see Federico climbing down the ladder, trying not to wake me. I struggle to hide my disappointment as I recall the night before. He sees that

I'm awake and tells me he has to go home because his mum needs the car. I smile, relieved. He gives me a peck on the nose and is on his way.

Everyone says hooking up with an Italian is the best way to learn the language. Speaking with Federico, I slowly gain confidence. We misunderstand each other continually and he sends me text messages that force me to pore over the dictionary. But it's all good fun. When we can't communicate a hug or small show of affection can do the trick.

Like finding the perfect bar to have coffee, one of my favourite things to do in Rome is to dine out, despite my minimal budget. Federico is generous, often treating me to *cena*, dinner, or *pranzo*, lunch, and taking me to places I would never find on my own. I adore the cosy atmosphere of a traditional eatery, devoid of swank modern frills. I relish reading a menu I can't fully understand, asking Federico lots of questions and getting to know the unpretentious, mouth-watering Roman cuisine.

Often we go to a hole-in-the-wall trattoria in San Lorenzo, the student *quartiere* that flanks one side of Termini station. Inside the kitchen, visible from the waist up from the dining area, two mother-and-daughter teams chatter as they cook, the sizzle of their fry pans also reducing the drone of the small TV mounted in the dining area.

Dining at the trattoria with Federico one night, I look down at my *carciofo*, artichoke, antipasto and get a rush of the guilts from the pre-Italy me. My artichoke is drowning in olive oil that is nutty and tasty but so plentiful it's like drinking soup.

Federico asks me what's wrong, noting the look on my face.

He listens patiently before pausing to reflect on my bumbling opinions.

'*Tu sei magra. Comunque, la ciccia non fa male.*'

He's told me I don't need to worry because I am skinny. *Hardly*.

'*Ma…cos'è la ciccia?* But what is *ciccia*?' I ask, repeating the word out loud as it sounds.

Federico grabs my love handles and says the word again. Bless, he's trying to tell me that something extra to hold on to is not a bad thing.

I order the *tiramisù* and sip a *Lucano,* my preferred liqueur, without a second thought.

Simone from Pasqualino tells me that his father is willing to sign me up for the 800-euro work visa. He hands me the paperwork and tells me to fill it out and bring it back in the next day.

At home, I grab the dictionary and spend a good hour filling out the form and trying to ignore niggling doubts about whether what I am doing is a good idea. Simone has reassured me that if I change jobs the visa is still valid – I just have to update the document. But something doesn't sit right. Flying by the seat of my lingual pants is often fun, but when it comes to life-changing decisions it's frightening being in the dark. I'd ask Federico for help but he's away in London to play a gig with his band, Cactus. I talk to Nina a little, but she has an EU passport and doesn't know how to advise me. I ring Geoffrey but he isn't really informed on the issue and doesn't know what to tell me. I don't want to go to the *Questura* or embassy again because they seem to contradict each other at every turn.

I finish the form and find some clean paper to write a letter to Federico in Italian, intending to ask him to correct it on his return. It takes me ninety minutes to write four pages. I tell him I would like these things: first, I would like to speak more Italian. Second, I would like to work somewhere new. Third, I would like to go on holiday with you, somewhere beautiful.

I cringe at the simplicity of my writing, knowing my letter is riddled with errors. But I have to start somewhere.

It's November and the weather starts to bite, putting a slight brake on Rome's continual tourist train. Federico returns from London with presents – a pebble from the seaside, a cute cotton shirt with tapering hippy sleeves and a CD with bad Irish folk songs. I look at the CD in amusement. What *was* he thinking? Who cares. It was a sweet gesture. All that matters is that he's back.

My joy soon dissolves when Federico is restless and depressed for days. I try to talk to him about what is wrong but he is reticent to explain what I will, no doubt, find linguistically and culturally difficult to understand. Living at home is getting him down. His parents don't get along well, despite the fact, to my enduring amazement, they live together. I think of Maria and Luca in Perugia, who live in the same less than ideal situation. Why do Italians seem to stay together even when unhappy? Later an Italian friend explains to me that in traditional quarters divorce is seen to be a public no-no, due to the influence of the Catholic Church. The family unit is so sacred that couples may stay together for the sake of their kids. And then financial dependency can come into play.

For a week I try to talk to Federico about his blues, suggesting he make the most of his rent-free life and save so he can move out. But my bad Italian falls on deaf ears until eventually I lose my patience with his wallowing. It's exhausting enough trying to keep my head above water in a foreign city. I can't carry him too.

My Italian stallion has, for now, been put out to pasture.

Circo Massimo is a sprawling, rectangular paddock where the Romans used to stage chariot races from around the fourth century BC. It is the nearest public space I can visit to go running. Ringed by major roads and containing more dirt and rubbish than grass, it's hardly the most scenic place to exercise when one is used to jogging around the Sydney Opera House. But I love the idea of what the Circo once was.

Standing on its hilly edge one morning, I look down at the long, flat basin and the two strips of dirt that were once racetracks. I imagine the Romans cheering and hurtling in chariots from one length to the other and Caesar, who rebuilt the space, yelling out to control a cheering audience of 300 000.

I set off at a slow canter, trying to ease myself into a rhythm. I can swim for kilometres without tiring, but jogging does not come naturally to me. I only do it because it's meant to be an effective fat burner. God knows I sweat copious amounts. It must be doing some good.

I complete a circuit, passing a guy who is searching a grassy slope, perhaps for a drug stash, and a group of hippies playing bongo drums at the base of some concrete steps. I am on my second lap when I hear voices. I look back to see two men jogging a short distance behind me. Dressed in marathon-style shorts and singlet tops, they look lean and professional. Wearing an old cotton skirt, my wobbling bum is in full view. My competitive streak flares and I try to pick up my pace.

I have just rounded the next corner when I trip over a tuft of grass. I try to regain my balance but it's too late. I tumble face-first towards the ground, littered with broken beer bottles. Pushing my hands out to break my fall, I somehow avoid scraping my face on the dirt before I hit the deck at full speed and body weight.

I lie motionless like a dummy for a few seconds before I pull myself up to a sitting position to assess the damage. Blood spills from small cuts on my legs but my hands are the worst, covered in gashes on both sides. Red is everywhere. I wriggle my ankles and move my legs. No sprains or broken limbs.

The patter of feet grows louder. I look up to see the two men, looking concerned.

'*Ti sei fatta male?* Have you hurt yourself badly?' asks one.

Humiliated, bleeding and trying to keep my legs together to avoid flashing my undies, I am too shocked to think straight.

'*No, va via!* No, go away!'

The men look at me with concern and amusement before turning on their heels. I pick myself up, gingerly. Pride makes me start running again, as if nothing has happened. It's no good. My nerves are shot and the blood won't stop running. Hobbling home, my injuries suddenly throbbing, I wait at some traffic lights near the Colosseum. People in passing cars gawk at me with amusement and horror. My hands are so bloody I look like I've killed someone who put up a good fight. A wailing ambulance abruptly swings around a corner and stops briefly beside me. I'm half tempted to knock on the back door until I see a flash of movement. The hand of a male medic juts out of the open window in the back of the van. The hand ashes a burning cigarette which is then pulled back inside as the ambulance speeds off.

Arriving at Pasqualino in the afternoon, I discover with dismay that the ladies' bathroom has flooded. I am lumped with the responsibility of unblocking a toilet with a suction pump. My hands are wrapped in bandage gauze provided by Tiziana, who works for a pharmaceutical company. Thankfully when I got home she came to my rescue.

Later, my hand throbs as I struggle to cut the bread for tables arriving for dinner. My mood only worsens when Simone pulls me aside at a busy moment.

'My father cannot help you with the work visa because he has discovered there is an official limit to how many people he can sign papers for and he's done too many,' he says quietly, looking at me apologetically. 'But you can try to get the domestic visa – my father knows someone who could help.'

When the dinner rush subsides, Simone accompanies me to a pizzeria around the corner, leading me out the back to a little courtyard off the kitchen. Resting on a chair, enjoying a rolled cigarette, is a man I recognize as the chef who took over at Pasqualino recently when Fabio was on holidays.

It seems Nicola has asked Agostino to act as my sponsor to get a *Permesso* based on a domestic worker's visa. I stare at Agostino with gratitude and suspicion. Just above my height, with thick horn-rimmed glasses, a complexion as white as the dough he kneads and a low-hanging gut, he remains quiet – so quiet I wonder if he's happy about what he's doing or if Nicola has pushed him into it. Nonetheless, he hands me a visa document he has filled out, leaving me the portion I have to complete and take to the local *Questura* within seventy-two hours, before the amnesty expires.

I smell a giant rat, but Simone assures me scores of illegal immigrants are finding sponsors to get the domestic work visa, which must be renewed after three months and can be upgraded to an open work visa. All I have to do is pay 349 euros. I don't have to set foot in Agostino's house. The authorities never check the system.

Lying in my loft bed after work, my face frighteningly close to the roof, I mull over the situation. Try as I might, I can't believe Agostino wants nothing in return. He seems pleasant enough. But so did Ted Bundy. I know Simone and Nicola are trying to help me, but I don't have a good feeling about it all. Trying to listen to my instinct, I am suddenly reminded of my last official appointment in Australia – with Carmen. So *this* is what her premonition about visa and immigration problems was all about.

A wave of tiredness and teariness washes over me. I have been working at Pasqualino for just over three months. I am not learning any new Italian, because I've exhausted the limited conversations I can have with my colleagues, with whom I have no great desire to socialise.

I may not possess a *Permesso di Soggiorno*, but I do have the health card I obtained in Perugia, which allows me to work in restaurants and bars. It's not that hard to find a job when you have English as a mother tongue. My personal savings have almost run out but I have enough money to pay two months' rent and cover expenses.

Questions, half-answers and confusion exhaust me enough to guarantee sleep.

The next morning, my mind is made up. I will never clean toilets again. I will never return to Pasqualino.

Dad always told me never to burn your bridges and leave a job without lining up another, but I need a break. I want to study as much as I can to get my Italian up to speed so I am more employable. With no immediate plans to travel – and therefore face passport control points – I tell myself it's okay to be *una clandestina.*

Holed up in my room studying one day, my phone rings. It's The President. He must have got my number from Pasqualino.

After the briefest of conversations, the phone cuts out. How odd – he's invited me to lunch. I was tempted to decline but he hardly gave me the chance. I have to put my study into action, and I'm always partial to a good lunch. And I promised myself I'd say yes to most things in Italy.

At 11.30 am I arrive at Bar Martini, as requested, to find The President alone at a table. A bottle of white wine rests in a fancy cooler. He pours me a glass and speaks slowly, asking me what happened at Pasqualino.

As I start to explain, I struggle to quell a creeping sensation of unease. What am I doing? The old man is half-cooked. Before I have time to plot an escape, The President has ushered me out of the bar and flagged a cab.

The taxi halts in a narrow cobbled street. The President pays the driver and leads me along the cobbled footpath and through a plastic flap of tarpaulin to a dining area that contains about fifteen white plastic tables and chairs.

A robust, attractive woman wearing a floral dress, white apron and a white linen head scarf that sweeps back her grey hair appears from the doorway of the cosy trattoria.

'*Holà. Ciao Paola,*' my host says, before introducing me.

Her eyes a steely grey, Paola looks at me with affection and concern. I bet she's wondering what a young filly like me is doing dining with an old man like The President.

Anch'io, I think silently. Me too.

She ushers us to a table inside Ristorante der Pallaro. Yellow lanterns light the entrance hall and the two smaller rooms leading off it. More plastic tables are set simply with checked tablecloths, cutlery and tumblers. Appetising aromas waft out of the kitchen where, thanks to a small serving window, I can see an old, stooped woman rolling mince into meatballs.

A few minutes later a forty-something couple join our table. Mauro is a member of the *carabinieri*, the police, and his chain-smoking wife, Valentina, is a teacher. The knot of unease in my belly unravels. There's safety in numbers.

Talking to The President about Pasqualino and my *Permesso,* I am surprised when he says he would have helped me with the domestic visa if he didn't already have a maid. But a bigger surprise is in store.

Mauro tells me with a warm, friendly smile that he will talk to a colleague to see if anything can be done to 'put everything in place'.

Before I have time to dwell on something that sounds naughtily exciting, a wave of antipasti plates arrive, followed by fresh fettucine and more *secondi*. Menus at the restaurant are non-existent. For 22 euros you get a spread fit for a bridal party with an endless jug of house wine.

Just when I think the meal is over, an old man appears with shot glasses of fresh mandarin juice and a slice of homemade *crostata* with apricot jam. His hands tremble with age as he pushes my hand to pick up the dessert, showing me to dip the pastry crust into the mandarin juice before me. The President introduces me to the man, Giovanni, Paola's husband.

The President picks up the tab for everyone and Paola kisses my cheeks multiple times and gives me a hug as we walk out the door. Drunk, I try to make a mental note of where I am so I can visit the trattoria again. Every bloody cobbled street looks the same.

I leap out of the cab at Colosseo, thanking The President profusely for lunch. His eyes glaze over and he gives me a drunken smile as he tells me he'll call me soon. Is he really an important ex-soccer boss or just a no-good boozer? Either way I have decided he's not sleazy. Just lonely.

Walking home, I giggle at the day's events. How do I tell my mother that I've had lunch with a man old enough to be my father and might be getting some bent cops to fix my visa situation? How surreal.

I love the sense of liberation that comes with being able to do whatever I please so far from home without the feeling that my friends or family are judging me. If I find myself in odd situations it's usually because I can't understand enough to know what I might be letting myself in for. But for now my instinct is bearing up fine.

My willpower is weak at the best of times, and worse when under the influence of lunch. Despite my determination not to get weighed down with other people's baggage, I suddenly pine for Federico.

I send him a convoluted text message – trying to ask him if he misses me – as I round the Colosseum and turn into my street. The reply bleeps instantly.

'Of course I mess you. *Facciamo cena insieme?*'

His innocent spelling mistake makes me grin madly as my heart swells. Guess who's coming to dinner!

Ti voglio bene

Cooking for anyone makes me nervous because I'm no Nigella. I blame my mother, who spent the 1970s buying Margaret Fulton bibles which looked suitably impressive on the kitchen shelf but gained more dust than dog-eared pages.

Catering for Italians, however, triples my anxiety – because most of them grew up watching their *mamma* and *nonna* cook and are capable cooks themselves. Almost without exception, they are opinionated about food, ingredients and how they are best married to create unfussy but scrumptious dishes. And if they don't like what they are tasting they'll tell you immediately.

Before I came to Rome I viewed pasta as a meal that could be made in ten minutes – dicing garlic finely and frying it in a pan to which I added tinned tomatoes and God knows what else before pouring it over whatever pasta was in the pantry. No wonder it was a bland sensation.

Watching an Italian cook pasta, I realise it can still be a quick meal but it requires a pinch more patience. First, garlic is never diced, rather a whole clove or half clove is thrown in the fry pan to help flavour the oil. Sometimes it's thrown out before serving, but usually left in the sauce – because it's so big, it's easy for the diner to avoid it. From what I can tell, Italian chefs use fewer ingredients to make a sauce but they cook them longer for maximum flavour (rather than fry the hell out of them to produce a dish more quickly). Finally, they choose a pasta that marries well with the sauce.

I was surprised to discover that Italians serve various types of pasta with specific sauces not just because of centuries-old tradition but because it tastes better. For example, fettuccine is served *alla Bolognese* or with a *ragù* because the long, flat strips of pasta absorb the flavour of the *sugo*, sauce, more readily. I quickly learned never to suggest to an Italian that all pasta tastes the same, as the detailed rebuttal feels like friendly fire. It's true I have never seen as many varieties of pasta in my life as I have in Italy. And while modern Italy means take-away and pre-prepared foods, it still bemuses me that some Italians consume pasta twice a day.

Federico and I agree to resolve our relationship issues over dinner at my house. As I buy salad ingredients and some brilliant red cherry tomatoes from the fresh produce market, I envisage the night ahead: I will delay my kitchen preparation until he has arrived, then slowly begin to go through the motions of making a pasta sauce. Little by little I will ask him strategic questions, until eventually he will grow tired of my demands and order me out of the kitchen.

Federico is a good cook, having experimented in the kitchen when his mother was working full-time in his youth. He worked as a chef in an Italian restaurant in London for a three-month working holiday and enjoyed the experience but hated the unsociable hours. The reason his English is so poor is because when he was in London he lived with and hung out with Italian friends. If Italians leave Italy – and many don't, because they love their country and its food so much it's hard to convince them there's a world outside their so called *Bel Paese*, beautiful country – they tend to move in packs. Federico is different because he travels on his own – but he usually has an Italian friend in his port of call.

My sometime squeeze arrives in a playful mood, giving me a huge hug and smooch at the door – enough to tell me in any language that our linguistically and culturally challenged relationship is miraculously back on.

'*Allora, che facciamo? Una pasta?* Well then, what will we make? A pasta?' I ask innocently, looking with exaggerated despair at the ingredients I have dragged onto the table.

Federico throws some olive oil, garlic, mushrooms and zucchini in a pan then opens the bottle of white wine he brought and splashes a little in the pan too. The conversation bubbles along with the penne as we stand in the little kitchen. Nina, Tiziana and Alberta stick their heads in to say hello every now and then, which sometimes makes me embarrassed. When I am having trouble communicating to Federico, I get more flustered when my flatmates witness it too, because I sense they are wondering how the heck we manage to stay together with such a language deficit. Sometimes I wonder the same thing. But *amore* is a peculiar beast.

Full of pasta and a tad tipsy, Federico and I head to bed. To my annoyance, I soon find tears welling in my eyes. What is wrong with me? I can't pinpoint why I am suddenly emotional. I am convinced it's a random byproduct of trying to create a world on my own someplace new. Every now and then I just need to have a few quiet tears to flush out the pressure I often don't even realise I am dealing with. Pressure that even comes with doing the most banal things I take for granted – from asking directions to ordering a coffee how I like it.

Federico hugs me until I have exhausted my tears and we slowly make love. Within a few minutes I think I hear Federico say *già* which means 'already'.

Shit. Has he got his rocks off already? More to the point, how do I ask him delicately?

'*Hai finito?*' Are you finished? My voice wobbles in the dark.

Federico starts to laugh uncontrollably.

'*Ho detto "ciao", non "già"!*' I said "hello", not "already"!' he says, still laughing.

The physical contact between Federico and me is more intense because we can't talk about sexual subtleties. It's show and tell without the tell. Sleeping with him ranges from being blisteringly embarrassing to downright funny – but it is always extra sweet, because we have to work harder to communicate in our own form of language.

Lying beside Federico in a state of exhausted bliss, I am busting to tell him that every time we sleep together I experience what until now has come around about as often as the Olympic Games. I give myself a reality check. If I was with an English-speaking bloke I probably wouldn't tell him, or at least for a while, for fear he'd think he was sex on a stick.

No, I won't give specifics. But I have to say something.

'It was beautiful,' I say, wincing at my limited choice of words.

'For me,' he says with childlike honesty in his timid English, 'it was best ever.'

In the dark my face is painted with a smirk. I bet that's what he tells all the girls.

Autumnal leaves litter the roads that line the mud-green Tiber, which Federico skirts in his car as we leave Rome to drive to Castello di Santa Severa, in Tuscany. As I watch the white dome of St Peter's Basilica at Vatican City disappear from sight Federico says there is a beach at our destination.

I'm annoyed he didn't reveal this information earlier so I could have packed my togs. Luckily, I'm wearing full-brief black undies and a black singlet that will pass as a costume.

'*Ma che dici, Penny? Tu sei matta, fa freddo.* What are you saying? You're mad, it's cold.'

It's a chilly November day, but it's not Arctic freezing. Federico has no concept of how desperate I am for a dip. In Australia, I went to the beach every chance I could, swimming until the coldest point of winter. Call me a hippy, but I have a spiritual connection to the sea. The last time I bathed in the ocean was three months ago in Croatia.

The wind is strong and grey clouds rumble as Federico swings his small car into a gravel car park. We walk around the *castello* to the sea, choppy and heading for high tide. Apart from a couple canoodling on the sand nearby, there is not a soul in sight. Federico watches in amusement as I strip out of my jeans and jumper and run into the water.

He's right. The freezing water leaves me gasping for air. But I can't back out now – who knows when I'll be seaside again? I duck-dive under the water and thrash a few laps, but the current is too strong to go further out. I make my way back to shore.

Walking along the sand to Federico, the wind whipping my legs, a group of Italians walking their dog look at me with incredulity. I grin at them and grab a jumper Federico has given me to wipe my body before I haul my jeans and top back on, my frozen fingers fumbling. My body is numb but my spirit has come back from the dead.

Later that day, Federico hands me the letter I wrote him when he was in London, having corrected it as I asked him to, plus a letter in reply. I begin reading immediately, 'I would also like to have a beautiful holiday with you, but the thing I want the most is to find a house, maybe we can search for it together. What do you think?'

Surprised, a sense of warmth and irony rush through me. I lived with my first serious boyfriend when I was twenty – way too young. As I have grown older, I've found myself in many a relationship where I would have moved in with my boyfriend at the drop of a hat just because it seemed natural at the time. But in most cases the boy was scared to make the jump, thinking the rental lease may have a hidden clause about marriage, mortgage, kids, retirement, then death by chronic boredom.

After barely three months together Federico is already keen to shack up. I suspect a great part of his reasoning is because he sees it as a way to escape the home life he loathes. Apart from the fact it feels too soon, I don't want to be just a convenient means for him to leave his version of hell. Not when he himself could still prove to be a devil in disguise.

'Maybe,' I say, thinking even if he's super keen it could take years to happen. The only time I have seen Italians hurry is when the first drop of rain falls. For some reason they adopt the panicked attitude that rain is like napalm. When I linger outside to enjoy the feel of the rain on my skin they stare at me like the foreigner I will always be.

It's almost December and signs of *Natale*, Christmas, are omnipresent: boxes of *panettone* cake are stacked high in supermarkets, festive market stalls and vendors of fairy floss and a surplus of helium balloons in animal shapes fill Piazza Navona, a huge pine tree with lights and a red star at the top is erected in Piazza Venezia. As if from nowhere hard-up immigrants appear, roasting chestnuts on small, round grills mounted above barbecues fuelled by glowing red coals. The men weigh the sweet, charred chestnuts on old-fashioned scales and tip them into a paper cone.

Christmas lights hang the length of our very long street and one weekend the surrounding streets were blocked off for a special market full of antiques, clothing and foods. Walking down my street one afternoon I watch fifteen motorbikes pass by driven by men dressed as *Babbo Natale* – or Santa Claus.

I am socialising more with my flatmates, but only on average once a week, because they lead frenetic lives that fly in the face of the cruise-control Italy I envisaged before my arrival. I don't want them to think I am desperate for company – even if I am. Federico's presence, for this somewhat unhealthy reason, is cherished. But when things aren't working I notice it more than I would if I had a bigger social circle.

Sunday dawns a crisp, blue sky. In Italy, Sunday is synonymous with lunch with the family. Tiziana is, as per usual, at Latina, an hour south of Rome, where her mother lives. Alberta's family live in Bari, in the south of Italy, otherwise she'd be there. Nina is out with Marcella, her friend who runs a beautiful boutique a few steps from our palazzo.

Even though my own family never treated Sunday as special, I can't help but think of home on Sundays. Secretly, I yearn to be included at a lunch with Romans anywhere in the city. If I could invite myself in off the street and find a place set at any family table, I would. I know I can visit Geoffrey, Anna and Bianca, but it's half a day's travel and I'm hopeless at organising myself.

I have tried to hint to Federico that I would love to meet his family and have a meal sometime, but he flatly refuses. Apart from the fact his parents are living under the same roof in disharmony, it seems the last time he invited a girlfriend to his house he rued his decision: when he split with her, his parents wouldn't stop hassling him about why the relationship ended. It seems there is a hell of a lot of family pressure to marry.

It's hard for me to understand Federico's reasoning – in Australia, my parents met a string of boyfriends presented over the years by my sisters and me without batting an eyelid – but I try to understand. Even if his refusal to introduce me to his family makes me feel he doesn't view our relationship as important – despite his desire to live together.

Perhaps sensing my disappointment, Federico suggests we take a road trip to have lunch at Capalbio, a small hilltop town in Tuscany, three hours' drive or so away.

On the *autostrada* by ten o'clock, we haven't gone far when we pull over at an Auto Grill service station to get a coffee. Inside, noise and espresso cups fly in every direction as motorists jostle to the bar, manned by two garrulous baristas. Nearby, racks of shelves stock the biggest range of chocolate merchandise I have ever seen.

Federico buys a Kinder chocolate cake and dips it in his coffee, into which he's already dropped two sugars. I look at his teeth, stained a slight brown from cigarettes and, arguably, multiple daily doses of caffeine. I love the fact he enjoys the smallest of things without a trace of guilt.

We take the turn to Capalbio and the road dips and curves through fields of red soil and lush crops I can't identify. Federico unwraps a packet of cigarettes as he drives. I watch in horror as he opens his car window and throws out the plastic wrapping, before I get a chance to protest. He mutters something about people being paid to clean the area. How can anyone think it's all right to throw rubbish into the countryside? *Dirty Italians!*

Soon I notice, every half kilometre or so, lone women standing near cars or sitting on vespas parked by the road. Wearing short skirts and skimpy tops despite the winter chill, they hold or talk on mobile phones and, despite the glaring spectacle they create, try to look nonchalant.

'*Puttane*,' says Federico seeing my expression of interest. Prostitutes. One of my favourite Italian curses is *porca puttana*, a particularly vulgar term but I hear it so often that I kid myself it has a softer meaning along the lines of 'bloody hell'.

Accustomed to seeing hookers roaming the grotty, syringe-littered backstreets of Kings Cross and Darlinghurst, it's decidedly odd seeing them with the gorgeous Tuscan countryside as a backdrop. Litterbug habits aside, is there anything the Italians don't do with some form of style?

We wind up into the town of Capalbio, the wind bitter against our faces as we get out of the car. Federico steers me to Trattoria da Maria, a rustic eatery nestled inside the stone walls of the medieval town. Tables covered in granny lace brim with well-dressed Italian families who chatter noisily and boss about waiters in black tuxedos.

We order antipasti of cured meats and salamis before Federico tucks into a mixed grill of meat. I order hare served in a chocolate, sage and tomato sauce. It's strange but it works. With a fluffy light sponge soaked in just the right amount of Marsala and the freshest of cream, the *tiramisù* is a knock-out.

Driving home, I take the opportunity to bombard Federico with more questions about his life. He left school and went to university to do a degree in philosophy and sociology, but dropped out when it wasn't his scene. He worked in a pasta shop, cooking and delivering stock, then worked as a hospital volunteer for six months. For the past six years – apart from his three-month chef stint in London – he's worked in the hotel.

I look at him and brew over what I understand to be his life: living at home, working six days a week part-time without showing any zealous drive to change the life he says he is unhappy with. I am in no position to judge him – I'm unemployed, and I know well the horrible feeling of indecision that comes with not being sure of where one's future lies. But I am starting to think I need to be with someone who is more... Driven? Inspired? Sometimes when I'm with him I feel like a Ferrari being forced to move into the slow lane.

As if responding to my angst about not having a job, the big guy upstairs gives me not one, but two, cracks at employment. The fact I don't have a *Permesso di Soggiorno* is irrelevant. There are scores of jobs in the black or illegal market and anyway, I have my health sanitation card.

Out of the blue Tim, an English businessman I met by chance while working at Pasqualino, calls me to say his American friend, Steve, is offering a receptionist job at The Beehive, a funky small hostel near Termini station. The idea appeals to me, since the job is not physically zapping like waitressing, and it should be a sociable job, meeting travellers from all over the world. I call Steve and arrange a trial run of a few hours. The same day I notice a job advertised in *Wanted In Rome,* an English language magazine published every two weeks.

'Busy law firm seeks mother-tongue English secretary for part-time work. Travel required.'

I call the number, nervous at having to speak Italian on the telephone. Easily flustered speaking in person, talking on the phone is far worse. I talk to a man identifying himself as Donatello who replies in fluent English. Repeating his name to myself I can't help but grin. I know Raffaello and now Donatello. I wonder when the two other two Ninja Turtles will surface.

Arranging an appointment that afternoon, I take the address of Donatello's law firm then prepare myself. I put on the dressiest of the increasingly worn clothes I have – black pants, T-shirt and sandals – and grab my CV, which has only clips of stories I have written and no reference to secretarial skills. But I'm willing to wing it. As in love, when you give an air of indifference about a potential partnership you are always infinitely more attractive to suitors.

I catch the train to Piazza di Spagna, or the Spanish Steps, and walk what I think is the short distance to a street near Villa Borghese. It is much further than I expected and I arrive late. I press the only buzzer that says *avvocato*, lawyer, and wait. No answer.

I am about to turn on my heels when the door clicks open. Standing before me is a short man dressed in an smart navy suit and tie and Mr Sheen-shiny shoes.

'Penelope? I am Donatello,' he says with the fixed smile of a game show host.

Donatello holds the door for me then leads me down the imposing entrance foyer. The ad said busy law firm. I had envisaged an Ally McBeal-style office with attractive legal eagles toiling for justice and groping in unisex toilets.

I stop at the impressive, shiny, brass-panelled elevator in anticipation but Donatello keeps walking past and down two flights of stairs. He stops and unlocks a door at basement level. Inside is a small, stuffy office that is almost devoid of natural light. There is a small window at one end and a few framed certificates hanging on the wall above a walnut desk covered in neat piles of paper. There is not a computer in sight.

I sit in the chair across the desk from where Donatello sits and try to make small talk in Italian as a way of introduction.

'If you like we can speak in English,' he says immediately, 'because it will help me to improve my bad English.'

Relieved though disappointed, I tell him that my journalistic skills include exemplary shorthand skills. This is a massive overstatement, since the 120 words per minute I could scribble upon graduating as a journalist has, at the very least, halved.

The phone rings.

'Could you please respond?' says Donatello, eyeing me with interest.

I can't understand what the babbling woman on the other end is saying so I cut her off as nicely as possible and hand the receiver immediately to Donatello. My bluff appears to work. Donatello palms off the call then hangs up.

He tells me he shares another studio nearby with colleagues, but he is based at the office we are in and requires a secretary to field work when he is in court. He specialises in divorce cases and the annulment of marriages in accordance with the Roman Catholic Church.

After twenty minutes of banter, Donatello clears his throat.

'Penelope, I have seen many girls today but you are the most qualified by far. I am applying to the British Bar and I want to speak more English and I need someone who is happy to travel to London with me. I can pay you 100 euros a week for twenty hours – 4 pm to 8 pm, Monday to Friday. What do you think?'

I reckon it's a pittance, but at least it's a slight improvement on Pasqualino for fewer hours. I look at Donatello, his steely blue eyes resting a fraction too long on my features for my liking. I don't have to imagine hard to see him trying to jump me in a hotel room in London. But it could be an interesting means of understanding another part of the Italian culture – the might of the Catholic Church, not to mention Italian relationships – and free trips to London wouldn't go astray.

'Perfect, I can come tomorrow,' I hear myself saying. 'Just one thing,' I add warily, 'I don't have a *Permesso di Soggiorno.*'

'Don't worry,' says Donatello, looking relaxed. 'I have a friend – we'll work it out.'

His comment reminds me I must call Mauro, The President's friend, to see if his 'friend' in the *carabinieri* is in a position to help me.

Saying goodbye to Donatello at the door he kisses me on both cheeks before I have time to suggest otherwise. Grimacing, I tell myself it's the Italian way before hurrying out the door.

Federico sends a text message asking me to have a coffee with him later that afternoon. Meeting at a bar, I find my guitarist lover as upbeat as Kurt Cobain in his final hours. After having a circular conversation about his woes, I suggest we have a break once more.

'Some people are happiest when they are sad because they prefer it, but if you *really* want to change your life you can. It's your choice,' I tell him as I kiss him on both cheeks and walk away.

As I stroll home I wonder if I have done the right thing. I've just cut off someone I have strong feelings for, whom I love as a human being at the very least, and who is a huge support to me. Not to mention *una bella trombata*, a fabulous shag.

At home I find Alberta, Nina and Tiziana in the kitchen, drinking herbal teas and nibbling sweets from our local *pasticceria*. Alberta leafs through a book that seems to be a kind of oracle. Someone asks a question and she consults the book, which gives a prophetic response, depending on key words in the sentence asked. I watch my three flatmates shriek and laugh in response to dippy answers. Alberta's tome is my first introduction to the Italians' strong superstitious streak and credence in a loftier power outside the Catholic Church. Other titles I've seen around friends' houses include *How To Interpret Your Dreams To Win Lotto*. Predictors, clairvoyants and those with the gift of garbled gabble make a healthy profit offering advice on how to win the game of life and Lotto, arguably as popular as soccer. Unable to follow the palaver in my flatmates' coven, I fake a cheery goodnight and go to bed, from where I can still hear their shrill cackling.

The beep of a text message wakes me early two days later.

I read it straightaway, '*Ciao Penny. Mi manchi. Sono stupido, ma ti voglio tanto bene. Credimi. Se vuoi* give me last opportunity. *Baci.*'

I can understand most of Federico's text message. He says he wants another opportunity because he misses me and he was stupid. Bless, he is a man after all. But what does *ti voglio tanto bene* mean?

'Italians use *ti amo* – I love you – when a relationship is really serious, like between husband and wife, and engaged couples,' explains Nina, as we have breakfast. '*Ti voglio bene* also means "I love you" but it's less serious – you can say it to your mother or sister or friend. *Tanto*, in this case, means *a lot*.'

Nina looks at me with a smirk. She knows that I know that she knows why I asked her.

I go to my room and reflect on Federico's message before I reply. I tell him to take a little time to think. I'm over confused blokes. He's got to get his shit together.

His response comes back within a minute. 'Listen, I don't need more time, I understand that you are really special, but maybe it's too late? I don't want to see you in a little bit of time, for me it's important now.'

I sigh inwardly and smile as I tap the keypad of my mobile phone. Without even realising, I have become addicted to SMS like every other Italian I know. At least it serves as an educational tool. Every time I don't understand something I check my dictionary and rewrite the words so I have more hope of remembering them.

I meet Federico later in the day and somehow he ends up in my bed that night. I curse my willpower for caving in to my libido, but it feels good to be together. While there's so much of his culture I can't understand, I can appreciate his restless state.

My trial job as a receptionist at The Beehive goes more smoothly. The office is in a private apartment on the fourth floor of a residential palazzo near Piazza Vittorio Emanuele II, where I go to the fruit and vegetable market once a week.

Andrea, a young Argentinian woman with an abrupt but pleasant manner, greets me. She explains that the job involves checking-in tourists booked to stay in the three private rooms inside the apartment, called Mille Fiori and two other apartments nearby, Acacia and Clover – all operated by the Beehive hostel.

When not checking-in guests, the main part of the job is working on Cross Pollinate, a website offering bed and breakfast accommodation in Rome, Venice and Florence. The website was set up by Beehive owners Linda and Steve, a married couple with two young kids, when they couldn't keep up with demand at The Beehive.

Andrea shows me how to use the computer for Cross Pollinate, receiving new client reservations and then telephoning or emailing the B&Bs listed on the site to check if they have availability for each booking.

My heart thuds with fear as Andrea hands the phone to me and tells me to ring a B&B in Florence to check availability for a booking. I write down the words I have to say on paper. With little exception, the Italians who respond are patient and warm in the face of my stutter rap.

I work for four hours and return the next day for the same duration before I have to jump on the Metro to reach lawyer Donatello's office. As I'm leaving, Andrea tells me she has already trialled two other girls but smiles at me kindly.

'Don't worry, your chances are good,' she says.

Hoping for the best, I thank her and rush off.

As I walk in the door of Donatello's office he shakes my hand and kisses me on both cheeks. Ew. I feel like I've been slimed *Ghostbuster*-style. The unease rising in my stomach solidifies when I am reminded of the dungeon-like work space. He hands me a document written in Italian and asks me to translate it. I smile and grasp it quickly, sitting down at a desk he has set up for me nearby.

My smile falters when I realise I can only understand one out of every four words written on the three-page document. It is dripping in what is obviously legal jargon.

There are days when I wake up and feel switched on and can understand most of what I hear on the street or see written in the paper, but there are days when I feel like I did when I first stepped off the plane in Rome – plain stupid. Today is one of those days.

The phone rings and Donatello, busy reading a document, asks me to answer. Thrown by the difficulty of my task, I return his gaze and find myself shaking my head. He looks at me in disbelief.

Blushing, I apologise profusely, saying I need to focus on translating the document. The paper he has given me to write on remains brilliant white before me.

The phone cuts out and the studio buzzer rings, saving me from explaining to Donatello why his secretary should not be obliged to answer phones if she is experiencing an off-day.

'Penelope, I am sorry, but my client wants to discuss matters privately,' says Donatello, smiling kindly at an anxious-looking elderly man sitting in the chair opposite him.

I exit gratefully, grabbing my bag as I walk out of the room. Still looking at me like I'm a freak, Donatello tells me to wait outside in a small room opposite his door with chipped paintwork and a broken chair. So much for a charming waiting area. It feels like death row.

Donatello closes his office door behind him and I pace the room, brewing over the situation. Who am I trying to kid? I don't feel confident enough to speak on the phone to ask for more than a hotel reservation and I can't translate Italian. And I can't stand my boss puckering up every time he sees me. Staring at the office door, my mind is made up before Donatello reappears.

For the third time since my arrival, I find myself fleeing from a workplace knowing I will never return.

Daydream believer

As I rushed from one appointment to the next during my last hectic months in Australia, there were times when I wanted to beg any one of the office receptionists I came across to swap roles for a day. Not because I thought they were indolent, gossiping eavesdroppers who had lingering lunch breaks. Or at least not all three. I just imagined if I sat where they were I would develop a new persona. I'd be more in control with unflappable librarian calm. And surely I'd have at least fifteen minutes a day to collect my thoughts.

I hang my head in shame. Having scored the Beehive job, I now know differently. It's true I have more bouts of idle time than I did as a do-all waitress. But I am quickly discovering that being a receptionist is more arduous than I had expected. Notwithstanding my woeful memory, I am not terribly pragmatic, usually choosing the most complicated means to achieve what should be a straightforward task. I am also hopeless with computers and my boss, Steve, a techno geek, laughs at my ignorance when I call him to resolve countless stand-offs with my screen.

While generally a cheery person, I sometimes have to muster all my energy to be welcoming to the tourists who walk through the door. No matter how many times I get asked if the Colosseum is open on a Sunday (yes) or if the Pope gives a public speech on Wednesday and Sunday at the Vatican (yes), I have to be pleasant – regardless of how much of an idiot I think the person before me is, or whether I am in a foul mood because I've had a day like Michael Douglas in the movie *Falling Down*. Because the difference between a good stay and a memorable one often comes down to the service you get from the person who greets you in a new city. Don't I know it.

Working in the Mille Fiori apartment reception is nice, because it has a quiet, cosy ambience. There are couches, a dining table setting and a picture of Audrey Hepburn in *Roman Holiday* that hides the safe in a wall. From my desk I can see the doors of the three private rooms rented to tourists. All ages, they hail from every corner, but are mostly from the United States, Canada, England, Germany and Australia.

The Americans arrive with too much luggage on wheels and are sometimes blissfully ignorant of the fact that travelling in another country means adjusting to situations they may not like and cannot change – slow-draining showers, paper-thin towels, the noisy Romans. The Canadians are super-friendly and often keen to make it known they are not American, especially since the Bush-led Iraq invasion. The Poms fly in for weekends on cheap airlines from London, with little luggage and a blasé attitude. Either painfully polite or abruptly rude, the Germans keep to themselves. I'm no doubt biased, but the Aussies are the most easygoing and keen to chat as soon as they hear my accent.

Simple in theory, working on the Cross Pollinate accommodation website can turn into a nightmare easily: if a B&B listed on the site calls at the last minute to say they are overbooked there's a scramble to find suitable digs for a guest in transit as yet unaware their accommodation has fallen through; if a guest is unhappy with a lodging and emails or calls to complain; if a breakdown in communication leaves Cross Pollinate or the B&B out of pocket. Great attention to detail is required to avoid small mistakes that can cause a loss of money, reputation or both. The problem is, I often say I have understood something in Italian when I haven't, because I don't want to appear daft.

My Italian is slowly blossoming. I don't have to speak in great detail with the B&B owners, but small conversations are improving my comprehension and vocabulary – not to mention pronunciation.

One afternoon I ring B&B Pascucci, one of the nicest and most popular lodgings on the website, located near Piazza Navona and run by a married couple, Luciano and Anna. Luciano answers the phone gruffly, seemingly irritated.

'*Buongiorno, Luciano, sono Penelope di Cross Pollinate. Vorrei fare una prenotazione con lei.* Good morning Luciano, it's Penelope at Cross Pollinate. I would like to make a booking with you.'

There is an exaggerated pause on the end of the telephone before Luciano responds, speaking very slowly and annunciating each word for effect.

'*Pen-el-op-e, devi pro-nun-cia-re le parole meglio altri-menti sembra che chiedi qualcosa di complet-a-mente diverso. Pre-no-ta-zione. Non è pe-ne-tra-zione. Sai la differenza?* Penelope, you must pronounce words better, otherwise it seems like you ask for something completely different. *Pre-no-ta-zione.* It's not *pe-ne-tra-zione.* Do you know the difference?'

I blush and get off the blower quickly. Damn that rolling 'r'. Instead of telling everyone I want a *prenotazione*, booking, I've been asking them for a quickie. Mortified, I sit at my desk trying to practise. *Porca puttana.* I sound like a gutless lawnmower that won't start.

The intercom buzzes. It's Paolo, who owns one of the Beehive apartments and manages all three. He's a gentle, kind man, but he always seems to fuss around the apartment for no apparent gain. Maybe he's got an unhappy marriage he's trying to hide from, maybe he just likes to feel occupied, but on days when I'm busy, his untimed visits can be distracting. I say hello and continue working as he walks into the kitchen and tinkers.

He reappears to place three huge *panettone* on the dining table behind me – gifts, he says, for myself, Andrea and Amy, our other colleague, a young American.

'*Buon Natale*. Merry Christmas,' he says simply.

I thank him profusely, feeling guilty for my earlier uncharitable thoughts.

Closing up the office at midnight after the afternoon shift, I wrap myself in layers, *come una cipolla*, or like an onion, as the Italians say. I walk home swinging my *panettone* by the ribbon on the box, watching the breath I blow out of my mouth with exaggerated force. Rounding Piazza Vittorio Emanuele II, I pass three flower markets which are open 24–7. One can always find a flower stall open in Rome.

Buckets of tulips and roses and and lilies sit on the pavement in front of the small covered work space where the flowers are cut and wrapped. An operator naps on a small bench inside his stall. I wonder if his stock ever gets stolen by thieves or passing romantics.

Even with two beanies I'm shivering, but I could walk for another two hours. Rome is stunningly beautiful at night. When I see the Colosseum at the end of my street, as I have every day since I arrived almost five months ago, I stop and gaze at it with undiluted rapture.

Christmas Day dawns and Federico and I drive to San Gimignano to have lunch and spend the day with Geoffrey, Anna and Bianca and some of their friends. A pleasant gust of warmth and roasting meat greets us when Geoffrey throws open the door. Anna is busy in the kitchen with a typically hyperactive Bianca biting at her heels. Set for eight, the dining table is decorated with bon-bons, a large decanter full of ruby red wine and bottles of *leggermente frizzante*, lightly fizzy water. Italians often drink bottled water in preference to tap water, which is drinkable but excessively calcified.

Dressed in smart tweed pants and a jumper, Geoffrey is in cheery form but miffed he hasn't yet received a telephone call from Australia, where his five brothers – including my father – gather on Christmas night for dinner.

'Our family is bloody hopeless, Penny,' he says. I keep silent, knowing it is an old axe he grinds and not wanting to let the festivity of the day be spoiled. Geoffrey is a highly sentimental and loving person and, like me, is often demanding and emotional when he feels wronged or let down.

Joining us for lunch are various friends of Geoffrey and Anna's: Harumi, a Japanese author living in France; Alice, an art gallery owner from Vienna; and David, a Spanish artist living in San Gimignano. Everyone has brought a nice bottle of wine as a contribution.

Christmas lunch is delicious – polenta drizzled with olive oil and parmesan, a creamy risotto with zucchini and then *capretto*, baby goat, roasted with potatoes and peas. I find room for Anna's home-made crème caramel and a wedge of *pandoro*, a spongy cake which, like *panettone*, comes packaged in a colourful box. Similar in mountainous form, the two traditional Christmas sweets vary in taste: the *panettone* cake contains candied fruit, while the *pandoro* is without spices but has an eggier, more buttery flavour. Packaged with a sachet of icing sugar, the fun trick with the *pandoro* is to open the plastic bag it's wrapped in, pour in the sachet of sugar, then reclose the bag and shake it violently to give the cake a snow coat of sugar. Cut into thick chunks, the *pandoro* is often served with *torrone*, large, rectangular chocolate bars which, as their Italian name translates, are shaped like big towers and are often laced with whole roasted hazelnuts or gooey fillings.

As I watch Bianca's face whiten with *pandoro* powder the conversation turns to foods traditionally eaten in Italy to mark festive and religious events. During *Carnevale*, in February, bakeries and bars sell the fried sweets *frappe* and *castagnole*. Weeks later you know Easter is on its way when bars and food stores overflow with colossal chocolate eggs, luxuriously packaged in coloured foil and containing a trinket inside. At *Pasqua*, too, butchers double the price of *agnello* as Italians stock up on lamb to roast for a long festive lunch. Just after the clock has struck midnight on New Year's Eve, continues Anna, it is customary to eat lentil stew with *zamponi* – pig's trotters stuffed with minced meat. The dish is supposed to bring good luck and fortune, the lentils representing coins. 'We pile our plates high every year but it never works, we just get fatter,' says Anna.

Federico and I drag ourselves out for a walk in the historic town centre. In the main piazza, framed by the gorgeous *duomo* and surrounded by some of San Gimignano's famous towers, stands a huge Christmas tree draped with red banners and a tinsel star.

My gloveless hands hurt from the cold and I snuggle up to Federico, thinking of my family, who spent the day in the sunshine near the sea in Sydney. While their company – not to mention some fat prawns and a body surf – would be a treat, I'm glad to be having a winter Christmas.

I stare at the tinsel star and think of the past five months in Rome. I still seem so far away from resolving my career crisis but I have enough to cover my rent and I feel happier than I was when I left home. Isn't that enough for now?

Squeezing my hand, Federico urges me to keep moving. His rosebud lips are tinged with blue.

Sascha, the now ex-girlfriend of Raffaello, is having a party for *Capodanno*, or New Year's Eve. Nina is in Germany and Tiziana and Alberta have been invited to dinner parties, so I have a shower and prepare myself for the party. Federico is going, but I haven't heard much from him since Christmas. He's in the grip of another maudlin period.

I take too long to get dressed, wanting to look cool but not having any clothes I like in my wardrobe. I can count on one hand the clothes I have bought since arriving in Italy. I'm earning about 60 euros more per week at The Beehive but I'd rather spend my still-small disposable income on dining out.

Sascha is throwing the party at the apartment of Sienna, an American artist friend who is spending Christmas in her native Seattle. She greets me at the door with her beautiful, full-lipped smile. Painfully slim, her long bottle-red hair clashes sensationally with some bright green clogs she has teamed with a flowing black dress. Dressed in jeans and boots, I suddenly feel like a sack of potatoes. I thrust a bottle of wine in her hand to disguise my lack of confidence.

The large apartment has beautiful high ceilings, and is filled with antique furniture and Sienna's art, including a stack of nude oil portraits of her friends, the theme of one of her recent exhibitions. In the main lounge area, where people are already jostling for space, is an enormous canvas mounted on an easel. It is a nude painting of Sascha, her back arched, her pubes and boobs thrust proudly out. Standing nearby, Sascha seems oblivious to the raw, sexual display.

I spy Federico in a corner with Raffaello and go over to say hello. Federico is distant and far from affectionate. I suddenly feel ill at ease, surrounded by people I don't know and with whom I am nervous about striking up a stilted conversation. I don't want to hang off Sascha's arm all night speaking English. Frustrated, I start one of many trips to the bench strewn with more than twenty wine bottles. When in doubt, get sozzled.

The night begins to get blurry and before I know it I have vague memories of telling Federico we're over because I can't tolerate his blues. And, yes, I will be fine, thank-you-very-much, because if I can move to Italy on my own without knowing a soul I can cope with anything that is thrown at me, relationship meltdowns included.

I stumble out of the party before midnight, just as Federico and Raffaello start to jam in one room. I can't do it. I can't face a room full of smiling strangers counting down for the New Year. For the first time since my arrival, I am *really* aching for the company of my circle of friends in Australia. Feeling both angry with and sorry for myself, I trudge home, sucking on a cigarette I'm too distracted to taste. I hear the occasional pump of party music as doors open and shut and horns tooting but the bitter cold has driven people indoors.

As is my habit, I turn to eyeball the Colosseum near home. For once, it does not fill me with joy and energy.

Vaffanculo!

I swear out loud at the monument and to anyone who cares to hear, which right now is no one. I seem to be the only person having a wobbly in Rome.

And then the obvious hits me. There is no 'r' in *vaffanculo*. I can say *fuck off* as convincingly as a local. There is a god.

Smirking drunkenly, I stumble up my street repeating the words to myself.

Checking my emails at work a few days later, I see Federico's name in my inbox. He's replying to an email I sent him on New Year's Day apologising for my party performance, suggesting we both know our relationship is doomed.

You are a special person, Penny, but I could never make you feel that way. I'm confused. I wish my problems hadn't influenced our relationship. Soon I hope to find the balance that will make me feel better. *Ti voglio molto bene.* I hope that you have the will to continue the road you have chosen. See you soon. One thousand kisses.

I swallow a lump in my throat and think of all the things I've shared with Federico and how my impressions of him and life in Rome are slowly shifting. At first, he seemed to personify the life I had romanticised well before I got to Italy, not letting work interfere with his quality of life. But reality is starting to sink in. Federico is close to his parents but his family life hardly mirrors my earlier impressions of the close unit I see on TV ads. He is also unhappy with his job, as are, no doubt, millions of other Italians. So why is it that they always appear cheerier to me? Am I simply imagining things that I want to see?

Disillusioned as I was with the daily grind of life in Australia, I suddenly suspect I've been painting the rosiest picture I can of Italy, blindly absorbing all the aesthetic positives of its culture – food, wine, history and more – in an effort to make myself happier. Boycotting English conversation and print wherever possible may have helped fast-track my language skills but it has conveniently allowed me to turn a blind eye to bigger and bleaker social issues which don't impinge on my everyday life – issues I've been content to ignore because it takes so long to read the Italian papers, and because I've been preoccupied with my fishpond life of work and *amore.* No wonder bemused locals treat foreigners like flippant fly-by-nighters. But is there anything wrong in holidaying with the pixies once in a while?

In an instant I reach a point where I want to – and know I must – get a grip on reality. Easier said than done when you live in a city as frightfully intoxicating as Rome, where it is so easy to be sucked into a vacuum of historical beauty and charm at the expense of the facts of daily life.

I stop myself from overanalysing things and send a quick but affectionate reply to Federico.

Almost 9 pm. I stare at the wall clock impatiently. Working from four o'clock to midnight is killing the social life I am so keen to create, because even though midnight is early by Italian standards, if there is a party on late I can't get there unless it's very close. Taxis are expensive and I hate taking them alone when I don't know the area. Roman drivers are notorious for taking the long way. I'm too scared to buy a Vespa – because if I get pulled over for anything I will be exposed as *una clandestina.*

Still, I am meeting interesting travellers via the apartment. I spend two enjoyable nights chatting to an Australian couple on their way to Florence to elope. A softly spoken, fifty-something Canadian couple surprise me by asking me to help them score some dope. Clad only in underpants, two rotund German men walk from their room to the shower, oblivious to the winter cold and the look of horror on my face.

One weekend the apartment is fully booked by a group comprising two adults and eight teenage children. I am on the phone to one of the Cross Pollinate B&Bs when I hear chanting voices. I swing my head to see that, behind me in the living room, the group has formed a standing circle. Linking hands, they repeat prayers before singing a hymn.

The next day they are gone. I check to see if they wrote in the guest book. My eyes widen as I read the last entry. They were a Bible group from Waco, Texas. They were probably praying to the ghost of David Koresh as well as God.

Working a rare morning shift one frosty Saturday, a petite woman with an impressively small backpack checks in. I see lots of mature women travelling in pairs, but I've never seen anyone of her grandmotherly age. From New Zealand, she must be at least sixty-five. Curious, I gently prod her for information.

It turns out Judy has been travelling for a few years, leaving New Zealand because she was sick of her children calling on her to be a babysitter.

'I kept on thinking,' she recalls, 'why don't you call me up to ask me to go to the movies or do something interesting, until finally I'd had enough!'

As Judy tells me about living in France and Spain, I look at her face, lined with wrinkles but somehow rendered young from a child-like curiosity. She has so much get-up-and-go she makes me want to repack my backpack and move on. I can't believe I thought I was potentially too old to be a backpacker before I left Australian shores.

Restless, I go for a walk into the historic centre and soon get lost in the maze of narrow streets shooting off Piazza Navona. My mind whirs with plans. I want to start organising little trips around Italy. I'm worried about crossing borders given my lack of visa, but there's nothing to stop me exploring regions of the country I suddenly have an insatiable desire to understand more thoroughly.

Rounding a corner I see an ornate sign, *Biancaneve e i Sette Nani*, which I soon figure out means 'Snow White and the Seven Dwarves'. The narrow shop is filled with carved wooden animals, painted in bright colours and mounted on stools. It's like a dismantled merry-go-round. Inside, a well-dressed, middle-aged man stands beside a young boy sitting on a stool, part of a bright red racing car. The man cuts the soft locks of the child, who is distracted by the spinning steering wheel of the car he sits in, as his mother looks on.

I enter the shop to admire the stools. Finishing his haircut, the man tells me they were sourced from a fun fair in Nuremberg in 1920, nine years before his hair salon opened. One of the framed newspaper clippings on the wall mentions Roberto Rossellini, once a customer. Grappling to understand what the man says, I take some notes on a scrap of paper and tell him I'll be back for more information. I have to email my *Corriere della Sera* contact to see if I can do a piece on the quaint store. Not only is it the first salon I've seen exclusively for kids, the magical charm it exudes is captivating.

I say farewell to the man and leave before I cave in to a strange temptation to leap on the elephant stool.

Uncle Geoffrey arrives in Rome to stay a few nights and see 'The Expressionists', a big exhibition held in the museum at Piazza Venezia. I collect him from Termini and we dump his bags at home before heading to the exhibition. We fill up on Kandinskys and Klees before we meet Federico, Raffaello and Sascha for dinner in San Lorenzo.

I'm nervous, not only because I haven't seen the others since my drunken performance on New Year's Eve, but also because I want Geoffrey to enjoy Rome. I figure he and Raffaello, at least, can bang on about arty-farty stuff.

My anxiety evaporates when Federico, Raffaello and Sascha greet me with warmth and affection. Geoffrey appears to have a fun night, engaging with Raffaello, whom I stare at with my usual fascination. I love his huge eyes, protruding lips and John Travolta chin dimple.

In pouring rain, I take Geoffrey around Rome to show him a few places where he may be able to exhibit. Winding up at Trastevere, we hole up in a cosy pizzeria and shoot the breeze. When I was in my teens, Geoffrey was already roaming the world and changing girlfriends like undies, unlike his five brothers, who took on careers and families. Twenty years older than me, Geoffrey and I have always had the black sheep label in common. He didn't sway my decision to come to Italy, but since I have arrived our relationship has changed from uncle–niece to one of friendship. We can have a laugh and a drink together but also dish out sobering home truths to each other.

On Geoffrey's final night in Rome I plan to take him to a cosy restaurant near home, but on the way, I am intercepted by a waiter I know by face at another eatery nearby. Somehow, I find myself agreeing to sit down at a table. I've never eaten there before and I am dismayed to discover the menu is average and the place is groaning with tourists.

I apologise to Geoffrey, who knows as well as I do I've got it wrong, but it's too late. He flattens his lips with displeasure and makes me suffer small silences before he pipes up.

'So, Penny, are you still with Federico?' he asks. I shake my head.

'I'm not surprised – when you came for Christmas it didn't seem like you were a couple.'

'Well, we're not. What do you think of Raffaello, by the way? I've got a bit of a crush on him.'

'He's nice. But Penny, what are you doing? You'll break up the band!' jokes Geoffrey, his good humour finally returning. 'You're so ephemeral. You're like flowers that spring up after rain then disappear two days later. You have a fairytale idea of love.'

Laughing, I struggle not to take offence. I know I'm a daydreamer, but that's my right as a Piscean.

'I'd love to be in a relationship, I just haven't met the right person,' I protest.

'Penny, right now, you are too selfish to love. Throw yourself into everything that you want to do, because you won't find anyone before you are thirty-five.'

Selfish, schmelfish! I've spent months trying to be Wonder Woman for boyfriends who ultimately didn't care enough about me to warrant us staying together. I can't be bothered arguing with Geoffrey who, like me, is fuelled with red wine. I bite my tongue and change the subject.

To make up for bungling our dinner venue, I take him to Café Café, a contemporary wine bar around the corner, where we share an orange-flavoured *tiramisù* and guzzle two rounds of port.

Hungover and sleep-deprived the next morning thanks to Geoffrey's chronic snoring, I walk my uncle to the station and give him a bear-hug before heading home. Passing bar after bar on the street, I fight a nostalgic craving for a fry-up breakfast and all the newspapers I used to read at home on a lazy, hazy Sunday.

McDonald's is my only hope of finding grease and eggs, the English papers are all two days old and I'm too seedy to try to absorb an Italian newspaper. Apart from the fact that I find the style of most papers convoluted, with story leads buried anywhere from the middle of the story down, Italian journalists often write for the elite section of their audience rather than for the fact-seeking public. And then there are pages and pages of Italian politics, as easy to piece together as a Rubik's cube. Italy has had fifty-nine governments – each with an average lifespan of eleven months – since declaring itself a republic in 1946. Both Silvio Berlusconi's centre-right party, *Forza Italia*, or Go Italy!, and the centre-left opposition coalition are so splintered that it's hard to follow party agendas.

When I asked Alberta to give me an overview of Italian politics one day she just sighed.

'*Un casino*,' she said, finally, shaking her right hand to emphasise her point. 'It's a mess. It's very hard to explain. No one, not even Italians, understand it.

Some things are obvious. Arguably as famous for his simplistic verbal blunders as George W. Bush is for tautology, Berlusconi has a Godfather-like grip on his country. The richest man in Italy, he enjoys a near monopoly of Italian television, with varying degrees of control over six of the seven main channels, and also owns the top-ranking Italian soccer club AC Milan. Legal proceedings that could expose dodgy business deals committed by some of his many companies are under way, however he has regularly won acquittals and, so far, managed to avoid prosecution on various charges including bribing judges.

At home, I flick on the TV to see a newsflash of Berlusconi showing Tony and Cherie Blair around his villa in southern Italy. I do a double take. Dressed in a glaringly white linen pants suit and sporting a rude tan, Berlusconi has completed his Julio Iglesias look by tying a white bandana around his head. Alexander Downer, take off your fishnets, this is true political style. As in daily life, politics is all about appearances.

Out of the blue, The President calls and asks me to lunch. Fighting a sinking feeling that it's not healthy to be accepting invitations from an older man with such a good appetite for booze, I tell myself not to be a snob. Everyone has their own vices. Lunch is never dull with The President, and besides, he says he has an Australian friend, Serena, he wants me to meet.

Arriving at Ristorante der Pallaro, where I first dined with him, I find my lunch date sitting with another middle-aged man. Dressed in a pinstripe navy suit, he introduces himself as Umberto.

Ending in an *o* or an *a* most often, I find it hard to remember names in Italian. To try to memorise them, I think of a rhyme that fits with both their name and their character. I look at Umberto eyeing me a little too lecherously for my liking. Umberto the perverto. *Perfetto.*

Five minutes later an attractive blonde with a film star aura approaches our table. Dressed elegantly in a long, flowing cotton skirt and blouse revealing a generous bosom, she accessorises with a colourful handbag and a small, white dog. She kisses The President and Umberto, whose attention is immediately diverted, before sitting down opposite me with grace.

In her mid-thirties, Serena moved to Italy to be with her boyfriend, a champion basketball player. She regales me with stories about the bizarre life she lived with her Italian ex in a small Mafia-controlled Sicilian town, where she was followed and gossiped about by the townfolk. She now lives in Rome but flits to New York regularly to work manic hours as a production designer for two- to three-month stretches. She then returns to Rome with her haul of American bucks to live *la dolce vita.*

Laughing hysterically at one of her anecdotes, I realise that it's been too long between belly laughs. God, it feels good. Serena is the first Aussie I have met who lives in Rome.

Small and annoyingly yappy with curly white hair, Serena's dog is named *Carlo il Terzo* – Charles the Third. Her brother and grandfather are also named Charlie. As Serena fusses over him I smile graciously while imagining him choking on his collar. I grew up around sheepdogs and labradors – bigger, barking dogs I could imagine saving my life one day, Lassie-style. Granted, Carlo III is only four months old, but he'll still be miniature when he's fully grown. To me, small dogs are whining wastes of space.

Before I rush off to work at the end of lunch, Serena and I arrange to have dinner at her place the following evening.

Serena lives about a twenty-minute walk from my house, further out into suburbia. Spoilt to be living so close to the historic centre, it's interesting to venture further out into another community. I walk with my eyes wide-open, taking note of good pastry shops and restaurants I might want to return to.

Beautifully decorated with antique and deco furniture and full of soft evening light, her apartment is gorgeous. Two bedrooms share a long, wide *terrazza*, which overflows with potplanted greenery. Both the kitchen and bathroom, with a huge bath, share another small *terrazza* full of plants. I look in the second bedroom, which has a big double bed with a high wooden frame. It's fit for a princess, albeit one who might need a small stool to hop up into bed.

'Are you searching for a flatmate?' I ask, despite the fact I have, until now, resolved not to live with an English-speaking person.

'An Italian girl is moving in the day after tomorrow,' she says. 'In a few weeks I leave for New York for three months so I'll rent that room to her and hang on to mine.'

Serena is a superb cook. We dine on a leg of lamb so tender and moist I could sob. Lamb always makes me think of home, imagining the roast dinners Mum would cook throughout my childhood and the juicy lamb chops we'd throw on the barbie.

Chatting with Serena, my resolution to minimise fraternising with English-speaking people weakens by the minute. It's comforting to have a cultural understanding of one another and to have a fluent, uninterrupted conversation. We laugh, drink, smoke and *facciamo le ore piccole* – stay up into the early hours.

Rolling out the door, I weave down the street, past a flower stall playing cheery radio music. Not far from home I see a homeless, African man wrapped in a rug and lying on the corner of an intersection. At night the streets of Rome are littered with human cargo covered in cardboard from empty boxes, garbage bags and stained, tatty rugs. As I pass by, the man's black pupils pop out from white sockets illuminated by his coal-black skin. In the bitter cold he looks at me with such serenity that my heart contracts with guilt.

I have no money in my wallet – not even change – so I do the next best thing. Reaching into my pocket I stretch out my hand to give the man my almost-full packet of cigarettes. To my surprise he shakes his head, not even bothering to raise his hand.

'*Non fumo*. I don't smoke.'

I blush with embarrassment. Of all the tramps in Rome I had to pick the one with more brains than me. I mumble my apologies that I don't have any change, and then toss my cigarettes in a bin as I walk past the rowdy pub beneath my house. The muffled strains of Axl Rose whining 'November Rain' accompany me up the staircase and all the way to my elevated cradle.

Life is (always) beautiful

Australia Day and I wake feeling like a disgrace to my nation, with the worst hangover I have had in Rome. *Madonna mia.* Damn those Italians and their teetotalling habits. Without even trying, I've become a two-pot screamer. Seedier than a vineyard, I spend the morning prostrate, willing myself back to rude health. I can't even contemplate the ladder.

At the end of my bed, my mobile phone beeps. It's a message from Raffaello, responding to one I sent him with my uncle's address. Raffaello plans to send his portfolio to Geoffrey, who will pass it on to a local gallery in San Gimignano that may be interested in taking on an exhibition. His friendly message ends with '*Un bacio*'. My hangover and my spirits lift. He's sent me a wet one. There's no time to waste.

Before I chicken out, I send Raffaello a message inviting him to my house for lunch, hoping I will develop an appetite. It will be a good incentive to get out of bed. I lie back waiting for a response, wondering what I have just done.

Actually, I know precisely what I am doing. Playing with sizeable firecrackers. Raffaello is not Federico's best mate – but they are good friends who play in the same band. Flirting with an ex's friend is just not cricket. But I've never had the patience to understand that dull game anyway. I can't help myself. Things didn't work out with Federico and Raffaello is, like me, newly single. So what's the big deal? I don't have evil intentions. I just want to live for the moment, as I promised myself I would when in Italy. When in Rome.

My phone beeps. Raffaello responds in the affirmative. I ease my head back onto my pillow and try to get some desperately needed beauty sleep between baby wails.

As I prepare a pasta sauce later, I wonder what my friends at home are doing for the public holiday long weekend. Maybe they've hired a house down on the south coast, no doubt enjoying weather as divine in January as it is ball-breaking in Rome. The door buzzer interrupts my hangover melancholy.

In Converse boots, black jeans, a green leather motorbike jacket and a tartan scarf, Raffaello is all punk spunk. As we move to kiss each other I blush when I go for the wrong side. Or is he wrong? I still seem to bumble my double-pecks.

I invite him into the kitchen, where I serve up penne with an *amatriciana* sauce. Watching Tizi one night I learned how to make the simple and apparently no-fail recipe.

'*È buono*. It's good,' says Raffaello, to my relief. God love bacon. It makes anything taste yummy and cures any hangover, for which there is no precise word in Italian, probably because it's considered such poor form to have one.

Raffaello is not a social animal, but when he speaks he has interesting things to say. He's preparing for an exhibition in Testaccio, and describes his experimentation with spray paint instead of his regular oils, working in a disused room he found in the apartment block he lives in. Not having seen any of Raffaello's works, I ask him to describe them. I throw around a few artists' names until I have a rough idea.

The conversation turns to Federico and Raffaello asks how I am. 'I'm fine. We still catch up now and then. It just didn't work out.' 'I understand,' he says. 'It was like that with Sascha and me.'

Sitting in the tiny kitchen, the house falls silent as we gaze at each other across the table. I often think in music, especially when I am over-tired. The lyrics of one of my favourite Smiths tunes drifts into my head and before I know it, Morrissey has convinced me to throw caution to the wind.

Bumbling over my words, I tell Raffaello that I was attracted to him when I met him at the first dinner Nina organised after she arrived home, but that I knew he was with Sascha and I put the issue aside, because I also had feelings for Federico. I blush at the raw manner in which I have explained things, watching Raffaello's eyes widen with surprise and, if I am not mistaken, delight. What I am doing? I don't even know the guy – and I haven't enough friends in Rome to start making enemies.

He smiles and asks me to see a film later in the evening, but I have to work until midnight. I suggest we catch up afterwards.

My stomach does a neat triple somersault with pike. I ignore the voice in my head that tells me I am about to create *un gran casino*, a big, fat mess.

After work I walk to meet Raffaello, who has just come out of a cinema with Federico and Sascha. We go to a bar nearby and I try to act normally – despite the fact I am sitting at a table with my ex, his mate, whom I have a crush on, and his only recently turned ex-girlfriend, who may have lingering issues with her ex. Talk about a bizarre love square.

Nervous, I talk to Sascha in our native language and she tells me about her job as a private English teacher, moving around Rome's outer suburbs by bus and working her own hours. I have considered doing the same thing because it's good money, but, despite the night work, I like the Beehive gig because I have to speak Italian for the Cross Pollinate work.

'*Guarda, Penny!*' says Federico, pointing at his teeth. They are brilliant white.

During our relationship he was forever telling me he was about to go to the dentist to get his tobacco-stained chompers cleaned. We grin at each other, sharing a silly ex-lovers' moment.

Raffaello interrupts my thoughts, asking me what the gold and ruby ring on my right hand signifies. Telling him it was a fortieth wedding anniversary gift from my grandfather to my grandmother, I stare at him for a moment too long. He responds in kind.

Walking home at 2 am, I send a text message to Federico, saying I'm glad we can still see one another and be mates. Easier said than done after any relationship. Fuelled with *vino*, I then send a text to Raffaello, asking him if I had imagined him being flirtatious. His reply comes back instantly, 'No, it's not imagination, however the situation with the others is a little embarrassing. I feel that I have to see you in secret! Kisses.'

I am still smirking as I read Federico's response, 'I'm also really content to have seen you again because I missed you heaps. Well then, see you soon. *Ti voglio bene.* 'Night. Kiss.'

What are you doing, Penny? You'll break up the band! Geoffrey's joke bounces around my head. I try to block everything out and get some sleep – in less than four hours the most important woman in my life lands in Rome.

It's just past 6.30 am when I see Mum standing alone at the baggage reclaim area at the airport. Her plane was early.

Love and pride wash over me as I race towards her. At fifty-three, with a small backpack on her shoulders and a tiny wheely bag at her feet, she's just spent twenty-four hours in the air, yet she looks as if she's set to go on the road. What a trooper.

We hug for ages before catching the train back to the city.

'Wow!' says Mum as we emerge from Colosseo Metro and step outside in full view of the hulking monument. 'I can't believe you live so close to the Colosseum!'

'Yeah,' I say, not looking up because I am busy texting Raffaello.

'Pen! Look out!' Mum yelps as I step onto the busy pedestrian crossing leading from the Metro to the monument.

'*Calma!* If you don't walk out aggressively like this you'll never cross, Mum,' I argue, not wanting to admit that my SMS habit is getting out of control. Pretty soon I am going to need a safe-texting room.

As I stride towards home, one of Mum's bags on my back, I force myself to slow down. Absence often makes people seem so much older. It's ten months since I last saw Mum and, for all her get-up-and-go, I cannot expect her to be the woman who, fifteen years ago, drove me to water polo practice at sparrow's five mornings a week, managed a household, a business and everything else besides.

We lunch at a neighbourhood trattoria, then have cups of tea all afternoon at home before I take her to see an art show by Sienna, the artist whose apartment I visited on New Year's Eve. Held at a funky café near the Spanish Steps, the exhibition consists of small, square portraits of some of Sienna's friends, including Federico and Raffaello, who are yet to arrive.

I introduce Mum to Sienna, then we wander the exhibition. I stare at the oiled faces of Federico and Raffaello hanging on the bright red walls of the café, trying not to linger too obviously in front of them. They are so different. With longish brown hair, striking blue eyes, a long, fine nose and angelic mouth, Federico stares blankly, revealing little of his personality. Raffaello's tight, black curls contrast against his pallid skin. His features – small nose, large black eyes and thin mouth – seem to snarl. Ironic, given the more I get to know him the sweeter he seems.

Explaining the status quo to Mum, she looks at Federico before stopping at Raffaello.

'He looks a bit scary,' she says bluntly, making me laugh.

Before Federico and Raffaello arrive, Mum succumbs to jet lag. Taking her home, I introduce her to my flatmates, with whom we have a light meal before Mum hops into the futon bed of Alberta's I've dragged into my room. I am handing her a cup of tea when my mobile buzzes with a message from Raffaello, asking me to meet him outside Al Vino Al Vino, a wine bar in Monti, a hip inner-city quarter within walking distance.

'Mum, do you mind if I go out?' I'm no longer a teen, but I feel guilty leaving my mother at home alone in Rome.

'No. I reckon I'll be out like a light in ten minutes.'

Bless the old girl.

At eleven o'clock Al Vino Al Vino is crammed with groups sitting at the marble-topped tables. Walking through the entrance hall, its walls lined with teak shelves stacked with hundreds of bottles of wine, we nab a table out the back and order two glasses of *Nero D'Avola,* a Sicilian red, and *caponata,* which Raffaello says also hails from Sicily. We smear the moreish blend of capsicum, tomato, eggplant, capers and onion on crusty bread.

Raffaello and I talk in circles, openly admitting the attraction between us but not wanting to start something that might hurt the feelings of Sascha and Federico, given barely a month has passed since our respective splits.

'I am scared to look at you too much when the others are around. You have such beautiful eyes,' he says.

If an Australian bloke said that I'd probably snort and tell him to save his energy for an audition on 'The Bold and the Beautiful'. I am awkward when it comes to accepting compliments, to the point where I must seem dismissive and rude at times. Uttered in Italian, however, such flattery is somehow more authentic.

Raffaello and I leave the wine bar and walk down the street, the Colosseum illuminated straight ahead of us. Perhaps swept away by the surrounding beauty and the second round of *vini rossi*, we finally give in to temptation and kiss like love-struck teens. Parting to give each other a sly grin, we head towards my place.

Raffaello compliments me on my name. Beautiful eyes, beautiful name. (Call me an ungrateful wench, but can't the Italians come up with new adjectives? They use forms of 'beautiful' – *bello, bel, bei, begli, bella* and *belle* – as frequently as they respond to *mamma* on their mobile phones.)

Raffaello is not the first Italian to gush about my full name, which has never raised any interest at home and which I loathed as a child for its formality. But Italians know well the tale of Penelope, wife of the Greek hero Ulysses. Besieged by suitors who told her that her husband was lying lifeless on a battlefield, Penelope insisted she could not choose a new husband until she had knitted a funereal shroud in memory of Ulysses. Knitting by day, each night she painstakingly unravelled her needlework, staving off her admirers for many years until her beloved finally returned.

While the romantic in me admires Penelope's faithfulness and swoons at the Cinderella finish, the cynic in me thinks she was a silly old duck for passing up some rumpy pumpy. Her warrior husband was probably waving more than one sword in his travels.

Stealing one last snog from my Ulysses of the moment, I stumble home, giddy with the thrill of what could, somewhat naughtily, be.

I give Mum a warm scarf before we head into the historic centre of Rome to Pascucci, the Cross Pollinate lodging run by Anna and Luciano, who has forgiven my phone gaffe. I've decided to

visit all the Cross Pollinate B&Bs in Rome so I can meet the
owners and, more importantly, personally see their lodgings,
enabling me to answer clients' questions in more detail. When I
called Luciano to say I had to cancel our appointment because
Mum was in town, he insisted that she come with me and Amy,
my American colleague – and that we all stay for lunch.

A pot-bellied man with a ringmaster's moustache and proud
disposition greets us at the door. Dressed in pressed cream pants
and a striped blue and white shirt, Luciano ushers us into an
elegant lounge room with two long, leather divans, impressive oil
portraits and Persian rugs resplendent in rich tones of red. Squat,
buxom and dripping in jewellery, Anna appears from the kitchen
to kiss us like orphans. The couple give us a tour of the one
bedroom they rent out, which has a similarly luxurious decor,
before we sit down at a round table in the light-filled dining room.

Amy speaks the best Italian so she acts as translator when
required. Poor Mum can't understand a word but Luciano's animated
gestures help break any boredom. Anna brings in some bruschetta
with juicy cherry tomatoes before Luciano carries in a huge bowl
of spaghetti with *vongole*, which he claims to have made. I suspect
there will be more and, sure enough, Anna presents us each with
a plate loaded with a whole sea bass, marinated with cloves and
slices of orange. Struggling even to finish the pasta, Amy and
Mum look at one another with alarm. Next Luciano passes around
a big bowl of fresh fava beans, showing us how to string and shell
the beans, then serves slices of fresh rockmelon, Swiss chocolate
and coffee.

'Don't tell me that they eat like this every day,' Mum says,
pulling a fat face when Luciano and Anna are out of the room.

'No, but when they do the trick is not to feel obliged to eat
everything and do as the locals do and have a walk after,' I say,

having learnt my lesson months earlier. Amy looks like she's on the brink of collapse.

Flabbergasted by Luciano and Anna's splendid home and generous hospitality, Mum asks to take a photo of the couple as we leave. Checking each other's appearance, they pose formally like a royal couple on one of the divans, Luciano cradling their two chubby Persian cats as the Queen might hold her corgis.

'*Mamma, mamma, vieni qui!*' Beckoning with his hands, Luciano calls out to Mum and practically drags her to sit between them and the fat cats.

As I take the photo on Mum's camera, I already can't wait to get the image back. Seeing her face, flushed with vino and happiness that comes from experiencing all things new, it reminds me of the very reason I dreamt of coming to Italy.

Rising early, Mum and I grab our small backpacks and board the train to Naples, a two-hour ride south of Rome and the first stop in a ten-day itinerary I have planned.

Looking at the front page of *City*, a commuter newspaper I grabbed at Termini, my eyes pop out of my head when I see the main picture – a close-up of the disfigured body of one of four men killed by *la camorra,* the Neapolitan mafia. The man died after being *incaprettato*, which I later learn means being tied up like a goat in such a manner that if you move an inch, the rope around you tightens. One burst of frustrated movement means you can kill yourself. There has been a surge in clan warfare in Napoli, with seven deaths and nine injured in ten days. In ten months the Mafia massacres have claimed over one hundred lives. It intrigues me that Italian papers publish such graphic pictures. It's common, too, to watch the nightly news and see lifeless limbs escaping from white sheets draped haphazardly over bodies at crime scenes, as if the cops want to publicise their dangerous profession.

'It's great that you're reading the papers, Pen – you'll be fluent in no time,' Mum says innocently, looking up from her Maeve Binchy book to see me poring over my dictionary.

Pushing the paper from view I smile, vowing silently to watch her like a hawk for the whole time we are south. Everyone has warned me about the seedy nature of Napoli, where a friend of mine had her bag swiped by a motorbike bandit and another mate paid 100 euros to a street vendor for a digital camera he personally inspected, only to open up the box later to find nothing but shredded paper and a small rock. The further south you go, the more poverty you encounter, with chronic unemployment and many communities tangled in Mafia networks. Successive boatloads of *clandestini*, illegal immigrants, washing up on the picturesque island of Lampedusa add to the murky minestrone.

My defences are slowly shot down as I take in the scene beyond Napoli train station: musty shops with dusty shelves stacked high with odd and seemingly obsolete objects; dirty street markets that burst with life; destitute people trying to flog contraband cigarettes; an ageing couple in threadbare clothes around a barbecue in the middle of a back street, trying to make a quick panino profit from bypassers; grotty, hilly streets that hide centuries of squalid secrets. People are doing anything to survive yet somehow the overall atmosphere isn't gloomy. An intangible buzz of energy oozes from every nook and dirty cranny. Like the Romans, the Neapolitans seem to put the sun into life whenever they can.

Disappointingly, we have less than three hours to explore before we hop on a train to Sorrento, our base for the next two days. But before we leave the birthplace of Italian pizza, we find time to devour an enormous plate of thin, crispy dough drizzled with fresh tomato sauce and mozzarella and, for good measure, sample the *misto di frittura*, or fried vegetables, sold at the ubiquitous makeshift street stalls. Naples seems three times grimier and noisier and less architecturally impressive than Rome, but it's loaded with raw fascination. Like the gory Mafia scene in the newspaper, it is both disturbing and compelling. Hooked, I decide to return as soon as I can.

Dumping our bags at our cheap hotel in Sorrento, we jump on a bus that winds around the precariously steep Amalfi Coast. Every two minutes the bus driver toots his horn a fraction of a second before rounding a hairpin bend, and I remember how scared I felt during my visit in 1997, when our bus scraped a small car on a narrow cliff pass. I hold Mum's hand like a child. At least if we go over the edge we won't see where we are going: fog and drizzle obscure the smattering of pretty villages and luxury hotels that draw a procession of celebrities and rich wannabes.

Alighting at Positano, we wander in and out of quaint boutiques selling resort fashion, gourmet foods and iridescent yellow bottles of *Limoncello* before the miserable weather forces us to head back to Sorrento. After hot showers to thaw our numb limbs, we go out to a café recommended in our guidebook that's close to our hotel.

As I try to talk to the waiter, a tall, lean and bookishly cute local who humours my slow Italian, I see Mum smiling at me.

'What?' I ask her when the waiter is out of earshot.

'Nothing…I'm just wondering if there's anyone you meet who you don't try and talk to – today you chatted to the woman in the pastry shop in Naples, the fisherman we saw on our walk in Sorrento, the newsagent in Positano and now the waiter,' she says.

It's official. I've become a raving lunatic.

'Sorry. I guess I want to speak as much as I can because I'm scared I'll lose what little I have during two weeks with you.'

'Don't apologise! I love hearing it. I think it's great you're trying.'

Standing in a bar the next morning, I order *cornetti* and *cappuccini* for Mum and me. Sure enough, our coffees come with love hearts on top. As I explain the 'love heart on coffee tourist service' to Mum I hear the old man who made our coffee sing out to the younger man at the cash register, '*Facciamogli un bel prezzo.*'

Am I going crazy, or did the barista just order the man at the till to 'do them a beautiful price' – or hike the bill of our breakfast? When I get to the cash register I find they've almost quadrupled the normal price.

Indignant, I struggle to think of what I can say before realising it's a lost cause. They'll only feign incomprehension. I've lived in Rome for half a year but in an instant I feel like one of the hapless tourists I have seen the locals rip off via nefarious means: refusing to display prices and quoting their own prices or fudging the change, hoping their swindle will go unnoticed. There is no sign in the bar showing prices. I don't have a leg to stand on. I pay and leave, feeling powerless and furious I can't argue in Italian.

After combing the ruins of Pompeii, buried in 79 AD by the eruption of the still active volcano Vesuvio that dominates the majestic skyline, Mum and I head north to Perugia, checking in to a hotel in the same street as Bar Papaia. It's a thrill to introduce Mum to Sanja, Piero and Ivo, who kiss her on the cheek and give us some coffee on the house. But the best is to come: Maria fusses over Mum like the *nonna* she is to me. Plying us with more coffee and Perugina chocolates, her face beams as she analyses Mum's face then mine, noting we are like chalk and cheese: Mum has blue eyes and grey hair, I have dark features with green-hazel eyes, like Dad.

After dining with Sanja at a pizzeria in town, Mum and I are about to turn off the light when my mobile phone beeps.

'What's that?'

'It's a message from Raffaello, sending me *tanti baci* – many kisses,' I say, blushing.

Rolling her eyes, Mum turns her back to me and goes to sleep.

Several cities later, including Venice where standing high on a *ponte* above the Grand Canal, we get caught up in a magical snowflake flurry, rendering us like figurines in a snowcone shaker, we reach San Gimignano for the final leg of our tour. Spending time with Geoffrey, Anna and Bianca restores our energy and before I know it we are back in Rome with thirty-six hours before Mum's departure. All of a sudden I feel an urge to show her as much of my new life as I can – so when she gets home she can put images to my words.

To that end, I take her to see Serena's apartment. She called when we were on the road to ask if I would be interested in renting the second bedroom at her place. The Italian girl she had lined up has pulled out. Seeing Mum's positive reaction to Serena's flat reinforces my feeling that I should accept the offer. The rent is more but the apartment is light-filled and spacious. Although I would have preferred to live with at least one Italian, Serena is a fab chick. In any case, she and Carlo III will be away for at least two months, giving me loads of time to study in peace.

The thought of leaving via di San Giovanni in Laterano fills me with sadness because, apart from my initial lonely month, our household is a lively one. Although Alberta, Tiziana, Nina and I don't socialise much together, there is always someone around to play with. But after six months in one home it feels like a good time for change. I tell Serena I'm in.

On our way to dinner on her last night, Mum and I stop briefly to say hello to Raffaello, who is on his way to jam with Cactus.

'He's nice, Pen,' says Mum, when Raffaello is out of sight. She doesn't have to add the line – I know she's thinking it. *Don't worry, we won't get our hopes up.* Though they have no expectations of me, my family tends to view my love life like a Lotto machine. We're all waiting for the right numbers to fall.

I fail in my effort to hold back tears as Mum gives me a lingering hug goodbye at the airport. In two weeks she has travelled the country without complaining of tiredness for a second and treated me to heavenly meals and sights I will never forget. Encouraging me to stay put and suck the juice out of Rome, she's given me the unconditional love and support I hadn't realised I needed to refuel my determination to stay in Italy.

As she disappears through the departure gates I wonder how I coped so long without seeing her, and how much time will pass before we'll meet again.

Saturday night *febbre*

Feeling sooky minus Mum, I return home from the airport to find my flatmates breakfasting in the kitchen. I stare at the makeshift cardboard noticeboard stuck on a wall near the fridge. A talented sketcher, Tiziana has drawn our household as cartoon characters, surrounded by random clippings and comments. I take a deep breath and announce that I am moving out within weeks, at the start of March. My flatties are sad but understanding – which only makes it harder to leave.

'I'm going to have a '70s party that week, so it can be your farewell too,' says Nina, whose clothes rack is bound to be loaded with garments of the era. Forever finding a reason to have a *festa*, Nina would celebrate the launch of a new toothbrush if she could. I love her pizzazz. She's a human Rice Bubble.

'Great – it's my birthday around then, too,' I say, feeling cheerier by the minute.

Putting on some lighter clothing, I decide to go out and soak up the day, unseasonably warm for February. Once upon a time I would have put on any old thing when leaving the house, but now I find myself making more of an effort whatever the hour. In Italy, just as those who dress well get treated better when entering a clothes store, you receive more courtesy, even admiration, if you take pride in your appearance.

Climate change breeds batty behaviour in Rome. In winter, women cling to their furs and puffy, feather-lined bomber jackets like life buoys, even when freak weather pushes the mercury well above average. I think of the mild, spring day in April when Jo and I arrived and I was subjected to unwanted attention near the Spanish Steps. Back then, I didn't realise my crime: showing bare shoulders in a top that was judged too summery by Italian women but drew wolf whistles from the men. Conversely, in summer, a cool spell is ignored by women, many of whom resemble 'Baywatch' extras, with slim limbs, plate-flat stomachs and boobs pumped up by push-up bras or silicon.

Slaves to *il tempo*, the weather, and *la moda*, fashion, the Italian attitude to illness amuses me just as much. At the slightest hint of *la febbre*, a fever, Tiziana locks herself in her room for three days, claiming she is too weak to work, while Alberta, wrestling with *influenza*, talks as if it's a new strain of SARS. Accustomed to overhearing Italians prattling about food at every turn, in winter the words I hear most are *febbre* and *influenza*. Both strike fear in the hearts of the alarmist, superstitious locals.

I grab the Metro freebie paper and sit and read in a park near home. More reader-friendly than other *giornali*, I also like the commuter papers because they are full of national surveys that hint at the complex make-up of Italy. Today the front-page splash of *Metro* is '*Più sani e più poveri*. More healthy and poorer', with census figures showing that while the life expectancy has increased, so too has the cost of living, with almost forty per cent of locals saying they have insufficient means to get by. Much is made of the disproportionate increase in daily living expenses with the introduction of the euro. I remember well the time when the Australian dollar held more or less the same value as the old lira, making travel for me in Italy affordable, so I understand the continuing local outrage at the euro. As gloomy as the statistics are, with the word 'recession' often appearing in the headlines, I can't help but smile at the colour photo illustrating the survey: a sixty-something man and woman clad in swimmers, looking tanned and lean as they lie back on their beach chairs – both with a cigarette in their hands. The shot screams Italy like Max Dupain's *The Bather* represents my homeland.

I meet Raffaello and we drive to collect his drum set and take it back to the home he shares with his father in Monte Verde Vecchio, a *quartiere* on the hill above Trastevere dwelled in by many a well-fed artist. Entering the spacious second-floor apartment, I see a small man who has the same large, dark eyes as Raffaello. Banned from ever meeting Federico's parents, it is heartening to be introduced to Alfredo, a published sage who is courteous and charming. Raffaello's parents are separated and his mother lives in Venice, returning to the family home in Rome for short sojourns.

Raffaello gives me a quick tour of the apartment – full of his artworks, some painted when he was a child, and offering views of the city skyline – before he takes me to his room, where a turntable and stereo surrounded by scores of vinyls and CDs take pride of place. I wonder what his Top Five worst break-ups are. Raffaello shows me some of his older oil paintings, with gloomy to black tones and intimidating, animalistic faces. His recent, sprayed works are more happy-crazy, featuring extra-terrestrial forms in fluorescent shades. They're unusual and I like them a lot. Looking at his bed I cheer silently. It may be a divan bed but it's *matrimoniale* – a double bed. But I wouldn't have been surprised if it were single in accordance with local trends.

We listen to some music then say *ciao* to Alfredo and walk down to Campo de' Fiori. Time for a quick coffee at Latteria del

Gallo, a tiny family bar run by a shrunken *nonna* who steadfastly refuses to let anyone take photos of the gorgeous vintage interior, including a wall stacked with beverage cans from all over the world. Raffaello gives me a quick but affectionate snog before I duck around the corner to Ristorante der Pallaro, where I usually dine with The President. My *Corriere della Sera* contact has said yes to a story on the restaurant, acknowledging it is a Roman institution frequented by pollies, Hollywood actors (including Mel Gibson most recently) and the public who are charmed by the home-style cooking.

Wearing her trademark floral dress, white cotton apron and matching hair band, Paola greets me with the overblown enthusiasm she dollops on every client. Getting her to stop fussing for a minute is difficult, but after explaining what I am doing – and dropping the name of the *Corriere della Sera,* the most widely read broadsheet in Italy – she plonks herself down at an empty table and looks at me impatiently. Her eyes dart about as I pepper her with questions and her answers are given in a heavy, Roman dialect.

I learn that she and her potbellied husband, Giovanni, whose shaking hands betray his age as he hovers nearby setting tables, have been married for forty years. Paola was sixteen years old when she met Giovanni. After they married she worked beside her new husband's late father, Mario, who founded the restaurant, to learn the family trade. Now she and Giovanni serve up their unwritten, fixed menu for lunch and dinner every day but Monday. In the morning Paola buys provisions at the daily produce market in Campo de' Fiori, then she and her small staff make everything fresh on the premises – from kilos of fettuccine to enormous *crostate*, tarts.

Fed up with being interrogated, Paola shoos me into the kitchen where olive oil bubbles and hisses in huge fry pans cooking hand-sliced potatoes into thin, curling crisps. Wearing what looks suspiciously like a shower cap, Paola's older sister stands rolling pasta dough. Paola opens one of two industrial ovens and pulls out a baking dish holding a fat roll of veal. She slices a thick hunk off the meat and puts it on a plate then adds two artichokes from a roasting tray nearby, making sure she drips plenty of juice and oil on them.

'*Mangia!* Eat!' she orders, shoving the plate into my hand.

It's only just gone midday, a good hour before Italians start to think about lunch, but I dare not be disobedient. Wrenching myself from Paola's chesty farewell, I walk home with a happy belly and heart. In the Internet café around the corner I file my story in record time.

On a biting Saturday afternoon I meet Raffaello in the main piazza of Trastevere. We buy some groceries for dinner and jump on a bus, which winds up Gianicolo, the beautiful park lookout over Rome, to his leafy suburb. Within half an hour of entering his apartment we've consummated our relationship. Ridiculously, until now, we haven't had a chance: I'm scared to invite Raffaello home because I haven't yet told Alberta I am seeing another one of her friends, and his dad, currently away on a business trip, is usually home.

One of the funniest statistics I've read claimed a high percentage of Italians admitted they had lost their virginity *in macchina*, in the car, and continue to have back seat quickies, because they don't have a chance at home – *mamma* or *la famiglia* is always waiting in the wings.

After dinner, we are watching television when, out of the blue, Raffaello complains of having *la febbre*. He plucks a thermometer from somewhere and sticks it under his armpit, watching it with concern.

'*Mi sento debole*. I feel weak,' he complains.

Not wanting to spread his infection, despite the fact we've just exchanged copious amounts of love germs, Raffaello insists I sleep in Alfredo's bed. If the unfamiliarity of lying in a new boyfriend's bed has occasionally robbed me of sleep, lying in my new boyfriend's father's bed feels doubly strange. Staring at the antique furniture, bookshelves and framed baby photos of Raffaello, who I hear padding to retrieve the thermometer, I take hours to nod off.

Tired the next morning, I go to say goodbye to Raffaello, having made lunch plans with Serena. Lying in bed with a woeful expression stamped on his face, he looks at me with unabashed need.

'Can you stay here today? I don't feel well and my father doesn't return until tomorrow.'

Quashing a conviction that all men are hypochondriacs, I agree reluctantly, not wanting to make my new squeeze think I'm a heartless wench. But I can't help but wonder how Raffaello would cope if he found himself, like me, alone in a country where he couldn't read the instructions on any pharmaceutical product and didn't have a trusted doctor at his fingertips.

He's the same age as me, but I suspect Raffaello, like most young Italians, is used to his mother doing everything for him, even though her decision to move to Venice in recent years would have had an impact. Granted, my own mum dedicated herself to raising three daughters and waited until I, the baby of her family, was an independent fifteen before she worked full-time. But when I finished school I couldn't wait to leave home and explore the world. My parents were always there in emergencies, but I relished my independence.

In Italy it's irrelevant whether *mamma* works or not. She still organises every facet of family life. But the thing I find most bizarre is how she continues to do everything for her children, even when they are grown adults. Single or attached, Italian men and women often live at home well into their thirties and often much longer, sometimes never leaving the family home until they get married. Even then it's not uncommon for them to live in the same palazzo as *mamma*. If young Italians do get a life and move out they drop in to to to see *mamma* regularly and eat her home-cooked lunches or dinners. And if they can't make it they know *mamma* will drop tasty parcels at their place when she has time – which she always does, because every good *mamma* has.

Alberta and Tizi return home as often as possible, Tizi almost every weekend since her family lives closest to Rome. When she arrives home late on Sunday I head straight for the kitchen to see what tasty treats her *mamma* has offloaded, praying she has my favourite: melt-in-your-mouth *ciambelline* biscuits.

'Nobody makes pasta like *mamma*,' an Italian friend, who lives at home at the age of twenty-eight, told me one day, admitting he hoped his future girlfriend would be just as talented as his mother. God help me. My culinary skills will never net me a catch.

Raffaello looks at me from his sheeted tomb, the thermometer resting at his fingertips.

'There's no aspirin left. Could you go and buy some more?'

Giving me an aggrieved look, he thrusts ten euros into my hand and gives me directions to the nearest *farmacia*.

Glad to get out of the flat, my joy fades when I discover the pharmacy is closed. Damn, it's Sunday. Only bars, the odd tobbaconist, cake shops and restaurants remain open to satisfy the locals' constant demand for coffee, cigarettes, a sweet to take to *mamma*'s for lunch, or a long meal.

I walk for what feels like hours around the suburb, asking baristas and newsagents for information about other 24–7 pharmacies that might be nearby, receiving directions I muddle time and time again. In the end I resort to begging friendly-looking bar staff and passers-by for some *aspirina*. I feel like a junkie.

Defeated and cold, I return back to Raffaello's house and tell him I have lucked out.

He asks me to knock on the front doors of the apartments in his palazzo. I look at him with dismay, but he looks so pathetic I find myself agreeing. Finally, an old woman on the level below, who knows Raffaello's family, shoves four aspirin in my hand. It's all I can do not to hug her.

I collapse on the bed beside Raffaello, exhausted and flat after the morning's events, and try to communicate random thoughts to him. Finally the patient pipes up.

'You know...I don't understand why I am not in love, because you are so nice, intelligent and beautiful.'

I look incredulously at Raffaello. At least one ex has uttered something similar as a kiss-off. But Raffaello's words seem totally leftfield and hit me like bullets – coming as they do after a morning in which I have felt humiliated trying to get him pain relief. The more I think about the situation, the angrier I get, for being such a doormat. If Raffaello thinks he's dying he can call the ambos.

Feigning indifference, I tell him that I have to go to work and leave.

I barely feel my feet hit the pavement as I march home, fists pushing into the corners of my white leather jacket. I am freezing, despite the fact I have a wool scarf wrapped tightly around my neck. Raffaello doesn't even *know* me, yet in a matter of weeks he's swung from saying he can't take his eyes off me to questioning whether he wants to see me again. *Cretino!*

Listening to 78 Saab on my Discman as I stride through the middle of the ancient Forum, majestic custodian of centuries of history laced with war, peace, romance and intrigue, I feel like I'm on the modern-day set of a romantic comedy. I go for a long walk until the music and street scenes wash away my anger, arriving home just in time for dinner with my flatties and two guests:

Agnese, a German friend of Nina's who is taking over my room, and Francesco, our landlord.

Dressed in his burgundy Dalai Lama smock, with a mobile phone cord hanging from each ear, Francesco's exaggerated personality cheers me up no end. He talks a million miles an hour, mumbling that he's high on the fumes of paint he's been using to renovate his apartment. After dinner he downs a generous glass of grappa and rolls a fat joint. I've rarely met or been on friendly terms with any of my landlords, let alone got high with them. I sleep soundly.

It's been a while since I have seen Federico, so we meet for dinner at a pizzeria near home. As soon as I see him I realise I've missed his friendship and regret being out of touch. In a positive mood, pretty soon he is hinting that I seem to have been spending a bit of time with Raffaello.

Unable to lie to him and suspecting he has guessed anyway, I tell him that I have been seeing his friend. Far from surprised, Federico says he and Sascha had put two and two together. Without going into great detail, confusion and dented ego have me confessing that the relationship with my *febbre*-ridden drummer boy appears over. Federico listens to me without seeming to form any obvious judgement.

I suddenly feel the need to apologise for my recent behaviour, which even I can't understand. I've been so distracted by Raffaello that I had forgotten how much Federico's companionship means to me. I miss my mates when they disappear into the lovey-dovey puff of a new relationship – but here I am doing the same thing. I don't want to lose – nor burn, if I can help it – the few, important people in my life right now.

Point blank, to my surprise, Federico asks me if I am in love with Raffaello. I respond with an automatic '*No*'. When I ask him if he was in love when we were together he shrugs and says when we were together he always felt love for me. We look at each other with affection, reading each other's thoughts. *Who knows what true love is anyway? How do you know if you are in love with someone or you just love them – and is there a big difference? I guess when it's right you don't even question it.*

Catching up with any ex where there is alcohol involved is not a good idea. I either want to thump them or jump them. Chatting with Federico, I battle nostalgia. More relaxed as my language skills improve, he makes me feel so happy that I wonder why we ever broke up. He hasn't lost his grunge-appeal.

I remind myself of why we split – but accept a warm embrace from him before we part. Taller than me, he still does good hug. I walk home feeling fuzzy but comforted.

I have just arrived at work the next day when an SMS message from Raffaello pops up on my mobile with a beep.

Hello. I wanted to tell you that I was wrong to tell you those things, I realise that now that I don't have the fever! Maybe you won't believe me and it's already too late, but I wanted to tell you immediately because I miss you. Sorry.

Try as I might to stubbornly maintain my annoyance, I smile to myself. *La febbre* is more serious than I thought. Not only does it weaken your body but it attacks your mental health. Silly me. I respond by telling him I'll be in touch tomorrow.

Checking my email I find an early happy birthday message from a scatty friend who mixed up her days. The day after tomorrow I'll be twenty-nine. It's almost a year since I left Australia and seven months since arriving in Rome. While I occasionally yearn for a magic carpet to transport me to Australia to see friends and family, my relationships here with the few people I see and trust the most are comforting, stimulating and entertaining. I'm not often lonely but when I crave company I can usually find it.

Whenever I do need a lift, I make a beeline for the Pantheon. Walking into the centre of the hulking building, I strain my neck to admire the beautiful panels that line the open-air dome then reread my guide book and immerse myself in a fraction of the stupefying beauty of the city I live in. A fat gelato with my favourite three flavours – *pistacchio, melone* and *Bacio* – ices my sensory joy.

Often dirty, crude and (now that I can understand enough to accept the realities in my existence) rude, the Romans unwittingly challenge me to stay put. I remain spellbound by their live-for-the-moment spirit and contradictory lifestyle – marrying mindboggling history and an inherently slow, hedonistic existence with the modern trappings of a European capital in the global economy. If they do something to put me offside, I often still can't help but laugh – either at their sheer cunning (bending rules is a national sport), or their theatrical skills, since they are all born actors.

If I could bottle the intense sensation of joy I get from standing in a bar listening to the locals banter, or being fed to my gills at an Italian family table, I'd be happy forever.

I'm doing what I always wanted to do, I conclude, and start to reply to my friend's email.

I have one year until I turn the big three-O. I have to make this year in Rome count. I really should try to get some more freelance writing going. The problem is I am finding it harder and harder to get motivated. At this rate, a decade will pass and I will still be a receptionist who writes the odd yarn on food and culture in Rome. *Allora.* Worse things have happened.

Cutting Raffaello some slack, I meet him at Al Vino Al Vino for wine and *caponata,* and he again apologises for his behaviour, insisting his Saturday night *febbre* was to blame. He's so sincere he's funny, and the wine just adds to the affection I feel for him. Walking out into the street we head towards my home, holding hands and exchanging coy smiles, forgetting the events of the past week.

As we near the Colosseum, Raffaello steers me until we are standing beneath its huge walls, faintly lit by the dim orange glow of nearby street lamps. He pins me by the arms to stop me and looks like he's on the verge of saying something important. I just hope this time *la febbre* won't be doing the talking.

'*Tanti auguri a te,*
Tanti auguri a te,
Tanti aug-uri cara Penelope,
Tanti auguri a te,' he sings.

I glance at my watch – it's midnight. It's my birthday.

I look from the Colosseum to the cute grin on Raffaello's face and feel – for the second time in as many days – like I'm on a film set. Girl re-gets guy. Cue drop-dead amazing monument, passionate kiss and sappy song. Roll credits.

Walking in the front door of home, another surprise is in store.

'*Buon compleanno! Tanti auguri!* Happy birthday, best wishes!'

Springing from the kitchen, Nina and Tiziana hug me and pop open a bottle of champagne. I am so touched by their gesture I could almost cry. Sensing I might be feeling a little displaced on my birthday, without my family and friends near, they have made an effort to be around. Some people don't raise an eyebrow when they have a birthday but I believe you only get to be the centre of attention once a year, so you may as well make it big. This one definitely rates.

Already tipsy, I manage to inhale a glass of champagne before Raffaello and I drag ourselves up the ladder to bed.

Ignoring a slight hangover, I set out to enjoy the first day of the last year of my twenties with more energy than I possess.

We buy bread rolls, fresh cheese and ham at the local deli then catch a bus to Testaccio, where Raffaello gives me a local's perspective of the *quartiere*, traditionally a bastion of the Centre-Left in Italy. We walk past the soccer club, one of the oldest and most vibrant associations in Rome, and the produce market, where we bump into Raffaello's aunt. Her short, frail figure is wrapped in a fur coat despite the warm weather. It is winter, after all.

We get on a bus to Villa Pamphili, the biggest park in Rome, which is brimming with well-dressed, solarium-bronzed Italians exercising or walking their dogs. Kids dressed in traditional costume for *Carnevale,* the famous festival held in Venice every year but celebrated in towns across Italy, play chasies as their parents chat nearby.

We stroll past beautifully manicured gardens until we find a lush hill strewn with daisies, where we eat lunch then lie in the sun, taking off our shoes and socks and lifting our shirts to attempt to get some sun on our lily-white bellies. Raffaello goes home to get changed before returning to my house with a small package wrapped in pretty pink paper with matching ribbon. In Italy, sweet treats bought at a *pasticceria* are often as beautifully wrapped as presents purchased from Tiffany's. Inside is a small ice-cream cake, which we tuck into immediately, since the freezer is frozen solid.

Our artist friend Sienna is having an exibition at Bar del Fico, near the Pantheon, and I've organised a birthday *aperitivo.* On our way, I stop off at Pallaro to give Paola the copy of my story on the restaurant, printed in the *Corriere della Sera* the previous Sunday. She doesn't speak a word of English but I want her to know I've done it all the same. Hugging me, she looks at Raffaello waiting outside and asks if he is my boyfriend.

'*Sì*,' I say smiling.

Paola tells me how happy she is to see me here without The President. The guts of her message is that it isn't pretty to see an old man with a girl young enough to be his daughter. I smile at her, grateful for her concern. I knew that all along, it's just that a few months ago I was a bit lost.

At Bar del Fico, named after the fig tree in the courtyard, I find Sienna, my Sicilian friends Carlo, Omar and Lucia, Serena, Tiziana, Nina and other faces.

Much later about ten of us make it home, where Omar and Lucia cook up a spicy pasta and the merriment continues until 3 am.

Raffaello and I have a late breakfast the next morning before he goes home to get his dad's car to help me move most of my stuff to Serena's apartment. In less than seventy-two hours I will depart via di San Giovanni in Laterano for good.

Later in the day I am cooking a meal to take to work when Alberta arrives home. Nina insinuated that Alberta was annoyed when Federico, though visiting our house more often to see me, treated her less attentively as a friend. I still haven't told her about Raffaello. I want to leave the house on good terms. But I also want to be honest at all costs.

When she comes into the kitchen to make a coffee I cut to the crazy chase and mention that Raffaello and I are seeing each other. I had assumed Nina had told her, but Alberta looks at me with surprise.

'You don't have to explain, do as you like, it's your life,' she says, eyeing the coffee percolator on the gas.

She's neither angry nor warm, just direct and unreadable. She probably thinks I am a tart, dating two of her mates for whom she may even have had feelings herself.

I stare at the table, wishing I hadn't opened my mouth. I can't articulate what I want to say. How do I explain what I have suddenly realised – that my relationships with Federico and Raffaello cannot be assessed on face value as normal, because so many things make them irregular: I can't communicate on my own terms, I am living in a foreign land and, as such, I am more vulnerable. Unconsciously, I am seeking support I would not normally require in a relationship conducted on home turf.

Defeated, I leave the kitchen and pack up the rest of my bags before racing to work.

The afternoon of the '70s party arrives. Even though I was born in that decade, my music memories are from the following decade. Getting up at 5 am most weekends to lie on my belly and record 'Rage', I watched Kylie chug her 'Locomotion' to number one and witnessed Michael Jackson when he was bad – but not infamous. Give me tickets to an AHA gig and I'll be your friend for life but, whatever you do, don't bother telling me Howard Jones was not cool. You just didn't understand him like I did.

We race around putting the house in order. As per usual, Tiziana's room is the junk room, crammed with excess furniture to create more corridor room and a dance space in Nina's room. My smaller room becomes a cloak room, Alberta's room, the lounge area, and the kitchen is the grog and munchies room. We light candles, put up streamers and arrange cheese and cabanossi platters. I pull on a chocolate-brown wool dress with a zip from top to bottom, bought for 5 euros at a market, fishnet stockings and chunky boots.

Before everyone arrives I stand with Nina, Tiziana and Alberta and we offer a toast to the party with the first of many martinis for the night. Looking at the made-up faces of my flatties I suppress a twinge of regret about leaving the household that made the initial, difficult months in Rome bearable.

At eleven o'clock the first of a stream of people walk through our front door. Federico, Sascha and Raffaello arrive, and I sneak moments of private conversation with the latter – even though our secret is out. Serena and The President, already merry from dinner, roll in the door. Soon drunk on the toxic sangria we have made, Serena waves her cigarette too close to Nina, accidentally burning a hole in her frock. Nina is not impressed.

Unable to hear, let alone infiltrate, the Italian conversations, I content myself with dancing and fall into bed at 4 am, listening to the last stragglers threaten to leave.

Four hours later I wake with a knotted stomach. It's my last day in the house and I have to get the rest of my stuff to Serena's before I start work. Alberta is out, but Nina and Tiziana are home. We pick up cigarette butts that litter the floor and spray disinfectant everywhere before I do a final clean of my room and grab my bags.

'This is still your house. We'll see one another really soon,' says Nina.

'You must come to my house in Latina for Easter – my mum will make the biscuits you adore and a fantastic lunch!' adds Tiziana.

Struggling with my emotions, I hug them and walk out the door.

As I walk up the street towards Serena's place, the shopkeepers I have come to know give me big smiles – Marcella, the lovely woman who runs a clothes shop with beautiful garments I can't afford; the Indian man who runs the fruit shop; the Pakistani who runs the Internet café where the computer connection crashes almost every time I use it; Francesco, the bearded old man from the postcard shop; the young couple who manage a bar I pop into occasionally, who goo and gaa over their new-born who is so pink and squashy, I can't tell if it's a boy or girl.

There goes my neighbourhood.

Nolano

I feel like Julia Roberts in *Pretty Woman*, though my mouth isn't big enough to house a fire truck and Richard Gere doesn't make me want to rip my robes off. Overnight I've gone from living in a dark house with no hot water in the kitchen and no room to swing a kitten to a luminous, voluminous apartment with mod cons including cable TV and DVD.

Waking in the house in via Biella, the first thing I notice is the ceiling. I can't touch it. In my old room, my loft bed finished barely a metre below the ceiling, invoking the odd claustrophobic fit or knock to the head or arm. I spread my arms across the wide, thick mattress and stretch my toes to touch the white timber bed frame at my feet, sculpted so it peaks in the centre like a wave. Rolling onto my left side, I stare out the French doors leading to the huge *terrazza*, which Serena has stylishly decorated with divans draped in colourful, Moroccan-style cloths and assorted plants sitting in terracotta pots.

I sit up and swing my legs over the side of the bed, which is so high my feet don't come close to brushing the floor. Hearing a panting noise, I look down. A small puddle lies on the marble floor beneath my dangling toes. Carlo III sits nearby, eyeing me with haughty indifference.

Che palle, as the Romans would say, which translated literally means 'what balls' but really means 'how annoying'. I'll have to shut the French doors and my bedroom door to prevent the pesky shag pile from invading my domain. I grab some toilet paper and, after mopping up the puddle and spraying the area with disinfectant, walk out of my room onto the *terrazza*. On the top floor opposite an old woman waters her garden of potted geraniums and palms. Two levels down another *casalinga*, housewife, throws a doona over the window ledge and begins beating it with a stick, removing excess dust but probably putting just as much back in. Dirt veils Rome no matter what the season.

Padding along the terrace and back into the living room, I go and poke my nose through the door to Serena's room. She lies on her back in her equally huge bed, an airline mask covering her eyes. I smile to myself. Unlike me, she's so Marilyn glam she doesn't have to make an effort to look better dressed, more *Italian*.

As I leave, I spot a bar on the street corner to my left. I'm looking for my new local. There is no one sitting at the two tables outside and, in any case, it just seems too convenient. I walk in the other direction and spend the next fifteen minutes discreetly sussing out bars, walking in to grab one of the free newspapers or buy some chewing gum – anything to justify entering. If I added up all the times I've bought something for the sake of using a bathroom in a bar, I'd have a home deposit. I don't know why I bother – eighty-five per cent of bar toilets are gross because there is never toilet paper. I've learnt to always carry tissues.

None of the bars grabs my interest – too modern, too masculine, too many pokies, boring or stale-looking *cornetti*. I don't really have that many requirements; I just like a place to have some form of charm and good *cornetti*. I've never had a bad brew in

Rome, so coffee quality doesn't even enter the equation like it would at home.

Exhausting all options within range that could be considered local, I loop back to the bar twenty steps from my new address. At a quarter to eight it's breakfast rush hour. Behind the bar running along one wall of the rectangular room, three men work in synchronicity, churning out espressos and cappuccinos for the throng. There is an old, bald man with a gentlemanly demeanour and two young men, one with a golden tan and a baby-face, the other with spiky hair and the fat, flattened nose of a footballer. Near the bar, which has Nastro Azzurro beer on tap, there are two pokie machines and two white plastic tables and chairs. On one wall is a board with the Lotto numbers attached. A few cabinets contain the usual range of confectionery near a drinks fridge.

And then I find the element that makes me want to come back, apart from the extensive pastry selection. An old woman sits behind the bar at the far end, her shoulders slightly hunched. About seventy years old, she tokes a cigarette when she's not tapping the cash register, accepting payment and giving out receipts. The fact that no one here seems to pay before they consume tells me this is a friendly operation.

The bar is nothing special to look at, but I like the fact it doesn't try to be anything it's not. Most of all I love the old bird at the till, a craggy island in the sea of madness around her. I watch her light another cigarette. She has probably smoked at least two packs a day for half a century. I wonder how she will cope when the threatened ban on smoking in public places comes into effect.

I grab a *cornetto* with a telltale blob of strawberry jam seeping from the centre and move to the bar.

'*Un cappuccino bollante, per favore,*' I say to the old man.

'*Un cappuccino* bollente *per la signorina,*' he repeats cheerily, subtly correcting my mispronounciation of the word 'boiling'.

The front-row forward, who upon closer inspection has a three-day growth and looks like he slept thirty minutes the night before, swings into action. Just as he is about to slide my coffee towards me he stops.

'*Vuoi del cacao?*' he asks, gesturing towards my cappuccino and holding a silver shaker.

I twig. He's asking me if I want cocoa on my coffee. It's the first time anyone has given me the option. Usually I get a love heart in two seconds flat. Could it be that I'm sounding more Italian?

Paying the old woman at the till, I tell her I have just moved in nearby and ask for her name, plus that of the man I have correctly guessed is her husband.

I leave, happy because I know I will be seeing Elide and Fausto once a day for the indefinite future, as the harsh clang of bells sounds from the belltower attached to an ugly brick and stone church opposite the bar. Accustomed to being kept awake in my old house by crap pub music, the bells are Chopin to my ears.

Serena and I settle into a bit of a routine in the week before she jets off to New York usually lunching together before I run to get the Metro to work. She's a great cook and humours my fear of the kitchen.

'It's not that hard, really,' she says, hinting I should add a bit of basil to a pasta sauce I am making and advising me never to put the cherry tomatoes I have bought in the fridge, because they retain better flavour and ripen at room temperature.

I mask my intolerance of Carlo III, whom Serena takes out for walks in one of those slings in which new parents carry their babies, because the vet has advised he can't walk on the ground and be exposed to potential lurgies, until he reaches a certain age.

It could be worse. At least the mutt has personality. It's just that he's hyperactive and his size bugs me. He runs around the apartment chewing anything he can sink his *denti* into, especially shoes. He also pisses with regularity on the marble floor and poos on the *terrazza*. '*Bravo*, Carlo!' exclaims Serena when her pup occasionally manages to do his business on the newspaper pages we leave scattered on the floor around the apartment. I think of my old home in San Giovanni in Laterano and wonder what's worse: the wailing baby or crapping Carlo III.

My new home is twenty minutes further from work than before, and since the Metro stops at 11.30 pm during the week, I have to return home on foot. That doesn't bother me, but when I am tired it's a drag. I decide a bike will cut the time by half and be safer. I'll also be able to move around Rome more comfortably in the invading heat of summer, which lurks around the corner.

Before I leave to meet Raffaello I grab some cash from the pages of *Out of This Century: Confessions of an Art Addict*. I store my money in the chunky book, written by Peggy Guggenheim, because I don't have a bank account in which I can deposit my slim earnings. Living illegally is forcing me into strange habits. Sometimes, when I grab funds, I wish I had the inimitable life of art benefactor Guggenheim, whose bank balance allowed her to change lovers, villas and countries with remarkable deftness.

Raffaello accompanies me to a street near Porta Portese, the biggest open market in Rome, held every Sunday. With shops offering a multitude of new and old bikes, I decide to buy the latter, reasoning it will be a good idea to gauge first if I like being on a bike before investing any serious money.

Being Monday, when most stores in Rome open well after lunch at four o'clock, many of the shops are shut, but I soon find one with a few old treadlies. The old man running it lets me test-ride a few before I set my heart on a lady's bike, spray-painted black, with a shiny bell.

'*Quanto costa?*' I ask him, preparing to haggle. A trained accountant, my father is also a used car dealer who is proud when his daughters 'crunch' someone, like I did at the age of fifteen when, standing in Harvey Norman, I offered $800 cash for a gleaming stereo that had a $999 price tag attached. Sold to the precocious girl in the school tunic.

'*Quaranta cinque*,' says the man. I check with Raffaello. It's 45 euros.

'*Quaranta*,' I offer, thinking a 5-euro discount is so low it's bound to be accepted.

'*Quaranta cinque e ti do questo*,' the man fires back; 45 euros and I'll give you this bike chain.

Damn. He's out-foxed me. Still, the bike chain looks like it's a good one.

'*Va bene*,' I say happily.

Saying goodbye to Raffaello, I ride home with glee, whizzing around corners. I'd forgotten how fun it is to have pedal power. I haven't had wheels since I was seven, when I had a mountain bike that made Nicole Kidman's machine in *BMX Bandits* look like a pram. I got around on it everywhere, trailblazing the rocky dirt roads that surrounded our property.

Once in Sydney, it simply never entered my mind to buy one – too many cars, too many hills, not very cool. Rome has just as much traffic, but the difference is Italian drivers are accustomed to sharing the roads with nine million motorbike riders – almost one million of them being in Rome. The roads are generally flatter – although the cobblestones give my bum an anti-cellulite treatment – and rather than feel like a dag, I feel Euro-chic.

At least I did until my friend James, in London, sensibly convinced me to get a helmet. I wasn't planning to buy one, since it's not mandatory and I have never seen a local with one. But when James was knocked off his bike by a black cab, the only thing that saved his life was the helmet.

'If you dare not buy one I am sending it to you,' he warned. I find a bike shop up the road and settle for a yellow number. It's the least offensive in an unattractive range but now I feel like Lance Armstrong instead of Audrey Hepburn.

The morning of Serena's departure for New York we hug goodbye and, while I'm elated to be by myself for three months, the house suddenly feels big and empty. I call my old household and invite Alberta, Tiziana and Nina over for dinner next week on my day off and then SMS Raffaello to see if he'd like to dine out that night.

Money is not that important to me, but dating a struggling artist can, I am discovering, be frustrating. I want to explore the city, which includes dining out and going out, but often Raffaello can't afford to. He has no concept of having a job that pays the bills. He paints and gets by on funds from the few works he sells, and his third of the pittance his band makes at the occasional gig, but he is otherwise supported by his parents. Having fended for myself since I left home, I struggle to comprehend how Raffaello lives a life so devoid of independence.

But for all our cultural differences, the boy is growing on me more and more. An affectionate person, every time he looks at me with his huge, black eyes I melt. When we're together the world is a very fun place to be.

He texts me later, having found a cheap ticket deal at a cinema in Prati, a conservative suburb full of legal offices near the Vatican. *La Dolce Vita* is screening. I'm excited if not embarrassed – I've been meaning to see the cult film for at least a decade.

Sitting in the quaint, tiny cinema, I am blown away by Fellini's bizarre but whimsically beautiful and decadent take on Rome in the 1950s. Seeing footage of places that are part of my everyday life – the Trevi Fountain and via Veneto – makes me realise how real my Roman existence has become.

Maybe it's the silence of Serena's flat, but I am itching to meet more people around my age, and more Italians, since I am speaking a lot of English at work. Some more money would help too. I jump on my bike and return to Bar della Pace, down a side street off Piazza Navona. One of the most famous bars in Rome, it's packed with rich foreigners who tip well. My English will no doubt be in demand, but most of the staff are Italian.

I talk to the pony-tailed manager, who takes my number and seems to be happy that I have the health sanitation card which allows me to do bar work. I don't mention the fact I don't have a *Permesso di Soggiorno,* and he doesn't ask if I have one. It's been months now since I've been living illegally in Italy and, while I wish I had a *Permesso,* I've decided to try to let it slide from my personal morals bank. Somehow I've become a *menefreghista* – someone who doesn't bat an eyelid about breaking, bending or evading rules.

I meet Raffaello for a beer in Campo de' Fiori, where we choose a bar with wooden deckchairs and tables outside plus a few sets of beautiful 1960s wooden chairs connected at the sides, with flip-up seats. They look like they were ripped out of a cinema, perhaps Cinema Farnese, within view across the Campo.

Inside, a long timber bar with a marble top runs the length of the room. There's a puddle of water on the uneven, cobbled floor. The walls are stacked with wine and at the back of the bar, visible through an oval porthole, is a curvaceous female mannequin. Illuminated by soft lighting, she is nude, apart from a pair of black shoes painted onto her feet. There is no big sign out the front of the wine bar, but a piece of paper attached to the door says 'Bottiglieria di Nolano'.

The place is dilapidated and arty. I love it.

We sit outside and a tall, lean man approaches our table. Bald with thin grey hair, a wispy moustache and small, fine spectacles, his friendly face is lined with anecdotes and intelligence. About sixty years old, he exudes poetic charm. As we order two *Peroni Gran Riserva* beers I tell the man I am looking for work.

I don't know why, but I feel we have an instant rapport. He introduces himself as Armando, and has the manners of a true gentleman. He reminds me of my grandfather. He takes my name and number, promising to pass on my message to the boss, Mario.

He bids us *arrivederci* with a smile and a twinkle in his eye.

Two days later Mario calls to ask me to work that evening. Delighted, I dress in jeans, jumper and sneakers, jump on my bike and head to the Campo, arriving at 6 pm sharp.

No one is sitting at the tables outside because, although spring, it's still nippy at night. Opening one of the two wooden-framed glass doors to the bar, I spy Armando, standing with his back to me holding a round tray upon which rests a flute glass of *prosecco* and a glass of red wine. He leans slowly to place the drinks on a table and then asks for money from the clients, two young men. Swinging around to walk to the cash register near the door, his face lights up when he sees me.

'*Penelope, ma che bello rivederti! Benvenuta!* Penelope, why how beautiful to see you again, welcome!'

I blush with embarrassment, feeling the eyes of a few clients on me, and wish I could return Armando's flirtatious overture.

Planting two kisses on my cheeks, Armando takes me by the arm and leads me to the bar to introduce me to Giusi, a small woman with rosy cheeks who is the bartender for the evening.

A cigarette burns in an ashtray to her left, hidden behind twenty bottles of opened and unopened red wine stacked haphazardly on the bar alongside other spirits – Aperol, Martini, Gordon's Gin, Campari Bitter and Italian liqueurs such as *Monte Negro* and *Lucano*.

Armed with a pen and yellow Post-it notes, I begin taking orders from each client and sticking them on the bar before Giusi, who prepares the drinks and utters the cost of each order out loud. I repeat the prices in my head as I reach each table to ask for money. There is no system of table numbers, so I write descriptions in English of the people sitting at the table, or rough directions of where the tables are located. Armando keeps an eye on me, helping me when I can't understand someone's order.

Most of the clients are Italian and, hearing my accent, ask where I am from. Stumbling over my words, they joke and help me along. I start to relax and laugh at myself too. In between running orders and fetching *noccioline*, peanuts, *pistacchi* and *taralli*, savoury biscuit snacks, I study the list of wines, most of which are Italian, and international beers. In quiet moments I stand in the doorway of the bar, staring across at the tall apartments lining the Campo opposite. Crumbling and painted rustic tones of orange and yellow, the buildings are so postcard-gorgeous they seem fake. If not for a few people who lean out of the windows, I could swear the whole facade was just a cardboard cut-out prop.

Two hours into my shift, a fit-looking man with wispy grey hair and black, rectangular glasses enters the bar and approaches me immediately with an outstretched hand.

'*Penelope? Piacere, sono Mario.*'

When there's a lull I try to talk to Mario, who isn't a chatterbox but seems to understand my desire to speak Italian. He explains to me that he opened the bar only five months earlier, after winding up a second-hand clothes store he operated in the same location for almost thirty years. Mario is nearing sixty, like my dad.

Spying a bottle of Noble One on a shelf, I ask him how he sourced the respected Australian dessert wine.

'I once had an Australian girlfriend and we still hear from each other now and then,' says Mario, his eyes wandering with nostalgia.

By nine o'clock, starving, I ask Armando if we can get something to eat as the crowd drifts off to dinner.

'*Certo, signorina*,' he says with a grin, taking some money from the cash register.

He disappears and returns promptly with a box filled with rectangular slices of pizza. In Italy, you can go into any pizzeria and choose from a big selection behind the counter. Cut to size on request, the pizza is placed in a huge industrial oven to reheat. It's such a civilised way of eating pizza – as much or as little as you feel like, rather than ordering a whole one if you are not famished.

As I finish my glass of red I accidentally knock it over on the bar. Armando appears from nowhere and dips his fingers into the wine and then pats it on his neck like a perfume. I soon learn the super-superstitious Italians believe the act keeps bad fortune away.

The wine bar is suddenly busy again as people pour into the Campo for a post-dinner tipple. The piazza swarms with young people dressed to the nines who walk around carrying beer bottles. At night the Campo is *the* place to be seen. Young couples wander holding hands or stand being gooey with each other. Men and women dressed in hip street gear and denim walk around in packs, sussing out the talent. The odd dog runs past. The cobblestones of the piazza glint in the yellow light of street lamps.

At midnight, a bald man with the ruddy, telltale face of an alcoholic walks in and orders a glass of the house white. There is no house white, just an extensive list of good wine. Giusi sighs and gives him the cheapest drop. The man takes a seat at the only spare table and within no more than two minutes is asleep, his head slumped on the table. Armando smiles sadly, telling me the man comes every night and sleeps until closing time.

The bar is buzzing and my head spins with the merriment around me. I feel like I am part of a circus troupe. Indian men selling roses and offering to take polaroids come in and out of the door in waves, trying to cajole clients to part with a few euros. Two young street kids carrying tiny dogs zipped into their tracksuit jumpers and cardboard cups for money work the crowd, begging with innocent smiles that betray a life full of sadness and poverty. Mario and Armando treat them with fatherly affection, giving them each some pistachio nuts to eat with a glass of apple juice. A jazz band arrives to busk out the front. The saxophonist is so fat I find it hard to believe anyone would pity him enough to give him change. Hungry-looking he is not.

Another rose seller appears to do the rounds. I wonder if he doubles as one of the men who appear on street corners the moment a drop of rain appears to flog battered umbrellas for exorbitant prices.

Our final busker of the night is a stooped, old man in beige pants, a blue turtleneck jumper and a worn but dapper navy jacket.

'*Buonasera maestro,*' says Armando, tipping an imaginary hat at the man.

The hunchback holds a ukulele above one shoulder and tilts his head towards it as he plays a series of tunes, which sound like Greek folk songs. He walks around the tables, asking for small contributions.

At 2 am we boot the last people out, stack the tables and chairs and fetch cases of beer and supplies to put in the fridge, ready for the next day. Finally, Mario and Armando ask me to join them in having a nightcap – a Bailey's on ice. I nod gratefully.

As the two men chat with Giusi, I listen, exhausted but still high from my new work experience, watching the Campo and speaking a little with the locals. I know I'll remember some faces should I get a chance to come back. It's a bar with a loyal following – Mario and Armando are constantly clapping someone on the back or kissing the cheeks of a new arrival.

When I make to leave, Mario thanks me with a smile and a fatherly pat on the back and gives me 40 euros. Armando divides up the tips, which work out to be 6 euros each, and kisses me with exaggerated affection that makes me laugh.

As I ride home along via dei Fori Imperiali, past the Forum, the Colosseum and my old house in via di San Giovanni in Laterano, my face flickers with smiles as I replay highlights of the evening in my head. It's early days, but Mario has asked me to work again next week.

In eight hours I feel like I have found a new foothold – maybe even a new family – in Rome.

Italian inquisition

I n less than two days I should be winging my way back to Sydney, according to the latest version of my perpetually postponed plane ticket. As part of the paper chase to get my study visa for Perugia, I had to buy a return air fare – proof I had no plans to set up stumps in Italy.

Before I left Australia I had a hunch I wouldn't want to return in a hurry – and I was right. My *stella* is on the rise. I've been promoted from being a waitering toilet doll to a receptionist and wine-bar lush. Life is just starting to get interesting.

I ring and cancel my ticket indefinitely after the bubbly travel agent on the phone assures me I can use the fare value as a credit towards a new ticket when '*I know what my plans are*'. If only.

Talking on the phone to Steve, my boss at The Beehive, he tells me that the next time I am in Australia I should get another study visa, then return to Rome and follow normal procedure and get a *Permesso di Soggiorno.* There are bound to be chronic bureaucratic delays in getting my *Permesso,* but if my six-month study visa expires in the interim I should be able to extend it easily enough in Rome.

'Staying legal is one thing,' he warns ominously, 'but getting legal is another.'

Once I have my *Permesso,* Steve and Linda are reasonably confident they can help me change my study visa to a permanent visa. But my chances ride on a loophole that could disappear without warning depending on constantly changing immigration quotas and laws.

Grateful and elated at the prospect of potentially being legal in Italy, I have to stop myself from whooping down the line at Steve, who remains realistic about the confusion and chaos surrounding visas, having been there himself as an American citizen.

'A lot of people feel the need to be legal because they need that sense of security, but so many people aren't – because the law here is easily evaded and impossible to respect. That's why people throw up their arms, give up and do things the illegal way – simply because all the doors are closed to those who want to follow the rules.'

As my hopes begin to fade Steve continues, laughing despite himself at the convoluted existence he has to face far more often than I do, because he has a business and family in Italy.

'Being legal is harder, not just because you start to pay taxes but because it's such a nightmare going through the process to get the proper documents. And then you have to *keep* them. It's a full-time job. By the time you work it out it's time to renew them and then the laws have all changed again. It never, *ever* ends.'

Hanging up from Steve, I glance at the television. My heart tightens when I see a lifestyle documentary on Sydney. It's the first time I have seen images of home since I left.

I watch in silence as footage of Kings Cross, Surry Hills and Centennial Park – places I worked, socialised and lived in – flashes across the screen. I feel strangely removed and yet so close to home at the same time. When the camera sweeps over Bondi Beach a small whimper escapes from my mouth. I can almost feel the surf wash over me as I swim at the Icebergs ocean pool. I even see the woman I passed on the beach at South Bondi every morning when I lived there.

I flick off the TV as the credits roll, feeling agitated and directionless. A seaside summer holiday in Sydney is suddenly incredibly appealing.

My parents have sent me Power of Attorney documents giving them the right to handle my affairs in my absence and I need a lawyer to act as a witness and sign the papers. Asking around, I'm given the number for Stefano, a lawyer who has an office in the historic centre. Making an appointment, I hop on my bike and have a straight run until I reach Piazza Venezia, where cars and motorbikes hurtle around a massive traffic island and rarely stop for pedestrians who venture out on the zebra crossing with justifiable trepidation.

I have learnt to use zebra crossings with ease, walking out as if I *own* the crossing. If a car slows too late or gets too close to me for comfort I roll up my fingers to touch my thumb and shake my cupped hand to say 'What the hell are you doing?' Usually the driver returns my sign language and we glower at each other – but I win on a technicality, having forced them to stop.

I pull up on the flank of the piazza and wait for the policeman standing on a mounted concrete block, directing traffic, to give me right of way. I look at the riders on fancy and dilapidated motorbikes beside me. There's usually at least one hottie to perve on in these situations, but for now my eyes are fixed on the traffic cop. Wearing a smart blue uniform with a white helmet, he holds a gleaming silver whistle in his mouth and moves his hands, covered in white gloves, like Marcel Marceau. Occasionally he stops to jot down the number plate of a driver who has proudly infringed the traffic code. The cop has a year-round job because traffic lights don't exist in Piazza Venezia, one of the busiest intersections in

Rome. Seeing the policeman in the peak evening rush-hour is even more memorable: with the hulking Vittoriano monument as a backdrop and a large spotlight illuminating the concrete block at his feet, he appears to be the lead in an outdoor opera. In fact, the spectacle draws a regular evening audience.

Pedalling down a one-way street in the wrong direction, I approach a *carabinieri* watch post. Of the numerous types of police services in Italy, including national, regional, financial and military, the *carabinieri* (military) are my favourites. They have the foxiest uniform I have ever seen: a black suit with pants that feature a smart red stripe down the leg, Helmut-Lang style. They make the Australian Federal Police look like garbos.

I arrive at Stefano's office, cluttered with teak furniture and an austere air, to be greeted by a well-built man in his early thirties dressed in an immaculate suit. His hair is slicked neatly with gel, his coal-black eyes like pits in his deeply tanned face. He shows me into his office and sits in a black leather swivel chair, his back to the window. An antique desk separates us.

Through casual conversation with my contact I know Stefano is married – so I just assume he's being friendly when he asks me what I do and why I came to Italy. When he asks me my age and marriage status I maintain my cool and answer politely, eyeing the documents suggestively so he'll get a wriggle on.

As smoke curls from the Marlboro Light in his ashtray, Stefano reads the paperwork and, after what seems like hours, signs various pages. I am ready to race out the door, but when he refuses to take payment the least I can do is offer to buy him a coffee on the fly.

We walk to Tazza D'Oro near the Pantheon and have an espresso at the characterful bar. Feeling grateful for a service for which I could have paid at least 100 euros, I tell Stefano that I will try to direct more legal work his way via my English contacts if I can.

Giving me two business cards, he insists on taking my mobile number.

I am at The Beehive reception four hours later when my phone beeps with an SMS message. 'Can I invite you to dinner or for a drink tonight? Stefano.'

I reply that I work until midnight, but thank him for the invitation. I am naked in my room the next morning, grabbing for underwear after a shower, when an SMS message arrives. 'You really are very pretty/nice, meeting you was really very exciting for me and I can't think of anything else. I hope to see you again soon.'

He's got to be kidding. I don't respond, but within forty-eight hours, Stefano strikes again, once more inviting me to dinner. Amused but now pissed off, I text back immediately. 'I don't work Wednesday. It would be a pleasure to have dinner with you and your wife. Let me know.'

That's the last I hear of Stefano.

I knew it was too good to be true. After less than a month on Rome's potholed roads and cobblestones my *bici* is dying, the pedals wobbling madly.

Before Serena skipped town she made a point of introducing me to uncle-and-nephew team Michele and Franco, who run the hardware store around the corner and have done the occasional odd job for her. I wheel my bike to their small store and stop outside the entrance, crammed with everything from power drills and garden equipment to water pistols. With spring almost over, the Italians are getting more jovial as their stop-work August looms.

Reintroducing myself to Michele, I point at my pedals and tell him they are not working. He grabs some secret men's tools and bends over my bike in concentration. Fastening the pedals, he warns they may not last long.

'Penelope,' he says, shaking his head, 'you bought a piece of iron.'

I tell him that in English one says, 'You've bought a lemon'.

The translation, like so many others I try to use, is lost on Michele, who looks at me with interest for a moment. 'But what are you doing here? Did you marry an Italian?'

Why is everyone so keen to marry me off? I study Michele's face. Surely he's not hitting on me. No. He's old enough to be my dad and he seems sweet. But if he asks for my mobile, I'll knee him in the nuts. Then he'll really learn how to use that spanner.

As I explain why I came to Italy, he smiles at me kindly before refusing to accept payment for his efforts. I go to a *pasticceria* up the street and buy a small tray of bite-size pastries. Accepting it with delight, Michele sings out as he shoos me out the door, 'Call me if you need something, okay? I can come to your house too.'

Looking back I see him wearing the face of a choirboy, which only makes me laugh. While Stefano was a sleazeball, Michele is just doing what so many Italian men do so well – flirt in the name of good, clean fun.

I text Raffaello suggesting we go to Ostia, the closest beach to the city. Borrowing his father's car, we head out of Rome, driving along a long road lined with private and public gates that lead to stretches of beach hidden from the road by thick scrub. Parking in the road, we give 2 euros to a greasy-haired man wearing no shirt who approaches us as we pull up. It is commonplace to pay vagrants for car 'security', even if you are in a free parking zone. And when you stop at a service station after standard working hours, chances are you'll pay a tramp to pump petrol for you.

As we walk towards a gate I struggle to contain my excitement as I think of beaches I miss most at home: Bondi and Bronte in Sydney for their ocean pools, the rugged beauty of Manyana, on the New South Wales south coast, and any of the isolated beaches that bridge the coastline south from Perth to Margaret River.

Finally I catch sight of the ocean. Disappointment has a bluebottle sting. At midday, the flat water is streaked with sunscreen and human flotsam and jetsam. Covered in fine dirt, the beach is divided up into lots of public (free) and private areas which reverberate with the shouts of vociferous bathers, many with cigarettes hooked to their lips. People loll on hired beach chairs or stand along the water's edge, talking into their mobile phones. Clad in tiny, fripperied bikinis, women of all sizes strut up a wooden walkway to a kiosk that plays pop music and sells panini, gelati, coffee and beer. Every so often a big boat decorated with banners and blaring disco tracks pulls close in to the shore and a man with a loud hailer invites everyone to join the party for a small trip down the coast.

Raffaello and I sunbake for a while before I venture into the water for a record-quick dip. Back on my towel, a man carrying a board pinned with cheap-looking jewellery approaches us for the third time. Within minutes another vendor calls out, this time selling *grattachecca.*

'*E' molto Romano.* It's very Roman,' says Raffaello, explaining that a *grattachecca* is a summer drink made of ice that is scraped by hand from a huge slab and drizzled with syrup. Pooling our change, we buy two sugary but pleasant flavours – melon and cherry. As I slurp my iced treat I mask the severe cultural shock I am experiencing. I don't want to seem ungrateful, so I don't even try to explain to Raffaello what the word *beach* means in my glorious, unhemmed homeland. When I learn that it can cost up to 50 euros to swim at some of Italy's more exclusive beaches, my outrage is amplified.

Back in town Raffaello helps me load my bike into his car. Despite Michele's very best efforts, my *pezzo di ferro* has died.

Peeved that the bike fell to bits in less than a month, we return to the stall where I bought it to take up my case with the old man. Needing moral support, I ask Raffaello to come with me.

Finding the stall shut, a nearby storekeeper says the old man's son works at a shop down the street. We go there and I ask to speak with Mimmo.

'That's me.' From behind the rows and rows of bikes stacked to the ceiling emerges a man whose T-shirted gut wobbles like trifle. Fighting intimidation, I take a deep breath and explain my situation – and tell him I want my money back.

'You can't. It's not possible. The bike is second-hand. It's your problem!' says Mimmo, looking at me without a skerrick of sympathy.

A stream of nonsensical objections come out of my mouth as my face flushes with frustration. Whenever I get emotional my Italian gets worse. Seemingly unflappable, Mimmo refutes everything I throw at him. I look in desperation at Raffaello, who remains silent. I know there's nothing he can say, but I wish he'd try.

Defeated, I walk away and dump my bike in a back alley. Mimmo may be a grumpy *stronzo*, arsehole, but he's right. You always take a gamble buying anything used, not to mention without a guarantee, so he's hardly culpable. I just hate not being able to stand up for myself more effectively.

Saying goodbye to Raffaello, I walk to a bike shop I have seen near Termini. A maternal, grey-haired woman approaches and we start chatting. Gabriella is the face of the business her husband started forty years ago. Now widowed, she runs the shop with her three sons. One of them, Andrea, stands nearby. Tall with long brown hair and his *mamma*'s eyes, he is good-looking but too much of a pretty boy for my tastes.

As soon as Gabriella discovers my nationality I wait for the inevitable.

'But why are you here? Are you engaged?' she asks.

Going through my standard spiel, I wonder silently why it appears out of the realms of reality for Italians to believe a single woman would choose to create an independent life in a foreign land.

Gabriella shows me some new bikes they have on display. Gleaming in the afternoon sun illuminating the showroom, a royal blue lady's bike catches my eye. Better still, it's on sale.

As I go to pay, Gabriella slashes another 10 euros off the price and tells me to come back at my leisure and one of her boys will attach a basket on the front. Wheeling my bike out of the shop, my eyes fix on the brand name painted on one side that I didn't see at first.

I may be a terribly single Muriel but I've now got one very handsome Romeo.

It's my second shift at Nolano and there's a new man making drinks behind the bar.

'*Ciao, sono Federico.*' He introduces himself as he smashes ice to make two mojitos.

Great. Another flipping Federico. In Italy kids are often christened with the names of saints. Through work and friends, I already know four Andreas, two Alessias, three Stefanos – and now two Federicos.

A freelance journalist, Federico II is lean with gingerish hair, somewhat of a rarity in a dark-haired population. He's not drop-dead gorgeous but his aloof air makes him damn sexy. I can't understand many of the jokes he cracks to clients and friends who walk in the door but it's obvious he's charming and gregariously witty. The Romans love to use words as weapons, rolling and rhyming them for effect. As a wordsmith, Federico's ability to show off is amplified.

As I wait for the pre-dinner *aperitivo* rush, I drink a *prosecco* and begin to smoke a Marlboro Light, bought in mini-packs of ten which continue to thwart my effort to quit social smoking. Enjoying an innocent flirt with Federico during the night, my phone later beeps with a message from Raffaello, who has just returned from London, where he played a gig with Cactus. I haven't seen him for at least a week. I feel a pang of guilt. I didn't – and don't – miss him terribly. It's not that I don't enjoy his company. I'm just not convinced he's the love of my life.

I'd like to believe love conquers all, but my relationships with Federico I and now Raffaello are convincing me otherwise. The cultural divide feels too great. The only two English girlfriends I know with Italian boyfriends met them in London, where they had no doubt fled to escape the grip of *la famiglia*. Unless I meet a local who is well travelled and outward looking, I am likely to keep tripping over the same thing – an Italian man living at home, eating at the family table most nights and dreaming of finding a girlfriend who is a mini-mum. True, Federico and Raffaello enjoy more independence than the norm, but their parents still help fill their mouths and wallets and fold their washed undies.

I help Mario and Federico II restock the fridges with beer and wine for the next day. We lock up the bar as a soccer ball is booted around the Campo by young Italians. Nightowls hang out of windows and catch the ball before hurling it back down into play. I hop on Romeo and take a detour through the piazza of the Pantheon. At night there is not a soul around. It's all mine.

At home I send a late response to Raffaello, trying not to think of Federico II.

I've barely woken up when Mario calls, saying someone has pulled out of work at the last minute. Despite all my best intentions to slow down, especially since I have more than enough work at The Beehive, I find myself saying yes. At Nolano I'm enjoying meeting the revolving staff, generally all students in their twenties, and speaking more and more Italian to clients whose faces are starting to look familiar.

As I pedal past the Colosseum on my way to Campo de' Fiori I see a crowd gathering below the massive monument. Police cars swarm and the *Vigili del Fuoco*, or fire service, arrives with a large trampoline like you might see in a Walt Disney cartoon.

I look up to the top of the Colosseum. There, standing and peering over one of the half-circle windows, is one of the costumed gladiators. Somehow he's scaled an area normally banned from the public. He stands stoically in costume, his arms crossed defiantly, covered in fake body armour.

I want to stop and watch the situation unfold but I can't be late for work. No one seems to know what's happening.

I've just started work when Federico II stops in, on his way to the launch of a new magazine for which he is freelancing. In a cheeky mood, I tell him to stop by the bar later. Right on closing time, he breezes in the door, drunk as a skunk. And flirtatiously adorable. Mario lets the roller door slam shut and walks off, leaving us to chat outside.

I am making motions to leave when Federico makes a pass at me, kissing me out of the blue. With a tipple of *prosecco* and an *Amaro* nightcap under my belt, I respond.

'*Due euro, due euro…*'

We stop and look around to see one of the ubiquitous rose sellers standing behind us, thrusting a bunch of long-stemmed but wilting pink roses in our nostrils.

'Please, I'm kissing Penelope!' quips Federico in a deliberately dramatic voice which makes me belly-laugh.

Pulling away, I tell him I have to go, giving the excuse I must work early so he doesn't try to invite himself home to my place. Riding off, my guilt deepens, thinking about Raffaello.

There are no excuses for my behaviour but I try desperately to find them. I'm not married – though everyone else seems to wish I was – and I came to Italy to have fun and not get seriously entangled with anyone barring The Man Of My Dreams. From the start, my relationship with Raffaello has been unbalanced: either I've been totally into him when he's been distant or vice versa. It's not like he's been beating down my door to see me either. Who knows, he might be feeling and acting exactly as I am.

The next morning I read in the paper that the gladiator didn't jump. His protest was at the fact the business he says he invented has spawned so many copycat gladiators that authorities are considering cutting the licences or banning the trade entirely.

The headline screams '*Fateci lavorare o mi butto*, Let us work or I'll throw myself over.'

Maybe I've watched too many cop shows but everyone knows that jumpers rarely jump. While not questioning the gladiator's desperation, his stunt seems like an ordinary part of the theatrical life in Rome.

Perhaps sensing my betrayal, I leave work at midnight the next evening to find Raffaello waiting for me at the door outside. Surprised, guilt seeps out of my pores.

Over a glass of wine back at mine, I try to get the nerve to tell him that I have snogged someone else but I chicken out. It was an innocent kiss, it's not like I have slept with someone. Instead, I tell him that I had been asked on a date by someone else, which made me think about the status quo.

'The other day I met a cute girl, but I consider that we are together,' he says.

Raffaello crashes at my place and before we sleep he tells me sweet things and why he likes to be with me. Because. Because. Because. Having learnt to accept compliments better since my arrival in Rome, I don't feel as embarrassed as I once might have. But rather than bring happiness, his words only make me more confused.

I'm not the only one.

An email from my sister Lisa repeats the same questions I am asking myself. *Who is Federico II? What happened with Raffaello? What's going on?*

Explaining that Federico *al Nolano* is a Don Juan who has a stream of women chasing him, thus nothing serious will ever happen between us, I try to explain the Raffaello situation.

Positives: he's really sweet. He's smart. He's interesting. Like me he loves music, reading and art. He plays in a cool band (satisfies tragic rock groupie streak). He's a fantastic cook. With him I can relax and be me, despite the language difficulty.

Negatives: there's an attraction, but my heart doesn't skip when I see him. I'm not materialistic, but he doesn't seem to care that he has no dosh, even if it impinges upon our social life. He's timid to the point of it being hard work.

I mull the situation over and convince myself I want to pursue things with Raffaello. On many levels we're very compatible. Sometimes love grows. Even as I say the words to myself, I know I am clutching at straws. I don't believe in hanging on to something that is fundamentally flawed.

Yet something won't let me cut the rope.

I grab Romeo and ride to the Bull Dog, a pub in San Lorenzo, the hippy student zone of Rome. On the eve of his departure for a three-month stint in London, Federico has organised an *aperitivo*. Greeted with kisses by Nina and Alberta, I spy Raffaello sitting in a corner across the table. Boxed in by people, he acknowledges me briefly. Appearing from somewhere in the crowd, Federico gives me a hug.

As I look at him, I suddenly feel emotional at the prospect of losing one of the pillars of my Roman existence. We may see each other only sporadically, but an ocean of affection built on trust remains between us. We rode a roller-coaster together at a time when I couldn't understand a word around me and was questioning my decision to come to Rome. I will forever be grateful for the sweetness and patience he showed me – not to mention his shagging prowess.

I stare at the ceiling, willing the tears welling in my eyes to sink back into my eye sockets. It's too hard. As discreetly as possible I make some excuses and say my goodbyes before asking Federico to accompany me outside.

I forage in my shoulder bag and hand him a small present – a book of poetry by Charles Bukowski, with translation in Italian, and a pocket English dictionary – before I start sobbing like a toddler robbed of their favourite toy.

Federico looks at me in bewilderment then gives me a lingering hug and assures me he'll be back soon. I apologise for my blubbering and give up trying to explain something I can't even articulate in my own language. Giving him a final hug, I find Romeo and scoot.

As I pedal my phone rings. I stop on a street corner.

'What happened?' Raffaello asks.

'I can't explain,' I say, unable to muffle the sound of my tears. My sense of belonging in Rome, my sense of being, is swinging on a pendulum I can't seem to regulate.

Pushing the door open at home, more change is afoot. Carlo III's tiny paws scratch at my shins before I even manage to close the door.

The full Monti

Spoilt as I am living alone – walking around starkers after showers when summer humidity makes it hard to justify dressing for any occasion, hogging the TV and stereo, and not having to be remotely pleasant if I roll out of the wrong side of my princess bed – Serena's return adds a welcome pinch of flavour to my Roman existence.

Her arrival means we are effectively a household of four: Norah Jones – too syrupy for my eardrums – wails daily in the lounge room, while Carlo III, appearing fatter from chomping too many bagels in the Big Apple, harmonises intermittently with short, sharp yaps.

Serena's passion for food, *vino* and dalliances – an Italian count, a millionaire Swedish yachtie and a good-looking Hungarian– Roman at least five years her junior are among her suitors – keep me in stitches, while her penchant for whipping up sumptuous meals we enjoy on the terrace together makes my second summer in Rome far more entertaining than the first.

For all the positives, I decide to move house.

First, because I want to live with an Italian. While my English boycott is a memory, I notice within days of Serena's return that my basic Italian is starting to deteriorate.

'We can do a language course together,' she says, knowing as well as I do that neither of us has the willpower to speak in Italian with one other, and the moment we start sinking *vino* we'll forget we're even in Italy.

The other reason I want to move is because I can't fake affection for Carlo III for a nano-second longer. If I had my druthers he'd mysteriously plunge from the heights of the *terrazza*, in a scene worthy of *A Fish Called Wanda*. Serena's last handbag fell to its death down a stairwell in her New York apartment. I don't think she'd recover if Carlo III suffered a similar fate. For everyone's safety, it's best I leave.

When I inform Serena of my decision she looks at me as if I am barking mad. I agree. But I'm a loony on a mission – however deluded it may prove to be.

I buy the magazine *Wanted in Rome*, full of news in English, circle a few ads in the rooms to let section and make a few calls. Most rooms have already been rented but I like the sound of one in Monti, the funky *quartiere* that rises up behind the Forum and spreads uphill towards Termini train station. I make an appointment with Daniella, the contact name listed in the advertisement, the next day.

As Romeo carries me over the cobblestones of Monti, I note all the new sights with glee. Grey-haired men in dustcoats labour over furniture in antique restoration stores while young whippersnappers in greasy overalls tinker with two-wheeled patients at the mechanics. A *gelateria* is already serving clients at 11 am, as are a few small food stores, the butcher and baker. There are two solariums, chic modern boutiques, hair and beauty salons, and scores of eateries – from traditional trattorias *alla Romana* to Mexican, Japanese, Indian and Chinese restaurants.

In the centre of the main piazza of Monti, tucked behind a huge church, there is a pretty fountain, where children are splashing water at one other. Bordering the piazza are three bars with tables and chairs outside, a fruit shop with stacked crates of colourful, fresh produce on display and the crusty headquarters of the Rione Monti, or community club, where tubby old men smoking cigarettes mill without serious motive.

Turning into via Urbana I whiz past a few shops and a music school before finally pulling up beside a quaint theatre, positioned almost directly beneath the palazzo I am searching for.

I ring the doorbell and Daniella buzzes me in. I walk down a long corridor paved with black and white tiles. An antiquated elevator rattles softly to the seventh and top floor. Waiting with her apartment door open is a slim, barefoot woman about forty years old, of medium height with long brown hair and earnest hazel eyes. Offering a polite handshake, Daniella immediately shows me the bedroom that is for rent, the first door to my right upon entry.

Tiny but full of character, the room has a rustic stone floor, a single bed with a funky, mint-green velvet bed-head, a small square desk, chair and narrow wardrobe. A map of the world that looks like it was stolen from an Italian high school in the '50s hangs on one wall.

The room's size is compensated by a surprisingly large window with two shutters. I drink in the magical view over Monti – including a rooftop terrace covered in a pergola twenty metres away – and a good chunk of the Roman skyline. Talk about *una bella vista.*

Airy and spotless, the rest of the house is stylish in an effortlessly arty way. Leading off the long timber-floored corridor running from the front door to the terrace at the front of the apartment are: a bathroom with a big tub and pretty stained-glass windows boasting more million-dollar views; a kitchen full of quaint deco furniture and a mirror bearing a message in lipstick *'Mangialo pure!'*, or *'Go ahead and eat it!'*; a big bedroom in hospital white, rented out by Emma, an English girl. At the end of the corridor is Daniella's bedroom and a small lounge room crammed with a divan and shelves of video cassettes and film and theatre history books. Both rooms flank the long terrace which runs from one side of the apartment to the other.

Gingerly opening the wooden French doors leading from the lounge room, Daniella invites me onto the narrow terrace, covered in pot plants of herbs and flowers. Heat rises off the tiles. I can't look down for more than a second without getting vertigo.

Daniella tells me a little about herself: once a journalist, she now writes scripts for theatre and television. She has lived in the apartment for six years and rents out the two other rooms sporadically, when she's low on funds. Practical, with a good sense of humour, I like her instantly. I tell her a little bit about myself, explaining my desire to speak more Italian. She says she likes living with Emma so she can practise her English, but adds that the pair speak mainly in Italian.

The rent is 150 euros more than I pay at Serena's, despite the fact my room is half the size. I can barely afford it, but I tell myself it will be a good incentive to start doing more freelancing. The rent rate reflects the fact Monti is one of the trendiest zones in the historic centre.

The bed in Daniella's house means I won't be able to bring anyone home, but a bit of enforced celibacy can't be a bad thing. Men are starting to complicate my life again. I leave my number with Daniella, who is still to meet a few other potential flatmates, and ride home to relax.

Serena has a hot date on a Saturday night and, after working all week, I'm looking forward to a fat steak, *vino rosso* and a good

DVD on my own. I'm halfway through dinner when my mobile phone rings. It's Mario *al Nolano* seeking my last-minute help. I bolt my steak before mounting Romeo. I've never worked at the bar on a Saturday night. It should be interesting. Within half an hour I am striding in the door of Nolano to be greeted with relief by two new faces – Marianna, Mario's daughter, and her partner, Alessio.

Tall, with a body like Sigourney Weaver in *Aliens*, Marianna fits my perception of the perfectly manicured Italian woman. Boasting a deep tan that covers every visible inch of her envy-inducing body, her pleasant face is made up with precision to render her a knock-out: her eyes are ringed with charcoal eyeliner, mascara separates every one of her long eyelashes, her full lips glisten with gloss and scream *baciami*, kiss me. Rose pink pants that are tight but not tarty – although she leaves a flash of her G-string showing on one hip – cover her gym-taut tush and long legs. Her shapely bosom is covered by a white top with one shoulder slashed to reveal fine clavicles. Marianna wears heels, despite the fact she darts behind the bar to do orders. Everything she does is performed with precision. Occasionally, she stops to suck discreetly on a cigarette.

Equally bronzed with a Popeye physique, Alessio wears a tight T-shirt, jeans and hippy beads around his neck and wrists. With a small goatee and beady dark eyes, he is quick with a joke and soon has me laughing at his antics, including the ability to spin anything – from a drinks tray to the menu – on top of his index finger. He's the bar jester.

The Campo heaves with heels and hormones as young people sit at tables or parade about carrying bottles of beer or mixers. Strange that in a land where getting drunk is often frowned upon it is legal to drink in the street. Serving a table outside, I watch as a young girl passing by gives a dainty shriek as one of her heels gets stuck in a crack between the uneven cobblestones. She smiles cutely at her tabled audience and wrests her shoe loose delicately before walking on, her dignity somehow intact.

Walking over to give a menu to a new table of people, I fix my eyes on the man before me and do a double-take. Without thinking, and with a strange surge of patriotism, I blurt out the name that enters my mind.

'Matt Day,' I say to the Australian actor whom I remember for his roles in 'A Country Practice' and home-grown films.

Acknowledging his identity, the actor looks as embarrassed as I feel ridiculous for declaring the obvious. Poor bloke. How was he to know he'd bump into a sheila working in one of the most popular watering holes in Rome? I take his money and rush off to serve the rowdy crowd.

A little later, I look up to see a moustached Indian man wearing a business shirt, tie and braces, standing on the pavement facing the outdoor tables, smoking a cigarette and eyeing the Campo and crowd as if waiting to pick the right moment. A few in the audience shout out to the man, having obviously seen his act before, as a small crowd forms a semi-circle around him.

His act, loaded with innuendo, includes magically making his tie erect by rubbing it with a pen, and turning a silver service tray loaded with flowers into a plate of flames.

'This magician is good...not for what he does, but how he does it,' says Alessio, grinning.

Whipping the audience up into a frenzy of jeers and hysterical laughter, the magician winds up his act by tapping his head a few times before whipping off a thick toupee. The audience bellows with appreciation and he goes in for the kill, flipping the toupee over to use as a cap for collecting coins. Hands reach into pockets everywhere.

Soon after the magician disappears into the throng, a man with his face painted white and wearing black pants, white gloves and a white and black striped singlet top appears. He turns on a small stereo which plays an eerie form of instrumental music.

He begins to perform a mime act, but, try as I might, I can't follow the meaning. I yell out to Alessio as we pass between tables.

'*Che fa lui?* What does he do?'

'*Una bella domanda. Io dico che non fa un cazzo.* Good question. I say he doesn't do a fucking thing.'

I watch the mime artist go around the tables after his act. Barely anyone gives him money and I wonder if that is because his act is indecipherable or because his white face paint fails to mask a sour expression.

I am standing at the bar waiting for Marianna to finish a drinks order when an earnest young man who has been sitting in a corner table all night writing notes by candlelight approaches. Serving him two glasses of red wine and two bowls of pistachio nuts in the past two hours, I've answered the usual questions and in a brief conversation learnt that he is a poet.

'What is your name?' he asks, pushing his glasses up the bridge of his nose.

I tell him quickly as I flush with embarrassment, feeling Marianna's eyes on me. He scribbles *A Penelope* on the top of a piece of paper and hands it to me.

'Good night. It was a pleasure to meet you,' he says as he walks out the door.

I glance at the paper and see the man has written a twenty-line poem describing the atmosphere of the wine bar and my movements, expressing in gallant exaggeration his desire to know my name. Unwittingly, I've been stalked in the most romantic of fashions. I can't understand every word, but Mario tells me it is impressive. I tuck it in my jeans pocket to decipher later. It makes a nice change from getting a hurriedly scribbled phone number.

Just before close, Mario sends me to rouse the drunk sleeping with his head atop a table. I giggle when I see someone, most likely Alessio, has placed candles all around the man's slumped body, creating a form of shrine. I touch the man gently and he stirs and swings an arm in annoyance. I keep prodding to no avail until Alessio finally comes to help me, raising his voice and clapping his hands to send the man grumbling on his way.

Without warning Raffaello walks in the door, offering me a lift home. I leave my other Romeo tied up to a pole in Piazza Farnese, where there is an all-night *carabinieri* post, and walk with him to his car.

Driving home, I am buzzing from the energy of the bar yet almost too tired to speak. It's nice to fall asleep as a pair.

Daniella from via Urbana rings me to say the room is mine. A few days later I say farewell to Serena as she rushes out the door for a lunch appointment and lock Carlo III in the kitchen so I can pack up my things in peace. I pull garments out of the wardrobe then stop to sit on my bed, suddenly weary. I think I am moving for the right reasons but all of a sudden I wonder what else is driving me. It's all very well to chase change, but I feel like I'm running in a million directions trying to find something to hold on to.

I keep packing until Raffaello arrives and helps me load my gear into his car. Even with its gussets expanded my backpack can no longer hold my belongings. Serena has generously given me pairs of shoes she never wears and I now have winter clothes, books, thirty extra CDs sent to me in various care packages and the laptop James bequeathed me.

Before we leave, I pop into my local to have one final cappuccino. When I tell Elide that I am moving, she offers me my last caffeine injection on the house. I accept it, sadly.

I wake the next day in my new home with aching muscles and a throat that feels slashed. Hauling myself out of the single bed, I look out my window over the city and suddenly fight nausea. It's the first time I've felt really crook since arriving.

I go to the pharmacy and blurt out *emicrania*, headache, and *muco*, mucus, to the grey-haired lady behind the counter. She gives me some medicine she says will take away my fever. Ah, yes. I bet the Italians have 246 products designed to battle the dreaded *febbre*. Ringing Steve to tell him I won't be able to come to work, I collapse in bed.

A sweaty ball of misery in a strange new house, I yearn for home. As kids, when my sisters and I were feeling sick, Mum used to give us lemonade and salty crackers smeared with Vegemite. My last stash of the sticky black stuff has run out. Suddenly everything seems worse, every anxiety amplified. I only have myself. I have to look after myself better. Right on cue, Daniella sticks her head in my door to deliver a parcel from Sascha, a good friend in Sydney.

I unwrap it eagerly to find the latest CD by my beloved Go-Betweens. Blame it on the *febbre,* but I am so touched by the gesture I find tears streaming down my cheeks. With my slimmer earnings, I haven't bought a CD since I arrived in Italy. Any package containing music is cherished while getting the latest home-grown CDs is a bonus.

I put the disc in my Discman and block out the world.

Later Emma, my other flatmate, arrives back from her native London. Breezy and pleasant with a plummy accent, she's in Italy frantically researching her doctorate on virgin martyrs from 1599 to 1670. In the coming weeks I will barely see her or Daniella, who bashes her keyboard in her room, working to deadlines for various writing projects. So much for my plan to speak more Italian at home. I'd learn more screaming swearwords at Carlo III.

Feeling empty and sick of lying in bed, I go outside to get some sunshine at noon the next day. Walking around the 'hood I pick my new local. Er Baretto is in via Boschetto, a long, sloping street full of shops close to home. Cosy small, the bar has a cheery ambience, with umbrella-covered tables outside and wooden bench seats inside. MTV plays and the coffee and *cornetti* are good. After a week I am on first name terms with the small staff – Ihmad, Marco and Mara.

As I pass Er Baretto one day, I notice a brightly coloured shop facade with a hot pink neon sign: Pulp. Curious, I head in. Immediately to my left, behind a small counter, is a small, delicate man with trendy glasses. He looks up from the magazine he is reading, smiles and says a feminine '*Ciao*'.

Illuminated by retro lighting, clothing racks groan with fabric remnants from the 1920s onwards. There are gorgeous handbags, diamond-studded evening dresses, psychedelic disco dresses, fabulous fifties swimming costumes and retro sunglasses.

I start to chat to the man, who introduces himself as Fabio. A stylist, he runs the store with his business partner, Fabrizio, who arrives a short time later. A nuggety man with a three-day growth, Fabrizio is the masculine force in their very camp operation.

Foraging through the racks, I find a gorgeous blue petticoat that I reckon I can get away with wearing as a day frock, even if I stand out a mile as *una straniera*. I imagine strolling down via Boschetto, chased by the butcher, the baker and the furniture maker.

In the next few months, all of my spare money will be channelled into Pulp, where Fabio and Fabrizio help me ignore my trivial worries, embroiling me in the large-scale drama of their lives: from going to the *palestra*, gym, to lose ten kilos and battling *la febbre* to going to the *casino* that is Napoli to source clothes from flea markets and making glittery costumes for demanding clients who work in theatre. There always seems to be a tizz to be had.

Every girl needs a good gay friend who will never trample on her heart and make her feel adored. Always available for a gossip, Fabio and Fabrizio give me small discounts and freebies – a scarf here or a belt there – to make me feel special.

After a few weeks in Monti I'm already feeling like part of the furniture, and I wonder if I am romanticising the sense of community that, for me, exists at every turn. I rack my brain to remember what kind of rapport I had with shopkeepers at home. Apart from occasional looks of recognition and general greetings at places I regularly bought lunch or had dinner, I was never addressed by my name – except, I realise with amusement, at a café run by Italians in inner-Sydney, where I'd get a take-away coffee most days.

July arrives, but it's so hot it already feels like August. When I heave open the big wooden door of the palazzo to face the day, a gush of heat covers my body in an instant. No one moves unless they are heading to the hills or the sea in the lead-up to *Ferragosto* and the holiday lull beyond.

'I keep cool by running a cold bath each morning that I keep full,' Mario tells me one night. 'Before I have to leave the house I immerse myself in it, and I keep doing that all day.'

I laugh out loud, but of course it makes perfect sense. Beside me Alessandro, one of my favourite colleagues, chuckles too. Slim and bespectacled with nose and eyebrow piercings, he's just finished a political science degree and is doing his final stint of compulsory military service. Within a few months he's off to Milan, where he's scored a three-month trial at MTV. Frightfully hip, with a memory for almost every genre of music, I know he'll dazzle the music giant's bigwigs.

Ale speaks English because he spent three months in the US as part of his university studies. Hearing an Italian speak phrases normally heard in a Spike Lee film is funny. A current affairs junkie, in Ale I have finally found someone who not only is interested in what's going on nationally and internationally but is happy to decode parts of the Italian culture and political landscape I can't grasp. At work we chat about the news of the day and outside work we catch up when we can for a beer.

I am starting to hang out with three other Nolano-ites – Christina, Susanna and Simona – albeit infrequently. All in their mid-twenties and finishing varying degrees, we keep in touch sporadically to organise *cenette*, little dinners, which start with an *aperitivo* anytime after eight at Nolano and finish early in the morning.

I am standing near the bar waiting for an order to be poured by Federico II, who is pretending, as I am, that nothing has happened between us, when a young woman about my age approaches me. She is tanned, with playful eyes, a generous mouth and happy face. I remember her because I totally mucked up her order half an hour ago and she tried to help me, speaking in broken English. Wearing a gorgeous loose-fitting cream top and an Indian-style skirt with slip-on shoes, her style is boho-chic. She's a breath of fresh air amid the Barbie dolls parading in the Campo.

Having introduced herself, and talking at knots in her excitement, Betta tells me she is about to go to Australia for the second time, to visit a Brazilian man she hooked up with during her first visit to Sydney. Her honesty and open-book approach is striking and, the more she chats about her love for the suburbs and places I adore in Sydney, the more I like her – and when she says she has a room to rent in her house in Monti my heart seesaws.

After barely two months, living with Daniella is becoming tedious – I often feel that I am staying in a hotel. She cleans fastidiously and is forever leaving helpful but annoying instructions about everything, from how to use the washing machine to placing laundry on the *terrazza*. It feels like her house, not a share house.

Curious, I accept Betta's invitation to see her apartment, a five-minute walk from my current address. She buzzes me into her first-floor apartment and I walk in to a space filled with antique and used furniture Betta proudly tells me she either bought at the Porta Portese market, or found on the street. A woman with obvious style, she has decorated the apartment with quirky objects that ooze character – a chaise covered in red and gold Chinese fabric, a fridge from the '50s, a chandelier in the kitchen. The apartment has a retro vibe I adore.

The room for rent is not as light as the one at Daniella's and has grey views of the interior walls of the palazzo. But it's twice as big with great shelving. I look at the double bed with surreptitious desire. Blow being celibate. It's one thing to live like a nun in suburban Perugia, another being in a capital city swarming with swarthy hunks.

Excited by both the apartment and the friendship I am quickly building with Betta, I tell her I will take the room when she returns from Australia in a month's time. Wishing her a fabulous holiday, I give her contact details for friends and family in Sydney and Melbourne.

Working up the courage to tell Daniella I'm moving out, I stop for a moment to people-watch on the edge of the piazza in Monti. There's always something going on.

Within minutes a young, attractive couple storm out of one of the bars, hissing at each other like feral cats. Dressed in designer jeans, a white linen shirt and shades, the man marches towards his motorbike as his lover tails him in fury. The eyes of every person seated and standing in the piazza discreetly watch as the couple stand near the man's bike, their angry but hushed voices rising by the second.

Resplendent in a colourful summer frock that illuminates her clear olive skin, the petite woman shakes her hands at the man in fury. Veins burst out of the temples of their reddening faces, which are separated by mere centimetres. Their argument builds to a crescendo. *This* is why I like Rome, I reflect. Life just always seems more interesting, somehow. There's always some little scene unfolding.

Suddenly the girl raises her hands and slaps the man, whose body jerks back in shock. Talk about tough love. More screaming and finger pointing ensues before the man kickstarts his bike and flees. My rapidly beating heart slows down as I exchange amused glances with total strangers.

My earliest impression of Roman women was that they were somehow vulnerable, pretty accessories who acquiesced to the demands of the man they invariably called *amore*, love, or *tesoro*, treasure, in gratingly cutesy tones. There are exceptions to every rule, but with time I see how I was hoodwinked by their feminine frailty. If Roman women seem like doormats it's all part of a clever show – so that when they strike they are even more formidable. Italian *donne* are more often than not ball-breakers: head-strong and demanding of their partners. As such, Italian men often view foreign girls as attractive because they are more relaxed – and more likely to put out.

Maybe that's why becoming a *mamma* commands such respect. Motherhood is a sign that after years of being a nut-cracking sweetie you've finally beaten your partner into submission. I think of Stefano the lawyer, the romantic poet *al Nolano* and the men who whistle and hiss at foreigners like me on the streets every day.

In the face of such constant attention it's no wonder I don't know how I feel about Raffaello.

Back at Daniella's, I tell her I have found another room. Surprised, she begins to talk me out of my decision, pointing out that for the same amount of rent it's hardly worth it. My resolve weakens when she says she will try to drop my rent in the future. And if she gets a few good jobs she might even buy a double bed for my room. Oh, a low blow. Smiling gratefully, I find myself telling her I'll stay put. All of a sudden the thought of hauling my gear metres down the road is exhausting.

I call Betta later as she is packing for Australia and tell her I've changed my mind. Totally relaxed, she says she'll be in contact when she returns so we can meet for an *aperitivo*.

Saturday night and I'm restless and dateless in Rome. Daniella has plans, Emma is in England, all of my numerous ex-flatmates and Nolano friends are either still on late-August holidays or on weekend trips away.

I scroll through the address book of my mobile phone, overwhelmed by a great desire to hit the turps. Hard. And then I see it. James II.

James I is my dear friend in London who came to visit me in Rome. James II is a witty British fellow I met one night at Nolano and have chatted to at the bar a few times since. At one point we were talking about house-hunting together, but then I found my room in via Urbana with Daniella.

I text him and am relieved to hear my mobile phone beep with an affirmative response. We agree to meet at Metro Cavour, just down the road.

Exiting the Metro I am surprised to see him wearing glasses, as he's always been without. Tall and lanky, James II is cute in a bookish kind of way.

We go and sit in the piazza in Monti and order a bottle of cheap red, watching the action around us. Spontaneous and knee-slappingly funny, James regales me with his impressions of the Italians and stories of his life in Rome, where he teaches English. Noticing my glum mood, he asks me what's wrong, but I can't pinpoint my feelings. We throw back two rounds of grappas that leave me well and truly *cotta* (cooked) then we leave the piazza and head in the direction of my house.

'The Metro's stopped and I don't have dosh for a cab – can I crash at yours?' James asks innocently, knowing as well as I do how the night may end.

Even in my sozzled state, I remember Daniella telling me when I moved in that, while it wasn't banned, she preferred not to have guests in the house. I blurt out my annoyance to James.

'That's ridiculous, you pay 550 euros rent,' he says. I think in Australian dollars that's about 1000 dollars. For God's sake, he's right. I can do what I want!

Stumbling in the door, I grab a bottle of Martini Bianco, a present from Nina, from my room and usher James to the kitchen, where we drink and smoke and chat some more before we tiptoe into the lounge room, which shares a common wall with Daniella's bedroom. Closing the sliding door, I pull out the divan to make a double bed for James. Tired and hammered, a grope is as serious as it gets before we crash.

In the morning, James is in the shower and I am lying on my bed in a comatose state when I look up to see Daniella standing in the doorway.

'What happened?' she asks frostily.

Giving her a brief spiel, she accepts the situation but reiterates her preference for not having strangers in the house. Peeved, I am nonetheless too tired to argue. Deep down I know telling James II he could stay would irritate the hell out of Daniella. I guess that's why I did it. I feel so hen-pecked living with her that I need to rebel.

James and I have a pastry and coffee before he gives me a peck on the cheek at the Metro stop.

'I'll call you soon, promise,' he says as he turns to walk away.

'Don't be a stranger,' I say just as warmly.

We both know we're unlikely to see each other again.

Le nonnette

I creep like a cat burglar from my room to the bathroom, managing to avoid Daniella for the rest of the day. In any case, I can't go near the *terrazza* or my bedroom window. With a hangover and vertigo I feel as stable as a patient in *One Flew Over the Cuckoo's Nest*.

I sit at the tiny table in my room and write Daniella a letter, placing it on the kitchen table as I leave for work that afternoon. As much as I would prefer a face-to-face chat, I am hopeless with confrontation – in any language. The more emotional I get, the more I lose my train of thought and sense of rationality. Plus, she's already talked me into staying once. I vent all of my thoughts as gently as possible – without the power of subtlety that fluency in a language allows. I tell Daniella I often feel like I am in a hotel; that, given the high rent I pay, it annoys me that it's a special request if a friend occasionally crashes in the house; that her fastidious cleaning and instructions are driving me potty.

Checking my email a few hours later, I am surprised to already find a response. From her corner of the ring, Daniella says I have brought a sense of agitation to the house and that I am rarely relaxed. That, even if I am the one member of the household with whom she feels she has the most in common, I am the person she least understands. If I feel like I am staying in a hotel it's because I haven't listened to the 'rhythm of the house' and observed how things function. That she had been forced to clean up more after me than any other flatmate who has dwelt in the house.

Tired and emotionally bankrupt, I don't know whether to laugh or cry. Either no one has ever told me I am Miss Piggy or Daniella has obsessive compulsive disorder – or we meet somewhere in the middle. Whatever, I feel like she has kept me under surveillance. I imagine she has plastic bags of evidence: crumbs I didn't clean off the kitchen table after dinner on August 5, the knife I used to stab the peach at 11.54 pm on August 28. She's got me on the ropes.

Daniella is right about one thing. I have been anxious – again – about my visa situation. But finally, after weeks of scouring Rome, I've found a language school willing to give me a certificate confirming my enrolment in a six-month language course – documentation I need to take to the Italian Embassy in Australia to apply for a study visa. The truth is, I may only be able to attend the school for two weeks, because paying for a six-month course will send me into debt. But I've managed to find a good school that is also very Italian – it bends the rules to get ahead.

I respond to Daniella's email and tell her I will be moving out as soon as possible but that I hope to see her in the future. We just can't live together. All of a sudden I feel so divorced.

I write an email to Betta, who is still in Australia.

I move into Betta's place a few weeks later, a day after she gets back. Dumping all my belongings in my new room, I sit on the couch and ask my jetlagged flatmate to explain the holiday disaster she referred to in her email.

I listen in amazement as she recounts the events of the month she spent in Sydney, where she flew to reunite with her lover, Rui. She met the strapping Brazilian a year earlier, during her first visit to Australia. Six months later, he flew to Rome and gave her an engagement ring, telling her he wanted to waltz her down the aisle and sire a family quick smart. Rui met Betta's mother, Ester, in order to assure her he wanted nothing but the best for her only child. Looking up at the tall, black, statuesque man with dreadlocks, Ester's eyes practically popped out of her head.

Landing in Sydney, Betta caught a cab to Rui's business, a gelateria in the city's western suburbs. The newlyweds-to-be spent a blissful first night together before Betta accompanied Rui to work the next day. Ten minutes later a woman walked into the gelateria. Turns out Rui had another lover.

'She was blonde with blue eyes,' says Betta, her black pupils widening with the drama of the memory, 'and she stood there and screamed at Rui – "Choose her or me!"'

Frantically calling the airline to unsuccessfully try to rebook her ticket to Rome, Betta remained at Rui's place for a few days to try to resolve the issue – to no avail. What else could she do? Sorting alternative accommodation, Betta made one final visit to the gelateria. Still fuming, when Rui wasn't looking, she did the only thing that came into her mind to make herself feel better. Spying a bulb of garlic, she separated the cloves and, one by one, popped them into the huge vats of flavoured syrups Rui used for toppings on the gelato he served his customers.

'*Ma quanto sei brava!* But how fantastic you are!'

Betta's face lights up with a proud little grin at my shriek of admiration. Dessert aside, Italians rarely cook a meal without incorporating garlic. It is entirely appropriate that she used the potent ingredient to exact a final act of revenge on her dastardly lover.

When he discovered the prank weeks later, Rui texted Betta to give her a ribbing. Whether his unsuspecting customers cottoned on that their sweet tooth was rather unsavoury is another thing entirely.

After chatting most of the day and sharing a pasta for dinner, I sleep for nine hours – at least three more hours than my nightly average in the last topsy-turvy month.

I haven't seen Raffaello for days. We meet for dinner at a restaurant near home and he fills me in on his news: he wants to go to Venice to paint, then perhaps do a show in Rome. And then he asks me about my impending trip to Australia.

Months ago I had imagined he might come with me, and indeed we had touched upon the subject as a possibility. I had romanticised the event in my usual fashion: my Italian lover charms my family and friends during a blissful summer holiday. We return to Rome, where things go from superb to divine. We move in together and not long after he drops onto his knees at the foot of the Pantheon and begs for my hand in marriage. I accept and we live happily – and I exist legally – ever after.

As I look at Raffaello across the table, I already know I want to go to Australia on my own. It's not that I don't feel at ease with him, I just don't feel like opening up my life at home to him. I tell him I haven't had time to book my ticket and the conversation moves on.

We walk to my apartment block, so I can show Raffaello my new home. Betta is in bed so we sit and whisper in the lounge room. I am walking him to the door when he suddenly swings around and kisses me passionately.

'*Ti amo*,' he says.

I look at him, confused, but he disappears without a glance before I can muster a response. Putting aside the fact I think

Raffaello is in love with the idea of being in love rather than in love with me, I think again of all the times I wished a boyfriend had said those same words. But the timing and situation are all wrong. Much to my frustration, I can't return the sentiment.

Do I feel so scared because Raffaello used the words Italians allegedly reserve for when a relationship is mighty serious? Or, could it be I've become that thing we heterosexual women love to hurl at men who don't return our feelings? Am I a Commitment Freak?

Living with Betta is a dream – despite the fact we are total opposites. I get up at sparrow's to go for a run or walk, she sleeps in as long as possible. I am always early for appointments, she is reliably late. I make plans constantly, she refuses to organise herself more than twenty minutes in advance. She is a fantastic chef who turns an onion into a five-course meal, I buy special ingredients I burn or ruin. She is attentive and coordinated, I break household objects because I am easily distracted and clumsy.

A law graduate, Betta works in a solicitor's office getting her practical hours up before she plans to sit an exam that, if she passes, will allow her to practise the full gamut of law. But her heart's not in it. Unsurprisingly, considering her great sense of style, she dreams of opening a boutique – but she's smart enough to know that the fashion industry is one of the fickler markets to ride.

Betta bought her flat when her father passed away some years ago. Fiercely independent, she nonetheless speaks to her mother twice a day on the telephone and visits her at least twice a week. Betta's relationship with Ester is close, but they bicker constantly. Occasionally, Betta screams at her mother then slams the phone down midsentence. Reassuring myself it's just their way of communicating, I am shocked nonetheless. The Italians love to argue. They treat a verbal stoush as sport.

Utterly pragmatic and level-headed, Betta has a fabulous sense of humour and the ridiculous.

'*Buongiorno, stupida,*' she says one morning, emerging from her bed dressed in a flannellette grandma nightie. Betta's way of greeting me is hurling affectionate insults. I return the compliment.

Sitting down at the table, she drops Cornflakes into her milky coffee instead of her usual sweet biscuits. When I ask her why, she reports that she went to the doctor the day before because she had slight constipation. The doctor told her to alter her diet and exercise more.

'Okay about the diet, but I told the doctor it is not possible for me to exercise. I *never* exercise,' she says with horror. 'The only thing I can do is fuck more.'

Belly-laughing at Betta's brutal command of the English language, I ask her how things are going with Paolo, her sometime squeeze of a few months.

'*Boh,*' she says, shrugging her shoulders.

A gentle man with a cheery disposition, Paolo comes to the house regularly, often bringing flowers, a carton of milk or the papers – and, once, a delicious apple and honey toffee made by, who else, his *mamma*. Handy with odd jobs, he has put up a shelf in the bathroom and tiles in the shower. Naturally, Betta hasn't told her mum Paolo is on the scene, so when Ester comes around to visit and notices alterations in the house Betta just says a friend helped her put them up.

I like Paolo a lot, even if I feel some pity for him, for as hard as he tries Betta is adamant that she will never be in love with him – no matter how much she cherishes his companionship and sweet ways.

'Invite Paolo for dinner tonight – I'm going to cook lamb,' I tell her, planning to also invite Sandro, a friend I met at Nolano. Quick with a joke, he's always fun to have around, although it can be dangerous. Twice as uncoordinated as me, he is forever dropping and losing things – ironic given he has a restoration business. We catch up only sporadically – perhaps knowing that when we are together we run the risk of accidentally killing each other.

I find the local butcher a few blocks away and enter the tiny shop for the first time. Standing at the counter are four locals waiting to be served. Watching the jovial young butcher wield his knife like a pirate and sing out to his customers asking for orders I suddenly feel nervous. I hate having to speak in front of strangers, paranoid about my accent. People standing behind me chat at speed. I am going to have to raise my voice to make myself heard.

I stare at the big slabs of meat in the counter. How do I tell the difference between beef, veal or lamb? It's all dead, red flesh to my eyes. I make my way to the cash register, where a young woman sits.

Explaining to her that I am Australian and I can't understand the language that well, I ask her to show me where the lamb is, trying not to draw attention to myself.

'*Stefano, 'sta ragazza Australiana vuole agnello ma è finito, vero?*'

I feel my cheeks catch fire. Yelling across the store to the butcher, the girl has announced that I am Australian and I want lamb.

'Unfortunately we don't have lamb, or kangaroo, but the *abbacchio* is tasty.'

I look around me to hear chuckling from the small crowd. Laughing at myself as much as they are, I stare at the *abbacchio* and lose my nerve to ask what the hell it is. It looks like lamb. So be it.

At home, I open the parcel in front of Betta, who explains that *abbacchio* is goat. I think of Gertrude, the baby kid we had when I was a toddler. At least I didn't select horse, available in most Italian supermarkets.

To avoid a culinary disaster, Betta helps me prepare the meal and as we tuck in to the perfectly cooked kid and sip red wine in good company, my mind wanders to my homeland. Soon I'll be savouring white wine in the summer heat and eating as much international cuisine as I can wrap my laughing gear around. Rome has some variety from Italian, but, apart from kebabs, anything that strays from the mainstream is often expensive.

With measurable dread, the next evening I meet Raffaello in the Monti piazza for a *vino* before we go to a party thrown by Tiziana in my old house.

Watching the action in the piazza around me – kids kicking a soccer ball, the newsagent selling papers at his octagonal kiosk and chatting to passers-by and people milling at the bars – I tell him what I should have told him weeks ago and chickened out of, instead trying to drop little clues that would stump the FBI. I explain I am not in love, as much as I love a lot of things about him. I talk about how, during our entire relationship, we've never been in sync emotionally, and that I am feeling a bit strange and detached from many things at the moment, on the eve of my trip home to Australia.

I look at Raffaello with guilt and regret, knowing that I could have handled things better if I had been more honest with myself from the start. But maybe we continued to be together, despite the fact that we saw each other less and less, because I was feeling insecure about so many things. Living with Betta has given me the confidence to face a few home truths.

Listening but saying little, Raffaello glowers. Equally frustrated with our own situations, we both go to the party and deal with the situation as best we can: we get drunk. I wander from room to room, taking in scenes of my old house, chatting to Nina, Tiziana and Alberta and trying to avoid Raffaello at all costs.

It's barely past midnight when I feel the need to escape. I jump on Romeo, glad to be returning to my room in a place that truly feels like home.

Situated directly above a mechanic shop and a shop specialising in the tuning of trombones, the lounge-room window of our first-floor apartment offers a bird's-eye view of the street below. I often find myself drawn to the windowsill, where I lean out to take in the action.

To my right, I can see a huge, grey marble church, which god-fearing people enter at all hours. To my left are two big green doors leading to a school of architecture, across from a beautiful nursery covered in thick vines. Below and to the right, I can see people dining *al fresco* at tables and chairs at La Pace, the Chinese restaurant in the palazzo next to ours. At lunchtime gypsies playing accordions compete with the sporadic din made by the man tuning his trombones and the roar of *motorini* engines revved by father-and-son mechanics Giancarlo and Fulvio.

On the street corner to my far right is La Licata, a small bar that is shaping up as my local, instead of Er Baretto. The bar is conveniently closer and, while not as quaint as Er Baretto, I like its rough and ready nature. Situated in a busier location, it attracts a strange crowd, from street sweepers and local shopkeepers to professionals and students. Every time I go there I am greeted by name or with a cheery '*Ciao, bella*' by Paola or Luigi, the sister and brother team who run the business, or Alessio, the young barista.

I have just returned home from La Licata for my mid-morning *macchiato* when Betta races out of her room. Dressed only in a G-string, she drags me to the window, covering her body at the last moment from street view.

'*Il bell' uomo di Monti! Il bell' uomo di Monti!*' She says excitedly, pointing below. A tall, tanned and woundingly good-looking man walks past casually, talking into his mobile phone.

He was drinking one night at Nolano, when Betta dropped in for a *prosecco*. We had both seen him around Monti – and we discovered we both fancied him. Egged on by Betta, I served the man and managed to strike up a thirty-second conversation, learning he did indeed live in Monti. Since we don't know his name, Betta and I simply refer to him as *il bell' uomo di Monti* – the beautiful man of Monti. We have no idea of his profession, which only adds to his intrigue.

'*Ma non è possible che sia così bello,* It's not possible that he is so beautiful,' sighs Betta, reluctantly dragging her almost naked butt back into her room to get dressed for work.

Riding Romeo past Er Baretto a few hours later, I look up to see *il bell' uomo di Monti* walking towards me. It's too late to pretend I haven't seen him and, when I draw near, I see that he does a double take, recognising me from the wine bar.

'Good morning. You live near here, right?'

Having already stopped my bike, I nod and scan my brain for conversation before realising the obvious: I am too nervous to speak and I have just remembered I am wearing my very ugly, bright yellow bicycle helmet. No Italian woman in her right mind would be seen dead in such garb. Too late to remove the helmet, I splutter out a few words about where I live and then ride off, cursing myself for not being more classy.

As I pull up below our apartment, I see Betta parking her *motorino*. Dressed in gorgeous pin-stripe pants, black and silver sneakers and a beautiful knit top, she looks designer cool. I gaze down at my jeans, jumper and rubber thongs and remind myself to lift my game and make more of an effort to be Italian foxy.

I've definitely become better groomed but being feminine just doesn't come naturally to me.

As I recount and lament my miserable performance to Betta, she gently suggests we go to a funky hair salon up the road. Two hours later I return with my long hair lopped and layered in a style that gives me a fringe for the first time in a decade.

Unsure if I like the style, Betta assures me I look fetching. Looking in the mirror the next morning all I see is Joan Jett. Thank God I have a stylist flatmate.

Two weeks before I am due to fly home to Australia I get an email from my good friend Bryce, whom I met thirteen years ago when we were both trying to get jobs as journalists in Sydney. Now based in Paris, he's been contacted by *marie claire* in Australia, who have asked him if he knows a freelance journo based in Italy. To my delight – and acute alarm – he has suggested me.

Within days I get an email from the magazine's editor-at-large, who explains she wants a story on a controversial school that has opened near Naples. The school offers limited places in a show-biz course, promising graduates jobs in what seems to be a bit like a work-for-the-dole scheme. Funded to the tune of one million euros by the European Community, the school has created global headlines, with critics branding it *la scuola delle veline* – the school of game-show bimbos.

In Italy, television is awash with *veline,* pretty girls who wear next to nothing and perform menial tasks on a range of game shows. When I first arrived, I was shocked by the young pieces of curvaceous flesh paid to flaunt themselves to sex up banal shows. If the same thing happened in Australia the switchboards of television stations would be jammed with complaints. But somehow it's an accepted part of society in Italy. Young girls dream of joining the ranks of the *veline,* whose fame escalates if they date a soccer hero.

A week later I meet Fabio, the freelance photographer assigned to do the job with me, and we hurtle south in his car. We take the turn-off to Frattemaggiore, a small hamlet on the outskirts of Naples, where youth unemployment peaks at 50 per cent. Driving around streets lined with rows of grey, graffitied apartment blocks to find the school, where I have organised an interview with the director and students, I feel desperation hanging in the air.

Fabio and I find the school in a dead-end street and buzz our way in. Chubby with a greasy pigtail and dressed in Johnny Cash black, the director ushers us into his office, a plain room with three chairs and a table bearing an ashtray full of extinguished cigarettes.

I hold my list of questions before me, turn on my tape recorder and commence the interview. Within minutes I realise with dismay it is extremely hard to understand the words coming out of the director's mouth. Betta told me the Neapolitan accent was thick, but I hadn't expected it to be so hard to comprehend. It's an entirely different dialect from the Roman language I am accustomed to hearing and speaking. Making the situation worse, the director is extremely defensive, since the school has attracted a tide of bad press.

I struggle to concentrate as panic rises in my throat. I calm myself with the thought that I have everything on tape and it will be easier to understand when I get home. I leave the director's office to talk to the students as they attend various classes, including the dance lesson. Dressed in designer tracksuit pants and boob tubes, they stretch and throw their bodies about. Some are born entertainers, others are so bad it's difficult to stifle a giggle.

Driving back to Rome in the evening, I voice my fears to Fabio, who reassures me that tomorrow, our final day, will be better.

Thankfully, he's right. Attending a music class, I watch as the students are called to perform songs and test their voices. I speak to some of them and slowly the story takes shape.

My relief is short-lived when I sit down at the table at home and start to transcribe the two mini-cassettes in my tape recorder. It's like listening to Russian. It takes me hours to transcribe, asking Betta for help when I stumble across chunks of dialogue I can't understand. I know I could pay someone to translate the tapes, but that defeats the purpose. I have to learn to cope on my own and understand the language – in any shape or form. Speaking with Betta in Italian each day is helping, but it seems I have a long way to go.

Finally I send the story off to Sydney, my heart in my mouth, hoping against all odds it is what *marie claire* wants. A few days later, I check my email as I prepare to go to the wine bar for my weekly shift. I yelp with excitement to learn that, apart from a few extra questions and adjustments, the magazine is happy with the story.

I've done it. I've cracked a story that will, hopefully, lead to other jobs. I write my good news in a note I leave on the kitchen table, addressed to 'Betta *la nonnetta*'.

As winter kicks in Betta and I have come to refer to each other as *le nonnette che fanno le cenette* – the little grannies who make little dinners. Cooking dinner and faffing around at home, we're in serious risk of rivalling the social habits of women three times our age. In fact, the last occupants of Betta's apartment were two sisters who never married. Ageing together, they literally died together in their home. Whenever Betta and I are becoming too house-bound we joke that our home is cursed.

At Nolano there are no longer tables outside. The November weather is too icy. I am standing at the bar taking orders when

Paolo II (as opposed to Betta's squeeze, Paolo I), an architect with a mad mutt called Gualdo, pops in for a drink. Betta knows Paolo II, since he dated one of her best friends for eight years a decade earlier. When I first came to Rome it seemed so huge, but the more people I meet at Nolano or through Betta it feels like everyone knows everyone via the tight connections of friends and family.

Still jubilant, I tell Paolo II my news.

'Come on, let's have dinner to celebrate!' he cries.

I accept readily. From the day I met Paolo II there has been chemistry between us. Just taller than me with short brown hair and gorgeous, mischievous brown eyes, he makes me laugh constantly. Always working on a few different projects at any time with great speed, he seems atypically Italian. He carries a digital camera, snapping pictures of Rome and his friends. Three beautiful images he took of Nolano hang from a wall opposite the bar.

The next day we meet outside my apartment and walk to a wine bar nearby. Paolo II tries to control Gualdo, who is strangely excitable. He strains on his leash, pulling Paolo in every direction. Somehow the bar manager seems happy to have the crazed animal in the restaurant. In general, dogs are accepted inside many stores, as many Italians and foreigners have dogs, often little yappy ones like Carlo III. It's not uncommon to see cushioned dog kennels inside a beauty centre or hair salon.

Paolo shoves Gualdo under one of the wooden tables where we take a seat. Wine bottles are stacked in shelves above us. The weight of two family bibles, the wine list is divided into the Italian regions, with extensive lists for white and red wine. The menu is similarly specialised in regional dishes. We order a plate of meats and cheese from Calabria, a region south of Rome known for its spicier produce, and a bottle of Sicilian red. Only one week remains before I head home, and I tell Paolo what I plan to do – spend time in Sydney with my mum and dad and sister Lisa and her family, fly to Perth to see my other sister, Sal, and her family, and cram in as much time as I can with friends.

'How long will you stay in Rome, Penny?' he asks.

'Maybe a life-time,' I quip, before trying to explain something I'm not so sure about. 'I don't know. I am only just starting to do what I hoped to do at work. It takes a long time to reach a point where you feel good. Right now, I feel like Rome is my home. We'll see.'

Paolo shakes his head in bemusement. He doesn't have to tell me what he's thinking: several Italians have queried my decision before, complaining about the bureaucratic chaos, Prime Minister Silvio Berlusconi's corrupt grip on the country, the spiralling economy, the high cost of living. The list goes on – but it doesn't extinguish my desire to stay. With one published magazine story up my sleeve, I suddenly feel confident and much more committed to remaining in Rome.

We have a nightcap at a bar in my street before Paolo walks me home, but not before he stops me in my tracks to kiss me goodnight. Suddenly we hear a noise and stop to turn around and see Gualdo vomiting violently on the pavement behind us. We both laugh hysterically. How romantic.

I stumble up the steps and crash tackle my bed, too tired even to undress.

Two days before my flight to Sydney I do my final shift at Nolano, telling Mario I will bring him back some nice red wine only if he lets me keep my regular Thursday shift.

I send a text message to friends asking them to pop in, and I am chuffed to see many familiar faces: Nolano staff including Ale, Federico II, Susanna, Simona, Christina, Eloi, Marianna and Alessio; Steve and Linda from The Beehive; and friends of mine – including Nina, Tiziana, Alberta and Federico I – and Betta's, whom I have come to know well. Raffaello doesn't respond to my SMS invitation.

Having organised someone to rent my room in my absence, my last twenty-four hours are spent stowing away my belongings, packing my backpack and saying goodbyes. I'm glad to spend my final night with Betta, who cooks me my favourite dish – *penne all' amatriciana* – and hands me a Christmas card.

Enjoy this beautiful period in Australia with family but here your home waits for you! I wish you a happy Christmas and fantastic 2004 (I hope in Italy!), that will give you the realisation of your dreams (also a man!). *Ti voglio bene.* A hug to the woman that moves always at a million miles an hour.

Betta thrusts a small package in my hand. Inside is an Estée Lauder blush, eye shadow and eyeliner.

'Since you arrived in this house you've become more of a woman...more Italian. Now you have your own make-up,' she says jubilantly, as if she is transforming me into a beauty queen.

I grin at Betta, thinking about all the times before we've gone out on the town together I've made her stand and do my face paint, because I'm incapable of doing it myself.

She drags me into the bathroom for a beauty session, and soon I've got it down pat.

'There! Now you're ready to go back to Australia!' Betta announces.

My stomach flips. Tomorrow I'll be walking through the arrivals gate at Sydney.

I have Betta's card tucked into my favourite Italian comic book in my hand-luggage when I meet Paolo, who insists on giving me a lift to Termini station, where I get a train to the airport. On the back of his large motorbike, my backpack strapped across my shoulders, I watch the streets of Rome I now know so well flash by.

Standing on platform 25, Paolo gives me a hug and turns to go.

'Give me another hug,' I say, suddenly feeling emotional.

He obliges then I disentangle myself and hop on the train.

At the airport, I walk around aimlessly staring at anything to distract myself – unsuccessfully. With a freelance career suddenly seeming attainable, a home where I finally feel settled and a growing social life, I am suddenly scared the small world that has taken me eighteen months to create will vanish in my absence – including my fetching new *amore*.

I am standing in line to board when my mobile phone beeps with a message from Paolo. It reads, 'I miss you! And…!' I reluctantly turn off my phone and begin the gangplank walk.

Home run

Sydney greets me with a cracker blue-sky Sunday and in my first twenty-four hours I feel like a kid clasping a gold ticket Willy Wonka chocolate bar. I relish everything: an early morning swim with my big sis and niece in marshmallow surf at Bondi Beach; a few soothing middies with close mates in Darlo; more quality family time over Thai take-away.

I wake in the dead of morning on Monday, jetlagged and glad to be home – but missing Italy. Rising with the sun, I grab the documents I need to get my study visa and leave my sister's inner-city house to stroll in the direction of the Italian Consulate at Circular Quay.

I walk along sleeping city streets, stopping to peer through shop windows. I'd forgotten what a hussy Sydney is, constantly changing appearance to tease and please a demanding crowd. New stores and restaurants have sprouted everywhere and everything is so shiny and chic compared to the centuries-old places to which I have grown accustomed.

Unsettled, I am glad to find my old local café open for breakfast. I had half feared it may have been bulldozed to make way for another bland bar full of blond timber and stainless steel. I approach the bar to find the Italian girl who used to take my coffee order every working day before I left home. When she looks at me with a flicker of recognition I remind her of my name and ask for hers. We are having a quick chat when I realise I'm holding up the queue. Oops. No standing brekkies here. Feeling strange, I order and sit at an outside table and read the papers.

At the Italian Consulate, I am told the reception does not open for another forty-five minutes so I find an Internet café to kill time. To my delight there's a message from Paolo II.

I miss you a lot. *Ti voglio bene* – maybe more than Gualdo but less than my mother. (-; Your return is always closer and I will keep strong until that date. Then we'll get married, okay?

Chuckling and blushing at once, I return to the consulate, hand in my papers and am told to return in a week to collect my visa. Bounding out of the office like a Jenny Craig success story, there's one last thing to do before I can embrace Sydney's balmy silly season. I find a mobile phone shop and get connected. I feel lost without my SMS lifeline to Roma.

As I start my social rounds, family and friends all seem more or less the same. But little by little I notice subtle and obvious changes that please and surprise me – and scare the life out of me. Visiting my grandfather, I do a double take when I see he keeps a cane on hand.

'Hey, Pa, what do you think about coming to Rome with me?' I joke, trying to quell guilt at not being able to spend time with him, and pain because I have missed him so much.

'You can spend your twilight years sitting in the sunny piazza in Monti. Don't worry about the lingo. I'll organise a *Sydney Morning Herald* subscription and get you cable TV.'

But Italy has no need for another old-timer. With one of the lowest birth rates in Europe and 20 per cent of the population over sixty-five, the country is sitting on a demographical time bomb. The Italian government is pushing to raise the legal retirement age – sometimes as low as forty-five – to avoid the inevitable meltdown of the generous pension system.

Still, I wish I could take Pa back with me. I reckon life expectancy is so high because the elderly there are engaged in life practically until the day they snuff it – rather than being shoved into a nursing home at the first sign that their body is not bearing up.

Each day my emotions swing erratically as I read Italian books, text Betta, Paolo II and other friends in Rome, and get seduced by a lazy Sydney summer, surrounded by my nearest and dearest friends, to whom I don't have to explain myself. I can't work out where I belong, or where I most want to be.

I fly and bus across country, seeing my sister and mates in Perth and my parents in country New South Wales, then find myself back in Bondi on New Year's Eve on the balcony of a friend's apartment. As fireworks burst across the sky I remember how upset I was this time last year in Rome, and think how much easier everything is in my homeland – so easy it's tempting to stay.

Yet while so many things are new, so much has stayed the same. Seeing my mates has helped me realise I'm still not ready to commit to any job or anyone. It's also helped reignite my ambitious streak, pushed aside during the initial struggle to settle in Rome then somehow forgotten as I found work that – however menial – allowed me to survive and adapt and explore a new city and country.

But now it's time for action.

In my last two days in Australia I tee up back-to-back interviews with as many magazine editors as I can, hoping this way they will be more responsive to emails from afar. I'll give myself six months in Rome to get some form of freelance writing caper going. And if I flounder I can always be a toilet scrubber until I figure out my next whimsical plan.

I feel good about leaving but my determination crumbles over dinner with friends on my last night in town. I can't quite believe my own ears when words borne from nostalgia spill from my mouth.

'I reckon I'll be home at the end of the year,' I say cheerily, looking from the surrounding faces to the Bondi sea I already miss. I take scores of polaroid photos I can already see stuck to the wall of my room millions of miles away.

Sitting on the plane the next day, I am reliving the night before when I hear an Italian accent a few aisles back. In an instant I realise my folly. I can't wait to get back to Rome.

A perfumed security officer stops me and asks me for my documents, including the letter from my Italian school. Confirming I have come to Italy to study in Rome, I look at the officer with unbridled happiness.

'*Okay. Tutto bene, arrivederci, signorina*,' he says with a hint of a flirtatious smile.

He's referred to me as a *young* lady rather than as the more mature *signora*. Easily flattered, I scurry off. Walking into the belly of the airport my heart beats to the chaos around me. I'd forgotten how much I had missed the constant cabaret. Italians make pouring a glass of water seem interesting.

I grab my luggage and jump on the train to Termini station, sending an SMS message to Betta warning her I'll be home within forty minutes. In her last email she promised to banish Paolo I from the house on my first night back so *le nonnette*, little grandmas, could catch up. Paolo II is in Paris for work, and I'll have to wait a week until he gets back.

Adjusting to the winter chill, I begin the ten-minute walk from Termini to home. With too many bags it seems to take two hours. But I'd rather see the city on foot than from a cab window. As I totter past waiters sneaking smokos outside restaurants they stare with uninhibited interest and within minutes I attract a '*Buonasera, bella*'. I'd forgotten I have foreigner written all over my face. My ego is set to skyrocket again.

Pushing open the heavy door to our palazzo, I heave myself up two flights of stairs and forage for my house key. In Italy, apartment door keys are usually archaic, long and heavy, reflecting the history of the buildings. I always feel like I am locking up a prisoner when I leave Betta's apartment, as I have to turn the key five times before the door fully locks.

I shove the enormous key in the front door and burst inside the apartment with as much kerfuffle as possible. Betta stands to my right in the kitchen, stirring what looks to be an *amatriciana* sauce.

'Good evening, ugly idiot, good evening,' she says in a quiet and deliberately prosaic tone, turning to face me. 'I'm making your preferred pasta, what do you say?'

I drop my arms to let my bags falls everywhere and pull a face. Shrieking at each other we bear-hug and the night dissolves into an overdue catch-up.

I thought being away from Rome for six weeks would wreak havoc on my Italian skills, but to my surprise – and joy – I feel more relaxed about speaking. I let go of my perfectionist streak and blurt out any old word, even if I know it's grammatically incorrect.

Thrilled to be back, I nonetheless feel decidedly strange – readjusting to the life I knew, thinking of what I left behind in Sydney and planning what I want to do in the coming months.

As I return to my local haunts – Er Baretto, Pulp and La Licata – I begin to feel more settled, greeted by familiar faces who sing out a cheery '*Ciao, Penelope! Bentornata!* Welcome back!'

My job at the hotel apartment has changed – I now work at the reception of the main Beehive hotel, which has a far more sociable environment. Better still, Steve and Linda are easygoing about cutting back my roster to give me the time I need to put my freelancing plan into action.

Now that I have my study visa, Steve reminds me to go to the *Questura* immediately to obtain my *Permesso di Soggiorno*, Permit to Stay, so we can clear the first hurdle towards trying to get me legal on a permanent basis. I am relieved to find I have to go to a different office, and one that is less crowded and nowhere near as depressing as the one I visited before. Directed to a waiting room, I am eventually told to go to the second floor.

A petite woman with a gentle, friendly demeanour greets me and tells me to take a seat opposite her desk. I hand over all my bits and bobs – my letter of enrolment for the Italian school, my study visa from Australia, my health insurance, my bank account details and more – and she fills out the necessary paper work. She mutters something I can't quite grasp and disappears.

I remain unfazed until the woman reappears dressed in a white coat, not unlike the one my doctor in Sydney wears when it's pap smear time, or the one the surgeon donned before ripping out my wisdom teeth. In an instant I am skittishly defensive.

Looking at me somewhat apologetically, she holds up her fingers and I cotton on she's telling me she needs to fingerprint me, as part of new immigration security measurements. She produces a mini-paint roller and a pad of black ink. I hold out the index finger of my right hand as a lone offering but she shakes her head and commands me to turn over my hand. I am surprised when she saturates my entire right hand in the sticky, viscous ink. Slowly and deftly, she grabs each finger to press onto a piece of paper. Then she places her two hands on the top of my hand and pumps my palm with force. She repeats the process with my left hand, which she is forced to re-do when the ink doesn't work thoroughly.

With bitter-sweet irony I think of how one of the things I love most about Italy is the welcoming populace. Right now I feel like a crook. When the job is finished I am directed to the bathroom. With only freezing cold water, skin rubs off my red hands as I scrub in vain to remove the thick ink.

My disillusion deepens when I hear there is a massive backlog of *Permesso di Soggiorno* applications. As such, I should expect to wait at least four months.

Thanking the woman for her time, I ask for her name and obtain her direct office number. Little do I know that it will come in handy to stay in touch with Francesca: my study visa will expire before my *Permesso* arrives and I will find myself visiting her, at Betta's suggestion, with small bribes (chocolates and beauty products) in a bid to jog her memory of my case and do what is within her power to speed up my application.

As I walk home, I already have a sinking feeling of the impending bureaucratic *incubo*, nightmare. I pop into the post office near home. Away for a few days, Betta has asked me for the first time to pay our phone bill. Inside it takes me a few minutes to cotton on to the drama unfolding.

A week earlier, the post office introduced a ticketing machine that issues alphabetic letters and numbers depending on the type of service offered. A veritable village of elderly people mill around on foot or sit in the waiting chairs. Suffering varying ranges of hearing, vision and technology disabilities, they grumble amongst themselves and jumble up the queue. Modernising life anywhere in Italy is asking for trouble. The locals hate change and regardless, are incapable of forming an orderly queue.

An overweight woman with botoxed lips and eyebrows plucked to the nth degree stands at one counter, berating the young female teller for treating her like a number after forty years of service. Behind her, old biddies tut-tut and exchange looks of superiority.

Forty minutes later I walk in the front door of our apartment, exhausted after a glimpse of the world I don't normally have to deal with. Spic and span, the house smells of floral cleaning products. My old flattie Daniella may find it hard to believe, but Betta and I take it in turns – with a dash of friendly competition – to vacuum, dust and mop the house each week.

Cranking up the stereo, I enjoy the dose of exercise. Yet try as I might, I can never seem to reach Betta's sparkling standards. When I tell her I can't get some grime off the bathroom sink, I smirk when she advises me to use some *olio di gomito* – literally 'oil of the elbow'. Italians use *olio* and *vino* for everything. Betta sometimes puts oil in her hair, claiming it strengthens it, and will gargle wine acid to make a sore throat go away. When it comes to domestic chores I reckon she'll always have the upper hand, because she's a *mamma's* girl.

I find a note from her on the small table in the kitchen.

Among the twelve things I must do in her brief absence to maintain the house are: try to break as few plates and glasses as possible, and not to open the door of the house to anyone except beautiful men. The last point makes me snort: if you can and you feel like it, respond to the telephone.

When I first moved in I didn't answer the phone because I get nervous speaking in Italian to strangers. Then I refused to respond simply because the telephone rings off the hook – Betta has bought a mobile phone that not only has the worst reception in Italy but misfunctions continually. Betta's mum calls about twice a day. Apologising each time she calls, usually when I am in the middle of making lunch and have something on the gas, she hangs up as soon as she has ascertained her *bimba*, little girl, is absent. Within the hour she'll call again. Some days I have to work hard not to tell Ester to *vaffanculo*.

I make pasta for lunch – which always guarantees at least a half-hour siesta – then read through a stockpile of Australian mags I lugged home from Sydney to familiarise myself with the content in view of pitching story ideas. I resolve to start buying Italian magazines, too, to get more of a feel for the hip things going on instead of walking around with my head in the clouds marvelling at ruins and dining in *nonna*-run trattorias.

All the things I am accustomed to in Sydney – funky new eateries or bars with minimalist cool design – are in vogue in Italy, where everything modern is desired and *esterofilia*, passion for all things foreign, rules. Paradoxically, one of the reasons I adore Rome is because it rudely snubs the digital age, the national passion for mobile phones aside, hanging on to tradition that is found in crusty restaurants and dusty artisan workships where time never seems to pass. It's no wonder that some locals can't get their head around the idea that a twenty-four-hour plane ride is required to reach Australia. '*Ma non è possibile!*' they exclaim with a violent shake of one hand.

Soon it's time to rock up for my regular Thursday shift at Nolano. Going straight back to The Beehive job, I haven't had time to call in beforehand. I grab the bottles of Riesling and Shiraz I bought in Australia for Mario and retrieve Romeo from the basement.

As I lug my bike up some stairs to the entrance, I force myself to say *buonasera* to our doorman, whom I have nicknamed *il rospo*, the toad, because he has a swollen gut, lumpy skin and an ugly face. Apart from the fact he seems to do zilch all day, he annoys me because he makes the smallest of requests difficult. He also banned Betta from having her thirtieth *festa* on the communal rooftop because there are too many old farts living in the building. I know the post between Italy and Australia is slow, but I swear when I tell him I am expecting a package he sits on it for days without croaking. I try to avoid him as much as possible, but when we meet I feign politeness. I never know when I may need a favour one day.

I chain my bike to a pole and, as I round the corner and enter Campo de' Fiori, find myself wanting to run into Nolano. Eloi, the Brazilian bartender I adore but often quarrel with, beams when he sees me. I've obviously been away too long.

'Hi, Penelope, did you see many kangaroos?' he says, giving me a hug. Soon Mario breezes in with fresh market-purchased mint for Elio to grind into mojito cocktails. He pecks me on the cheeks and I rummage in my bag.

'*Ecco!* Here!' I say, handing the wine to Mario, who slides his glasses down the bridge of his nose to peer at the labels.

I tell him about my holiday before the evening rush starts. As I work I look nervously about the Campo, waiting for Paolo II to show. He returned from Paris today. Although we have bombarded each other with flowery SMS messages, I'm suddenly nervous about the prospect of seeing him again.

Finally he sweeps in the door and gives me a big hug. Smelling his aftershave, which he applies somewhat too liberally, I am taken back to other moments we have spent together – lunching near Piazza Navona and dinner the night Gualdo comically interrupted our street smooch.

With the bar almost deserted as tables of people head off to dinner, I have time to sit down with him for a quick glass of wine and a chat. I sense within minutes that something has changed and ask him if I am imagining things. Without giving any explanation, he looks at me guiltily and blurts out random excuses.

'I'm sorry. I am a bit stressed with work at the moment – I can't see you now.'

'But what are you trying to tell me?' I ask, failing to hide my disappointment.

'I don't know, Penny. I'm not well. I'm sorry...'

When Betta returns home and sees my glum face she lets out a sad sigh. When I update her, she is not surprised. It seems Paolo has a habit of energetically wooing a string of her girlfriends then offering strange explanations and apologies before vanishing.

I read aloud the reams of SMS messages he sent me when I was in Australia and she shakes her head.

'He is really fabulous, but totally crazy.'

Feeling reassured that Paolo's strange behaviour has got nothing to do with anything I might have done, I try not to be disillusioned. I can't blame him. It's natural to play the dating game until you find someone you think or hope will be the love of your life. At least he's been honest, if a little evasive. It's just weird to have been dumped before anything began.

But then my dysfunctional love-life knows no boundaries.

Buon compleanno

Facing thirty, the average female will make it well known that she is a member of the Age-Schmage Club, claiming with indifference that she doesn't consider her looming birthday to be different to any other.

Bullshit.

She may look as cheerily in control as Mary Poppins but, deep down, you can bet she is, like me, having a self-analytical, mini-life crisis, asking herself any one of the following questions: Am I truly happy? Should I be thinking of what I want to be doing in another decade? Do I have the job of my dreams? Is it within my creative capacity to invent a new gadget and become a squillionaire? Do I really want to be with the snoring, belching log that lies beside me most nights for the rest of my life? Should I be clucky? Why can't I get a shag?

My pre-thirty angst is momentarily forgotten when an email arrives from *marie claire*. They want me to go to Venice to do a story on *Carnevale*, the hedonistic festival held in the water-logged city every February. The two-week extravaganza dates back to the Middle Ages, when Venetians donned masks to defy strict class distinctions and roamed the city to indulge in lusty forbidden fantasies.

I accept the brief immediately, happy to learn the photographer assigned to the job is an Australian, Carla, who lives in Florence. I'm curious to know her story.

On a grey, blustery day, I rise early and catch the Venice-bound Eurostar, which stops at Santa Maria Novella Stazione in Florence. I make my way up to Carla's seat number a few minutes after the train has pulled out of the station to find a striking brunette smiling at me.

Down-to-earth, positive and fun, Carla has been shooting in Italy for four years. Talking about our separate but often similar experiences, we agree we are both still in love with our new lives – to the point that we sometimes wonder when the romance will wear off.

'I've met some foreign women who have lived in Italy a lot longer than us – some of them have married, been divorced and so forth – and they are so bitter about aspects of life here,' Carla says. 'Everyone's experience is different, and maybe it's because I don't have to deal with the things they have had to, but I still feel incredibly glad to be here.'

Like me, Carla has stayed in Italy for the main part illegally, avoiding suspicion by rarely crossing a border. She jokes that the worst thing that can happen is that she is deported, however admits a recent incident scared her: she was on a train in northern Italy when it was stopped and all travellers who looked obviously foreign were told to alight to have their papers checked by the police. Imagining one of the final scenes of *The Great Escape,* I am amazed when Carla says she was not even asked to leave the train – because she looked Italian enough to avoid suspicion. I knew I had been dyeing my hair darker of late for good reason.

We arrive in Venice to rain and fog, which adds to the tangible air of mystery that seeps from cobblestone cracks in San Marco's pigeon-covered piazza and flows into anonymous backstreets. *Carnevale* is in full swing, with tourists and locals wearing masquerade costumes that range from beautiful to butt-ugly. The weather has dented crowd numbers but those on show seem oblivious to the sleety conditions.

Checked into our hotel, Carla and I interview the brains behind a ball touted to be the most risqué in the traditional, seductive spirit of *Carnevale*. To attend, we must dress up in full costume, generously loaned to us by the organisers.

As I put on an embroidered, apple-green dress, my Cinderella joy evaporates rapidly. First I haul a wire frame covered with linen binding shaped like a bread loaf over my shoulders, swivelling it down to sit on my hips. Next I drag the weighty frock over my head and arrange it to fan out over the wire frame. I look like a cross between Laura from 'Little House on the Prairie' and a life-sized toilet-roll doll. As Carla pulls my stringed corset tight I look at my milk-pale boobs – wobbling like *panna cotta* and threatening to spill over the neckline of my dress – with a mixture of pride and horror.

That night, Carla and I make our way to the ball venue – a magnificent, seventeenth-century palazzo on the Grand Canal. We squeeze into our gowns and tie on our colourful masks in a temporary dressing room then edge slowly down a flight of marble stairs to interview guests arriving on foot or in gondolas which slide in to a small jetty then push off into the wet, gusty night.

Shortly after the formal dinner commences, I make my way to the bathroom. With a dress as wide as a Mini Minor, remaining elegant isn't easy. I bump into tables and knock over the odd champagne glass as I make my way across the crowded ballroom.

Inside a toilet cubicle I giggle at the absurdity of the situation, wrestling with my dress as I try to hoist up the heavy layers. The wire underlay rips holes in my new wool stockings and pierces my skin, drawing blood. I am starting to wonder why the hell women of the epoch bothered to even get out of bed let alone managed to strip quickly enough to maintain the interest of a horny suitor.

In between courses, the ballroom ignites with provocative, choreographed shows performed by near-naked dancers wearing masks. It's so very *Eyes Wide Shut*. Carla and I watch as the dancers drag guests from tables and entice them to cavort beneath sheets and other titillating props.

As I interview faceless guests behind the safety of my own mask, I get the impression I am surrounded by normal thrill-seekers and rich couples trying to spice up their marriages. As I stand watching a raunchy performance, I feel caressing hands slide around my waist. Spinning around, I see the husband of a gorgeously costumed woman I interviewed earlier in the evening.

'I bet you haven't seen your breasts looking so good for a long time,' he murmurs as the music on the dance floor climaxes in a drum-beating orgy. Praying one of my nipples hasn't inched out to watch the peep show, I excuse myself abruptly and scurry like an elephant in a tutu toward Carla, who's also feeling the heat.

'I can't get rid of them,' she hisses of a Swiss couple who are hoping she'll act as an extra bedroom power point.

Before too long we make our excuses and trudge home in the rain, so exhausted from work and the costumes that we can barely speak. We get up the next day to do it all again, but this time we borrow black capes for the evening. Neither of us has the stamina for the frocks.

When we can, Carla and I indulge in the delicious range of fried, icing-sugar dusted pastries made during *Carnevale*. On our last night we meet Alex, a local who runs one of the B&Bs listed on the Cross Pollinate accommodation site, who takes us down alleys and across bridges to dimly lit bars serving *cicchetti*, small glasses of wine, and tasty tapas-style snacks. Accustomed to the harsher, if not aggressive, Roman dialect, hearing the soft, more melodic Venetian vernacular makes me swoon.

Back in Rome I file the story, and my contact at *marie claire* replies a week later, saying they love it. The magazine sends me the issue on publication and I am thrilled to see our story in a colourful, eight-page opening spread.

This is why I am living in Italy, I think, answering one of the many questions jockeying at the back of my mind.

One morning I am woken by the beep of a message from Sanja, my Croatian friend who works at Bar Papaia in Perugia. I'm elated when I read she's catching the train to Rome after she finishes work on Saturday afternoon to spend the evening and Sunday, her one day off, with me. I haven't seen her for months and since she doesn't have a home phone and both of us are always low on mobile credit we communicate via SMS.

I walk up to Termini station and see Sanja walking towards me along Platform Two, where the Eurostar has just pulled in. Wearing a white bomber jacket in the classic winter style of Italian women, she lights up a Marlboro Red. Locked up for hours in non-smoking purgatory, most of the Italians streaming past me are fumbling for a cigarette or lighter.

Sanja looks fantastic, having added weight to her bony frame.

'I can't stop eating,' she says, patting her stomach.

I ask, with a wink, if she is pregnant.

'Are you kidding? Worse, I haven't had any good romps for ages – *porca miseria!*'

We dump her bags at my house and have dinner at a pizzeria around the corner then head to Nolano, where I am annoyed to find Eloi, the Brazilian bartender, in a venomous mood. When he started working at the bar, I clashed with him for reasons I still struggle to understand but which are largely due to cultural differences. For example, when I thanked him one night for making me an order I quickly learnt niceties don't fly.

'But why do you say thank you so formally, you want to put a wall between us?' he snapped.

Looking at him in disbelief, I tried to explain that saying a simple 'thanks' in my own country is just a way of being courteous. My words fell on deaf ears.

As a fellow foreigner, I thought Eloi would be more sympathetic to the things we have both experienced – arriving in a new city without a friend or a home and making a life. Instead, he often treats me with contempt that dampens my enjoyment of a job I would do for love not money.

I order a beer for Sanja and ask Eloi for a nice red wine. When I ask him what he has served me he refuses to tell me, saying it's not important.

'It is important, I want to know so I can learn about our wines,' I reply angrily.

Eloi pretends not to hear. I sit down and vent my frustration to Sanja, who sucks successive Marlboro Reds and looks at me with the air of Yoda.

'Penny, my dear, don't be a victim – treat him like he treats you.'

Watching Eloi behind the bar, pounding ice to make his hundredth mojito, I realise I will never be able to comprehend fully what he has been through to get here, just as he can't understand my experience. And suddenly it's not so bad that we are often at loggerheads. Sometimes the best friendships, like the one I have with Sanja, have difficult beginnings. Eloi and I may never see eye to eye, but at least I'll learn some new swearwords in Portuguese.

Finishing my wine, I motion to Sanja and start to make my way out the door. '*Ciao, stronzo,*' I say to Eloi, following my insult with a wink. Even saying 'Goodbye, arsehole' sounds sweeter in Italian.

'*Ciao, stronza,*' he replies, his face lighting up in a cheeky grin.

I am glad when, the next morning, Sanja suggests we walk to the Vatican, where I haven't been for almost two years. When you start to assimilate into life in any major city you often don't do the most obvious, touristy things on offer. I've seen the Sistine Chapel but I haven't witnessed *Il Papa* – the Pope – give a papal audience.

Our timing is perfect. Standing in the huge piazza below the columned, ostentatious might of the Vatican, I watch in amazement as a speck of human flesh dressed in cream robes fringed with gold appears on a tiny balcony. A voice that slurs and wobbles in volume wafts from loudspeakers.

The crowd, thick with banners, stands in silence and as I look at the confused faces around me I know I'm not the only one who can't understand a word that is coming out of the mouth of the Pope. For someone with the whole, wide world in his hands, John Paul II sounds incredibly fragile.

Exchanging bemused glances, Sanja and I edge out of the piazza and go to lunch at Pallaro, where Paola greets me with her habitual, bosom-crushing hug. After the four-course lunch, we wander home to gossip the afternoon away until I hug her goodbye on a platform at Termini.

'*Stammi bene e tieniti in forma.* Take care and keep strong,' she says with a wink.

As I walk into my apartment I see Paolo I and Betta having dinner at the table. I resist the urge to make a wisecrack, remembering a conversation a week ago when Betta admitted her feelings had grown for the big-hearted chap. Without even realising it, I feel confident enough to make a stupid joke. Because I don't care anymore if it comes out wrong, I'll try.

'*Ho visto il Papa!*' I say casually, as if to infer I'd just bumped into His Holiness at my local bar.

Betta and Paolo I break into hysterics not remotely provoked by my lame wit. They inform me that, depending on how I pronounce the word *papa*, I could either be saying the Pope, the father or the pimp. Unfortunately I picked the latter, a word that is very, vulgarly Roman.

Reassuring them that I haven't started a new career, I put cotton wool into my ears before I fall into bed. Yet another palazzo is being refurbished nearby and between jackhammering and the chatter of old biddies hanging out their laundry to dry on small terraces across the courtyard, my sleep has been far from *tranquillo*.

After pestering magazines for replies to my emails, I call Carla in Florence with some good news – the editor of the Qantas inflight magazine *The Australian Way* has greenlighted a piece on Monti, the suburb I live in, and I need her to take the pictures. Just as keen to knock over work, Carla tells me she needs a story to accompany photos she has shot of a historic health and beauty salon in Florence.

Shoring up the story with another Australian magazine, I call the salon to make an appointment with the director, Augusto. As it happens, he is going to be in Rome in two days, so we agree to meet for an introductory chat before I visit the Florence salon.

On the morning of our meeting I exit my house to approach a tall, well-built man in his fifties with a Peter Sellers moustache and a rich lamp tan. Wearing a brown corduroy suit, a blue shirt and a caramel and orange-striped tie, Augusto carries a tan briefcase and reeks of aftershave. After shaking my hand he pushes on Gucci shades as we hail a taxi.

It's just gone eleven when we pull up at Piazza del Popolo, a short walk from the Spanish Steps. We take an outdoor table at a swank bar to enjoy a non-alcoholic *aperitivo*. Filling me in on the salon business, the conversation soon turns more general, Augusto peppering me with questions: How long have I been in Italy? Am I married? Why did I come to Italy? What do I miss about home?

As I talk of fabulous Australian beaches, Augusto reaches into his briefcase and produces a brochure with a range of impressive yachts. Ranting about his passion for sailing, he points at one of the most luxuriously large vessels and tells me he owns it.

'I have always dreamed of going to Australia. We could do a sailing tour of the world together, then go there,' he says.

Fobbing the comment off light-heartedly, I find myself accepting Augusto's offer to take me to lunch. Apart from the fact I am having fun deflecting his cat and mouse advances, I never turn down an opportunity to eat out in Rome.

As we walk out of the bar, Augusto stops abruptly and tells me to wait for a moment. I watch as he reaches into his jacket pocket and pulls out a small, gleaming silver pistol, which he slides quickly into his briefcase.

Closing my gaping mouth, I accept his characteristically Italian performance as a blatant effort to impress me with his masculinity. But I can't help but ask him why on earth he has a gun in his jacket pocket.

'For security,' he says, eyes darting from side to side to check no one has seen his Magnum PI moves. Mumbling something about Florence being a dangerous city to live in, he reassures me by flashing his gun licence before ushering me into Dal Bolognese, a chic restaurant next door with waiters in white tuxedos.

With rich timber panelling and gilded fittings, the restaurant – one of the city's most prestigious – is full of an ageing Armani set. Moments after we are ushered to a table, Augusto nods in the direction of a good-looking, middle-aged man dressed in trendily worn jeans and green velvet jacket, telling me he's a well-known actor.

Dressed in black pants, denim jacket and flat boots, I don't feel shabby – until I notice, at other tables, the jewels dripping off women wearing enough make-up to keep Lancôme afloat for a year. Observing a series of tables with older men dining with women half their age, I have a feeling Augusto has invited me to lunch to *fare una bella figura*, make a good impression, among Rome's society set.

We've just poured two glasses from a bottle of San Giovese when I see a rose-seller approaching. Half dreading an Augusto stunt, I am relieved when he refuses flatly. Careful not to drink too much in the company of the frisky, gun-toting Florentine, I struggle to understand his accent. Carla had warned me that 'c' is pronounced as 'h'.

Picking up the tab, Augusto walks me to the salon's outlet shop and I am half-relieved and half-sad to part company – he's full of wind, but his whacky enthusiasm for life is almost infectious.

'We'll see one another in Florence,' he says. 'And don't forget to call me if you would like to go to Sardinia – I have a beautiful house there and you will be my guest.'

I thank him and titter to myself as I race to The Beehive. I finish work at midnight – on my thirtieth birthday. Between my three jobs I had almost forgotten about it. I hurtle home on Romeo, expecting Betta to be awake. Turning the lock on the door once is enough to tell me she is home, but, to my disappointment, all the lights in the house are out.

I tiptoe past her room to mine, where I find a small gift in wrapping paper and a note.

'Buon compleanno! Scusami per non averti aspettato ma sono distrutta. Sogni d'oro, brutta. Happy Birthday! Sorry for not having waited for you but I'm destroyed. Sweet dreams, ugly.'

Standing with my back to the door I have just started to untie the ribbon on the gift when a ball of human flesh jumps on my back.

'Hey, little grandma! I wasn't sleeping, I wanted to surprise you!' shrieks Betta.

Unwrapping the gift I find a sexy, sheer, white nightslip and a beautiful velvet and silver jewellery box.

'You already have make-up and you're more like a woman – now you have something sexy to wear to bed.'

'*Speriamo che funziona.* Let's hope it works,' I say, giving her a hug.

I go to the kitchen and grab two shot glasses I fill with an *Amaro* for a late night toast. Looking at the slip, I tell Betta about a present a girlfriend and I once gave to our other perennially single female flatmate. Ken was a life-sized, inflatable doll who we at first propped in boxer shorts in the lounge room for a cheap laugh. As time passed, however, Ken became a loved member of our household, emerging in countless outfits and accompanying us on picnics and weekend trips away. He provoked interesting debates at dinner parties and, as a good listener, was an excellent friend.

I wonder if I should email my friend and ask her to send Ken over for a holiday.

Betta takes me on her *motorino* for breakfast at a Sicilian pastry shop, then I send off an SMS invitation for drinks on Saturday, when a few friends living in Europe are flying in. Soon my mobile phone starts beeping like a car alarm.

Many best wishes, most beautiful! You thought I had forgotten?
A million big wishes and a huge big kiss.

The affectionate message from Simona, the vivacious professional dancer I work with at Nolano, is melting in its warmth.

Best wishes! I'm just waking up now, like a lethargic bear. Big kiss.

At 2 pm, Federico I has just rolled out of bed.

Happy birthday! For your 30 years of food, sleep, school, work, love, socialising, friends, joy and pain . . . in summary of life! A huge hug from Venice.

The sweet message from Raffaello, whom I haven't seen for months, brings a lump to my throat. Maybe our friendship will survive after all.

Happy birthday! Thanks for having believed in me, even if for only a little time. See you tomorrow for a little while. Kiss.

Reading Paolo's exaggerated message makes me want to give him a sharp clout about the ears.

My Penny, happy birthday! Forgive me but I can't come. Dear wishes from the heart.

Daniella's sincere message smooths over the more difficult times in our relationship.

Arriving at Bottiglieria di Nolano I see the muscle-bound frames of Eloi and Alessio rubbing moisturising cream into their hands – I can't remember the last time I paid attention to my nails or hands.

As he often does on a Thursday, Armando pops in for a chat and *aperitivo* and, on learning it is my birthday, disappears only to return with a bunch of apricot tulips before commencing to sing a Roman folksong to me. Listening to his lyrical voice, I find myself, not for the first time, wishing he was half his age.

Eloi, already becoming a firm friend, passes me glasses of *prosecco* all night while Alessio, ever the clown, keeps me in fits of hysterics. We watch the usual performance artists – the Indian with the toupee, the strange mime artist with the painted white face and two guys who play the longest version of 'Knocking on Heaven's Door' on an electric guitar I have ever had the misfortune of hearing. At 2 am we close the bar and restock the fridges before having a few nightcaps.

Somehow I manage to balance my bag and my tulips as I steer Romeo home.

I haven't got time for a hangover as friends living in Spain, London and Paris fly in for the weekend, arriving at all hours. I spend my time playing host.

As we walk to Nolano for my birthday *aperitivo* on Saturday evening I have pre-party nerves. Away from the support base of friends I'd usually celebrate with, I wonder if my notoriously laid-back and somewhat unpredictable Italian friends will make an appearance.

Rounding the corner of Campo de' Fiori I see a small table already gathered and as the minutes pass a stream of friends arrives. Walking into the bar, I kiss my hellos to Mario and Eloi, who sings 'Happy Birthday' to me in Portuguese. I think of the acquaintances and friendships I have forged with people of all ages, backgrounds and nationalities since arriving in Italy: the elderly but poetically playful Armando; the young Moroccan street urchins who beg at the wine bar; Farshad, the Iranian–Roman who flogs carpets in the historic centre; Sanja, my tough-as-nails Croatian chum; Christina, the spirited Eritrean–Italian student who works at Nolano; my effervescent German friend and ex-flatmate Nina; the Sicilian mob, including the gorgeous Viviana, older than me but boasting a teenager-taut body with the most beautiful tattoos I have ever seen; Marco, Mario and Fabio, the Egyptians who run the show at Pasqualino. The list continues.

We take over three tables and are struggling to find chairs for everyone when it starts to rain lightly. With too many of us to expect to find a restaurant to fit us, I suggest to my Paris-based, Aussie mate Bryce we get wine and pizzas and retreat to the large apartment he has rented near the Pantheon.

Like mice following the Pied Piper, everyone tails Bryce and me as we head back to the apartment, skirting through Piazza della Rotunda, where soft lights illuminate the full splendour of the Pantheon.

Standing with my back to a wall in the apartment, taking in the scene, my memory wanders back to the day I arrived in Rome and the good, bad and shitty moments of my struggle to create a new life in a land I didn't understand and often didn't want to understand, drunk on the romance of simply being in Roma and living my dream.

There is still so much I don't comprehend about Italy and its complicated web of history, politics, culture and art, and the language I find so beguiling and so frustrating.

But that's precisely the point.

I've never felt happier because I am so challenged. Each day brings a new reality to face and a new subject to wrap my head around linguistically and culturally. I don't know how long I will stay here or how long my visa saga will stretch on. Maybe in a year I'll be tearing my hair out and booking a plane ticket home. But for now I can't get enough of Rome.

So this is the big three-0. What the hell is all the fuss about? I feel younger in spirit than the upstart I was a decade ago, when I treated my job far too earnestly in a bid to impress the pants off anyone within a two-metre range. I've slowly sidelined the two things I thought were important – a serious career and men – to chase a whim or a dream. Dealing with the realities of my decisions, not to mention the insecurity that comes with them, has often been excruciatingly hard.

But I've never felt more alive.

'*Ehi nonnetta! Svegliati!* Hey, little grandma! Wake up!'

Pushing her beaming face into mine, Betta drags me back into the party.

Acknowledgements

Special thanks to my family: Lisa, for wisdom and encouragement on tap; Nel, for 1974 favours and care packages; Sal, for positivity and potions; Roberto, for advice and genes, and Pa, for inspiring my wanderlust; and to Geoffrey, Anna and Bianca, for good counsel and hospitality *alle grande*.

To Betta Pannucci for *la casa nostra* and much, much more. To Deb Callaghan, Bernadette Foley, Siobhan Gooley and Emma Rusher for their endless patience and expert guidance. To Kirsten Galliott and Larry Writer, for the kick-start, to Iain Shedden, for timely opinions; to Charlotte Owen for generosity and wizardry; and to Alessandro D'Ottavi and Aruna de Sole for translations. To Federico and Raffaello, for understanding; and to Mario Tozzi, Armando Mella and *tutti al Nolano,* for buckets of fun and an extended family in Rome.

Big thanks also to: James Waller, Bryce Corbett, Peter Trute, Steve and Linda, Samantha, Michelle Coffey, John McCartney, Nicolas Parkhill, Rob Kelly, Vivienne Stanton, David Whittaker, Mark Whittaker, Amy Willesee, Pat McGuiness, Rebecca Aduckiewicz, Charlie Edwards, Simonne Carvin, Nicki Clark, Gabriele Cagnetta, the Beehive gals, Patrizia Romeo, Tim and

Dianne Adams, Sandra Lee, Josephine McKenna, Belinda Hughes, Peter Metzner and the Arcettes, Emma Cooper, Sascha Keen, Nina, Tiziana and Alberta, Sanja Susak, Sandro Bonfanti, Ester Pannucci, Fabio Cuttica, Vivianna Famulari, Paolo Mori, Paolo II, Giulia, Piero and Ivo, Fabio and Fabrizio at Pulp, and staff at Pallaro, La Licata, Pasqualino, Café' Café' and Ditirambo. And to Carmen, for extraordinary vision.

Penelope Green was born in Sydney and worked as a print journalist around Australia for a decade before moving to Rome in 2002. She writes for various publications including *Gourmet Traveller*, *marie claire* and *Harper's Bazaar*. Usually too lazy to study Italian, she prefers to put it into practice by working in a Roman wine bar once a week and waitressing sporadically.